UNILATERALISM, IDEOLOGY, & U.S. FOREIGN POLICY

The United States In and Out of UNESCO

ROGER A. COATE

Foreword by John E. Fobes

Lynne Rienner Publishers • Boulder & London

To Jean and Leonard

AS
4
.U83C58
1988

Published in the United States of America in 1988 by
Lynne Rienner Publishers, Inc.
948 North Street, Boulder, Colorado 80302

and in the United Kingdom by
Lynne Rienner Publishers, Inc.
3 Henrietta Street, Covent Garden, London WC2E 8LU

Library of Congress Cataloging-in-Publication Data

Coate, Roger A.
   Unilateralism, ideology, and U.S. foreign policy.

   Bibliography: p.
   Includes index.
   1. Unesco—United States. I. Title.
AS4.U83C58   1988   341.7'67   87-32225
ISBN   1-55587-088-0 (lib. bdg.)

British Library Cataloguing in Publication Data

A Cataloguing in Publication record for this book
is available from the British Library.

Printed and bound in the United States of America

The paper used in this publication meets
the requirements of the American National
Standard for Permanence of Paper for
Printed Library Materials Z39.48-1984.

Contents

Illustrations

Foreword

This book is about more than the United Nations Educational, Scientific and Cultural Organization (UNESCO) and U.S. participation in that organization. It has meaning for our attitudes toward and relationships with all United Nations agencies. Moreover, the author goes beyond a recounting of U.S. difficulties with multilateral institutions. He helps us understand weaknesses in the formulation of U.S. foreign (read "world") policies.

It has been said that there is a crisis of multilateralism, and, in the United States, a twilight in that form of international cooperation. Some see the problems of multilateralism in the light of a more profound multifaceted crisis of civilization. They refer to the tangle of global problems confronting societies, which give rise to ferment and uncertainty. From this perspective, it is natural that the international institutions should need reexamination. If the United States wishes to retain a leadership role in the world, it will need to be an active and constructive partner in that reexamination, including of UNESCO. In addition to pressing its own values and views in international organizations, the United States ought to help those organizations to be vehicles for understanding what is happening in the world. The United States must work actively with others to arrange new forms of international cooperation that will be commensurate with the challenges.

Professor Coate tells a story of policy made in a fragmented, partial manner and of a withdrawal of U.S. collaboration. Consultations among Washington agencies, with the Congress, with concerned public groups and with other governments were inadequate; responses received were sometimes ignored. It was claimed that the U.S. government's attitudes toward UNESCO were developed within the framework of an overall and comparative review of the effectiveness of all UN agencies; it now appears that this broader assessment may have been a formality.

This book is addressed to more than a scholarly audience. It has value for practitioners of international cooperation (governmental and private), for policymakers, members of Congress, civic leaders, teachers, researchers, and decisionmakers. The scholars will be able to discern the areas of research and teaching that need investigation and airing. Leaders of private voluntary organizations will perceive that their groups have a greater stake in the family of institutions of world order than they had realized. The voices of those organizations have been muffled. Their members are beginning to sense that they have broader ethical and practical responsibilities for multilateral cooperation than are covered by the usual definition of their professional, business, religious, or local community interests.

Here is a story that needs to be told—fascinating but disturbing, from which we all can learn. To some extent, the United State did not keep faith with itself, with its values and goals, nor with the favorable image that many in the world have of this country. The think tanks should have been commissioning studies in depth of the type this book represents. Developments in intergovernmental organizations, as well as in international nongovernmental associations, have been so many and so rapid in the past forty years that we only dimly comprehend the road we have traveled, or how and why. The social sciences could well furnish us with more analysis incorporating current history, like this book.

For many years, it may have been possible to treat policy toward intergovernmental organizations (IGOs) as a subject largely separate and apart from other domestic and foreign policies. Positions vis-à-vis the UN agencies were too often seen to require only an occasional gloss from basic foreign policy so as to avoid complications for that policy. Now that IGOs have become so numerous and pervasive, however, this distinct and partial treatment appears unsatisfactory. In addition, multilateral intergovernmental relations must be set against a vast and growing array of private, transnational relationships for which there is little policy as yet.

Professor Coate was privileged to have direct contact with some of the actors in multilateral cooperation in the last five years and to have been present at critical moments in the relations of the United States to UNESCO. He accepted a responsibility to observe carefully and to take notes. Fortunately, he had a strong base of research and teaching for such observation of current affairs. He has used his background and these experiences to produce a rare combination of scholarship and reporting; his book informs and analyzes in ways that should prove useful in a changing world.

Coate's review of the history of UNESCO and of the administration of one aspect of foreign policy comes at a strategic moment. The United Nations system is passing through a difficult period—and not only because the United States is withholding a substantial part of its assessed contribution. In the recent past, the United States may have taken strong initiatives at the UN in and its associated agencies for selected changes that it believed were in its interest. Others also have an agenda for change; reforms and adjustments are being proposed by many member states. In UNESCO, however, the United States walked away from the reform process before it had proceeded very far, resulting in doubts about negotiating in good faith.

In all the international agencies, there is an acute need for a long-term perspective to guide the consideration of structural and procedural changes that will make the UN system more responsive to a world much different from the one that existed at the creation of the system in 1945. The global issues confronting humankind have evolved and are increasingly complex. The process of adaptation will stumble along unless the United States learns from the experience of the past few years. The United States must also be seen to have learned, to have an integrated policy, and to display a willingness to stay the course.

Still to be examined—and this book provides a good beginning—is the story of the reactions of others to U.S. policy (or lack of it), to the U.S. withdrawal from UNESCO, to our withholding of contributions from the UN and its agencies. What damage has been done to the standing of the United States, our credibility, and our ability to pursue a constructive policy in the future?

Still to be examined also is whether there is a new oversight role for the U.S. Congress to play in respect to our participation in the complex array of international organizations. Moreover, for all forms of international cooperation in education, science, culture, and communications—the fields of UNESCO—what should be the nature of the mechanisms in the United States to cultivate the widest possible public understanding, support, and advice for such cooperation? What additional roles are appropriate for the private sector in an active, decentralized U.S. participation in international programs?

Roger Coate's book suggests to me that the United States must take strong measures to avoid privatized, narrow judgments in the formulation of the global policies to be pursued by this nation. At the same time, we can take fuller advantage of the intellectual, scientific, technological, and spiritual resources of our culture so as to bring them to bear in every possible avenue of worldwide cooperative problem solving.

These observations on an interesting book are based on my work experience with the United Nations at the time of its founding. Thereafter, I was privileged to deal with various instruments of international cooperation during service with the Bureau of the Budget, the Marshall Plan, and the Bureau of International Organization Affairs of the Department of State, as well as with the Foreign Service. Fourteen years were spent in senior posts with UNESCO, and I have been chairman of the U.S. National Commission for UNESCO.

These experiences confirm my belief that we have not heard the last word on U.S. participation in UNESCO and the UN generally. Opinion in this country, after the current period of uncertainty and partial withdrawal, will swing back to an insistence upon an active role for the United States. This book will not only help to turn the tide and activate positive U.S. attitudes; it will provide guidance for rebuilding that activist role and for greater wisdom in the formulation of national policies adequate to the world of the twenty-first century.

John E. Fobes
former Deputy-Director General, UNESCO

Preface

Around the halls of the UNESCO House, people—Secretariat staffers, delegates, and even reporters—were beginning to smile again. The occasion was the installation of a new Director-General; the date, November 16, 1987. While two long weeks earlier anxiety and gloom had pervaded these Paris headquarters, hope and anticipation of a brighter future were now rapidly bubbling to the surface. As stated by one observer, it was like watching a Cheshire cat after a satisfying meal. The smiles formed slowly at first but then grew and grew. It became even clearer in the weeks that followed that most member states of the organization were ready to start afresh.

Such expectations, however, were cushioned by what appeared to be a healthy dose of realism. The United Nations Educational, Scientific and Cultural Organization was still in the midst of a severe crisis. In assuming his new leadership role Federico Mayor made it clear that realism would guide his efforts to bring about changes in UNESCO to bring it "into step with the new reality" of global relations (UNESCO Doc. 24 C/INF.22, November 16, 1987). The new Director-General challenged:

> The founding objectives [of UNESCO] were not beyond the means of mankind nor were they erroneously formulated. It is true that the goals still look very distant. Furthermore, it sometimes seems that they move away more quickly than we can pursue them. We are now struggling amidst growing and insidious complexity that weakens the effectiveness of action, when it does not dissipate it altogether. Complexity, however, can be neither avoided nor concealed. Complexity, fragility and acceleration seem to me to be the three overriding characteristics of our time. These characteristics, far from serving as a pretext for inaction or as an excuse for being left behind, are a major argument for strengthening our determination and redoubling our energy, although this must be done by redefining the definition of objectives in order to align, with demanding realism, our aims with the resources available to us. It is precisely in the 'universal village,' whose outlines we are beginning to make out, that we must assess the total cost . . . of doing without UNESCO, without the dense web of interdependence that enwraps our entire human experience, without the intellectual frame on which the invisible but essential networks of harmony can be woven (Federico Mayor, UNESCO Doc. 24 C/INF.22:2–3).

While such a new sense of realism seems to have surfaced at UNESCO House in Paris, the situation is much less clear across the Atlantic Ocean, where ideological idealism appears to continue to dominate official U.S. multilateral relations in education, science, culture, and communications. Far from acknowledging complexity and attempting to work effectively within international institutions to deal with it, the tendency has been to deny its existence and to conduct U.S. foreign relations in these areas in a largely unilateral manner.

UNESCO seems well on the way to putting its house in order. Yet, as the study presented in the following pages reveals, U.S. foreign policy processes and structures, at least as they are related to multilateral relations in the areas of UNESCO's competence, remain very much in a state of disorder. Those aspects of U.S. foreign policymaking that contributed to the creation and intensification of UNESCO's problems in the first place are still present. Moreover, little seems to have been done so far to redress such a situation. It is my hope that this book will contribute to the emerging policy debate over this issue.

In writing this book, I am indebted to many people who have aided me in many ways. I am most deeply indebted to Jim Holderman, who gave me the opportunity to become a participant-observer in the UNESCO reform process. While in no way meaning to associate him with the content of this volume, he is to be commended for his initiative in providing his colleagues with opportunities to become involved in national and international service activities in order to foster their research programs. I hope that Jim Holderman's example will serve as a model for other academic administrators.

Jonathan Davidson and Jack Fobes have provided me with two extra sets of eyes and ears and have served well both as technical and substantive advisors. Indeed, many of the ideas in this volume are theirs. Given our close associations, however, I have found it impossible in many cases to distinguish my own thinking from theirs—I am certain that in far too many instances their ideas have gone uncited. For this I apologize and wish to give them a general acknowledgment now.

Other colleagues who have commented on various parts of this manuscript include Chad Alger, Larry Finkelstein, Peggy Galey, Harold Jacobson, Charles Kegley, Karen Mingst, Craig Murphy, Dick Nobbe, Jerel Rosati, Michael Schechter, and Pat Sewell. In this regard, special thanks go to Don Puchala, who convinced me that the most important story to be told from my studies of the crisis in UNESCO was that of the role of ideology in the U.S. foreign policy process. None of these individuals, of course, bears any responsibility for my views or for any mistakes contained in this volume.

Individuals who have given me inspiration or assistance in numerous other ways include Richard Aherne, Earl Black, Hershelle Challenor, Sam DePalma, Tom Duffy, Larry Eagleburger, Tom Forstenzer, Mike Genau, George Haley, Sandra Hall, Ed Hennelly, Tahlman Krumm, Scott Lawson, Millie Leatherman, Karl Lidstrom, Yemi Lijadu, Lois McHugh, Leonard Marks, Ivo Margan, Ursula Messe, Jamie Miller, Bill Mishler, Patty

Mitchell, Cassandra Pyle, Joe Rawley, Nancy Risser, Lee Sanders, Robert Schaaf, Cynthia Sprunger, Ralph Staiger, Judith Torney-Purta, Leonard Sussman, Gough Whitlam, David Wiley, David Wilson, Robert Woody, and others who must remain nameless. Also, my work was greatly aided by the skilled and conscientious research assistance of Rob Breckinridge, Robert Phillips, Gratzia Smeall, and Kurt Will. The contributions and sacrifices of Pat and Jessica Coate would take pages to recount, I will note simply that this study would not have possible without them. Finally, the research and drafting of this book have been aided or otherwise supported in part by the Department of Government and International Studies, the Institute of International Studies, and the James F. Byrnes International Center of the University of South Carolina, the United States National Commission for UNESCO, and Americans for the Universality of UNESCO.

My debt to all of the above is tremendous.

Roger A. Coate

CHAPTER ONE

Crisis in U.S./UNESCO Relations

On December 28, 1983, the U.S. government without formal consultation with its Western Group partners announced its intent to withdraw from the United Nations Educational, Scientific and Cultural Organization (UNESCO). At the end of 1984, after a twelve-month obligatory waiting period, the Reagan administration officially terminated U.S. membership in the organization. Twelve months later the United Kingdom followed the U.S. lead and also withdrew.[1] Thus, within a two-year period UNESCO had lost nearly 30 percent of its assessed budgetary base, as well as two of the member states that had been most responsible for the creation of the organization four decades earlier. UNESCO was clearly in the midst of a major crisis.

This state of affairs, however, should not be viewed as an isolated phenomenon.[2] As such events were occurring in UNESCO, there were mounting signs that financial and other problems were rapidly approaching crisis proportions in numerous institutions of international cooperation, including the United Nations (UN), itself. Symptoms of such troubled conditions abounded and even UN Secretary-General Javier Perez de Cuellar (1984) voiced public concern in this regard.

In the United States, government officials were reassessing their financial and other commitments to the United Nations and other multilateral institutions. An amendment to cut the U.S. contribution to the UN by $500 million over four years (that is, the Kassebaum Amendment) had passed the Senate by a two-thirds majority, failing only temporarily in the House. In the meantime financial problems in the United Nations had reached a point at which a special session of the General Assembly was to be convened in April 1986, devoted solely to financial questions. In addition, the viability of the international public legal order was being challenged as the Reagan

1

administration continued to disassociate itself with the Convention on the Law of the Sea, as well as with the legal jurisdiction of the International Court of Justice (ICJ) in political cases in general.

As these symptoms would seem to imply, at the core of this evolving "crisis in multilateralism" was the deteriorating relationship between international institutions and their largest contributor, the U.S. government. Indeed, it would seem to be more appropriate to describe the conditions not as a crisis in multilateralism but as a crisis of U.S. participation in multilateral relations. An evolving retreat from internationalism appeared to be rapidly giving way to full-scale unilateralism.

In the United States and elsewhere such conditions enlivened an ongoing policy debate over the future of U.S. participation in institutions of international cooperation. Traditional opponents of the United Nations have been intensifying their attacks. Especially active in this regard has been the Heritage Foundation. Its United Nations Assessment Project Study has produced numerous anti-UN tracts, such as Burton Yale Pines's (1984) edited study, *A World Without the U.N.: What Would Happen if the U.N. Shut Down*, and Roger A. Brooks's (1985) "The United Nations at 40: Myth and Reality." From another perspective supporters of the UN, such as United Nations Association (UNA-USA) President Edward Luck (1984–1985), have also been taking a critical look at the organization and the future of U.S. participation in it.

Yet, as John Ruggie (1985:344) has been quick to point out, "The academic community, from which one would hope for the dispassionate analyses that should inform policy debates, has barely been heard from at all." Relatively little systematic analysis has been conducted of the nature and causes of the evolving breakdown in multilateral cooperation and the role of U.S. participation therein.[3] Thus, we are hard pressed when asked to explain the phenomena. Moreover, there does not appear to exist a sound foundation in empirical research from which to provide the kind of policy-relevant knowledge called for by Ruggie.

This study endeavors to contribute to the building of a foundation by investigating one of the more dramatic episodes in recent U.S. multilateral relations—the evolving U.S. alienation and withdrawal from UNESCO. Why and how had the U.S. government become so alienated from this organization, which U.S. officials had been instrumental in designing at its creation? In both the proximate and more general sense how can we explain U.S. withdrawal? What lessons can we learn from the UNESCO experience for guiding future U.S. multilateral participation in science, education, culture, and communications? A desire to find answers to these and related questions provided the intitial impetus for this study. However, as research progressed it rapidly became apparent that at the center of the U.S. withdrawal from UNESCO was a phenomenon the implications of which extended far beyond a crisis in U.S. multilateral participation in UNESCO's spheres of interest—the capture of the U.S./UNESCO policy process by ideological forces.

BACKGROUND TO THE STUDY

It was on December 23, 1983, that National Security Advisor Robert McFarlane communicated President Reagan's approval of the State Department's recommendation to withdraw from UNESCO. In that memorandum McFarlane stressed the president's wish to expend every effort to "reform" UNESCO.[4]

> In pursuing the effort he wishes you to consider significant upgrading of our representation in UNESCO and appointment of a panel consisting of senior representatives of the academic community, the media and the corporate world to advise us over the next year. He is prepared to review the decision to withdraw should concrete changes materialize.[5]

In a follow-up memorandum of February 11, 1984, McFarlane outlined what he foresaw as a "major campaign to turn UNESCO around during 1984" and once again stressed the president's desire to upgrade U.S. representation and to establish a panel of experts "to provide the government with private counsel" concerning continued U.S. participation in the organization.[6] The call was reiterated on 2 March when the House Foreign Affairs Committee amended the Foreign Aid Bill to request that the president create a bipartisan panel.[7]

The formation of an advisory body made up of individuals from the press, academic, and business communities was officially announced on March 23, 1984. This Monitoring Panel on UNESCO was mandated the task of observing the activities and practices of, and developments within, UNESCO during 1984. The findings of the panel in this regard were to be reported to the secretary of state near the end of the year. James Holderman, the chairman of the U.S. National Commission for UNESCO and president of the University of South Carolina, was appointed by the president to serve as panel chairman.[8] In all, the advisory group consisted of fourteen members.[9] With the creation of the Monitoring Panel one element of the strategy that National Security Advisor McFarlane had outlined was initiated.

It was in the context of working with this panel that a possible paradox related to the Reagan administration's explanation of withdrawal first became apparent.[10] In reviewing government documents and interviewing numerous key participants both in Washington and Paris, including congressional staff members and State Department personnel, the official explanation did not seem to wash.[11] By most accounts, conditions in UNESCO in those problem areas cited as justification of withdrawal had improved markedly in recent years. Furthermore, although much talk about the need for reform in UNESCO was heard, high-level administration officials who were involved in the issue seemed to do little constructively to bring about organizational change. In practice the official policy toward UNESCO appeared to be one of getting the United States and other member states to quit the organization, not a policy of reforming UNESCO.

Congressional staffers, various Western diplomats in Paris, and numerous nongovernmental observers in the United States were beginning to arrive at a common conclusion: U.S. policy toward UNESCO had been captured by a small group of ideologues, who seemed to know or care little about UNESCO and its problems. In response, this study took on an additional, and to the author, a rather intriguing research question—how could such a small group of ideologically committed individuals have so completely captured and manipulated the foreign policy process? As suggested in the way this book has been organized, the answer to this question requires a thorough understanding of the evolution of U.S./UNESCO relations, as well as the ideological underpinnings of the administration's assault on UNESCO.

ORGANIZATION OF THE BOOK

The study begins with an examination of the justification for withdrawal that was given by Reagan administration officials. As mentioned earlier, when the official explanation is analyzed in the context of the various official documents and other sources upon which it was claimed to have been based, a paradox is evident. The United States withdrew from UNESCO at a time when the situation in the organization had been improving markedly from a U.S. perspective. Moreover, there was extremely little support in the official documentation for such a unilateral action. How then can the withdrawal be explained?

Chapter 3 explores this question by analyzing the evolution of U.S./UNESCO relations with specific regard to several deep-seated frustrations that appear to have existed within the administration. These frustrations came more clearly into focus midway through 1984, as U.S. officials presented UNESCO and its member states with a substantially revised statement of fundamental concerns about the organization. Again, however, an official explanation is found to be problematic: Much of the frustration inherent in the "fundamental" concerns appears to have resulted from confusion and/or misinformation regarding conditions within UNESCO and relations between the U.S. and UNESCO. The situation was such that no other member of the Western Group, not even the British, was willing to support the major structural changes proposed by the United States.

How then can the U.S. withdrawal best be explained? Was the announcement of the U.S. government's intent to withdraw part of a larger coherent strategy to force organizational change (that is, reform) within UNESCO? Or were administration officials simply determined, for whatever reasons, to get the United States out of what they perceived to be a totally unsalvageable international institution?

To answer these questions an analysis of U.S. participation in the reform process within UNESCO during 1984–1985 and an assessment of the outcomes of that process are undertaken in chapters 4 and 5. More specifically, U.S. participation is analyzed in the context of National Security Advisor McFarlane's requests that a major campaign be launched during 1984 to turn UNESCO around. This analysis is given further structure by comparing the actions and nonactions of Reagan administration officials in UNESCO with the strategy of boycott diplomacy employed in the case of U.S. withdrawal from the International Labor Organization (ILO) in the mid-1970s. Little evidence is found to support the hypothesis that U.S. withdrawal was in practice part of some larger coherent strategy to reform UNESCO. Although such a strategy might have been envisioned by Mr. McFarlane, the actions of others within the administration appear to have inhibited or prevented the strategy from materializing. Yet, given the constraints within which the reform process operated, a substantial amount of change was agreed upon and/or initiated during this period. But how can we account for the results, especially in the face of the feeble efforts of administration officials to secure any change? Furthermore, given the extent of reform and various other considerations, how can we best explain the U.S. withdrawal from UNESCO?

Chapter 6 expands the analysis of reform politics in order to answer these questions. The role of consensus within the Western Group, as well as the relative position of the United States therein, emerges as an important factor in explaining reform outcomes. There was a broad consensus in the Western Group on a variety of reform issues, and on those items where consensus existed reform outcomes were generally positive. However, with respect to a number of reform demands, U.S. officials were well outside that circle of consensus. Furthermore, an underlying tension existed within the Western Group over the nature of U.S. participation in the reform negotiations; U.S. involvement was not generally viewed as having been a constructive force.

When the findings of this analysis are added to those from previous chapters, a picture of the withdrawal process emerges that suggests the action was a predetermined move to terminate membership in UNESCO based largely on ideological grounds. As this analysis is expanded, it becomes clear that a small group of ideologues had captured and successfully manipulated the policy process with regard to U.S./UNESCO relations. The remainder of Chapter 6 endeavors to identify and explain the evolution of those factors and conditions that made an ideological takeover possible.

Chapter 7 builds on the results of the analysis in Chapter 6 and suggests various lessons to be learned from the UNESCO case for informing the policy debate over the future of U.S. multilateral relations in education, science, culture, and communications. Chapter 7 also explores various implications of the UNESCO case (especially as related to the impact of ideology on the policy process) for rethinking how we study, as well as conduct, U.S. multilateral relations. Under what conditions is the foreign policy process likely to be susceptible to ideological control and manipulation? What can be done to avoid such an outcome? Before attempting to address these questions, it is instructive to return to the beginning of the U.S. withdrawal from UNESCO and, at least in part, to reconstruct the events as they evolved.

NOTES

1. The government of Singapore, which had not been actively engaged in UNESCO for some years, also withdrew at the end of 1985.
2. I wish to thank Margaret Galey for drawing to my attention a number of years ago the need to place the UNESCO reform issue in the larger perspective of calls for comprehensive reform throughout the United Nations system. Such calls have been frequent over the last several decades. Furthermore, in the mid-1970s several actions were taken in an attempt to make the United Nations a more effective instrument for promoting international economic and social cooperation and development. A group of experts was appointed to consider the question in 1974. The following year they issued a report: *A New United Nations Structure for Global Economic Cooperation: Report of the Group of Experts on the Structure of the United Nations System* (UN Document E/AC.62/9). In addition, the Ad Hoc Committee on the Restructuring of the Economic and Social Sector of the United Nations System was created in 1975 (Resolution 3362(S-VII), September 16, 1975). A report was also issued by this body, whose conclusions and recommendations were endorsed by UN General Assembly (Resolution 32/197). Since that time various UN bodies, including the General Assembly, Economic and Social Council (ECOSOC), and the ILO, have confronted directly the issue of reform. In September 1986 a group of high-level intergovernmental experts ("Group of 18"), appointed by the president of the 40th General Assembly, issued a comprehensive report on administrative and budgetary reforms in the United Nations. The findings presented in this report were considered by the 41st General Assembly and there was agreement on a number of significant reforms, including the adoption of the budget by consensus. For a discussion of early United Nations efforts in this regard, see Meltzer (1978).
3. One notable exception has been the "United States Participation in International Organizations Study," directed by Margaret Karnes and Karen Mingst (1988). This project brings together nine social scientists

systematically focusing their attention on explaining changing patterns of U.S. participation in a wide variety of international organizations.

4. Robert C. McFarlane, NSC Memorandum of December 23, 1983, "Subject: Withdrawal from UNESCO."

5. Ibid.

6. Robert C. McFarlane, NSC Memorandum of February 11, 1984, "Subject: A Strategy for UNESCO."

7. Specifically, this amendment requested the president to do the following: (1) create a bipartisan panel of experts to review the question of future U.S. participation in UNESCO; (2) upgrade the U.S. mission to UNESCO and the appropriate office of the Department of State; and (3) consult the relevant committees of Congress before making or announcing a final decision (McHugh, 1984:10). It should also be noted that the intensity of action in Congress was far from routine for an issue related to a UN agency. Subcommittees of the foreign affairs and science and technology committees of the House of Representatives held numerous hearings about withdrawal and sent staff study missions to Paris. Also, these two committees requested the General Accounting Office (GAO) to review UNESCO's personnel, program, budget, and financial management. GAO investigators took up temporary residence in Paris between April 1 and July 15, producing a draft report with controlled circulation in mid-September and a final report, *Improvements Needed in UNESCO's Management, Personnel, Financial, and Budgetary Practices*, on November 30, 1984.

8. The U.S. National Commission for UNESCO was established by Congress (Public Law 565) in 1946 in fulfillment of an international legal obligation under Article VII of the UNESCO constitution. The commission provided liaison between UNESCO and its programs and the major American organizations interested in education, science, culture, and communications. Its role was to (1) disseminate information about UNESCO to the private sector, (2) prepare position papers for various U.S. governmental agencies, (3) initiate conferences and seminars on UNESCO themes, (4) ensure U.S. representation in UNESCO activities, (5) consult with the State Department concerning U.S. representation in UNESCO, and (6) conduct joint projects with other national commissions (U.S. National Commission for UNESCO, 1984:1).

9. The other panelists included Harold Anderson, Wendy Borcherdt, W. Glenn Campbell, Linda Chavez, George Haley, Marta Istomin, Leonard Marks, Ursula Meese, James Michener, Michael Novak, Arthur Ross, Frederick Seitz, and Jaques Torczyner.

10. In March 1984 the chairman of the Monitoring Panel asked the author to provide counsel to the panel on a private staff to operate in conjunction with, but external to, the staff provided by the Bureau of International Organization Affairs (IO Bureau) of the State Department. Duties included assisting the chairman in the construction of a set of specific criteria against which to measure and assess change in UNESCO, as well as representing the chairman on two field-study missions to UNESCO headquarters in Paris. Following the dissolution of the panel in December 1984, the author served as a consultant to the Executive Committee of the U.S. National Commission for UNESCO. In that capacity a special field-study mission was conducted to the 122nd Executive Board of UNESCO in September 1985.

11. Participant observation and elite interviewing were the main techniques used to gather data for this analysis. These activities were

undertaken between April 1984 and August 1987. During this period formal interviews and informal discussions were held with numerous current and former officials of the U.S. government, UNESCO, other member states of UNESCO, and various nongovernmental organizations. All interviews and discussions were conducted on the basis of anonymity, except in those cases where the interviewees voluntarily gave permission to be identified or quoted. Accordingly, such anonymity has been respected throughout this text.

These interviews and discussions included individuals from the Bureau of International Organization Affairs of the Department of State, the U.S. Mission to UNESCO in Paris, the Staff of the House of Representatives' Committee on Foreign Affairs, the General Accounting Office, and the U.S. National Commission for UNESCO, as well as former White House and other officials. Also, numerous other interviews and discussions were held during three trips to UNESCO Headquarters in Paris in July 1984, October 1984, and September 1985. Included were the Director-General and his immediate staff; most of the other highest-level UNESCO officials, as well as dozens of lower-level UNESCO personnel; numerous permanent delegates, Executive Board members, and/or mission staff of other Western Information Group member states, including participants most closely associated with the reform movement therein; selected officials of UNESCO's governing bodies, including the chairmen of the Executive Board and the Temporary Committee; and various permanent delegates and Executive Board members from Asia, Africa, and Latin America.

In addition to interviews and discussions, the visits to UNESCO headquarters provided the opportunity to observe formal and informal decision processes within UNESCO. Portions of the formal proceedings of the 120th and 122nd Session of the Executive Board, were monitored, as well as selected meetings of the Western Information Group. Also, informal exchanges between delegates within and around UNESCO headquarters were selectively observed. Information from participant observation experiences and the interviews and discussions provided the primary data base for the subsequent analysis of reform processes and outcomes.

CHAPTER TWO

Fog at Foggy Bottom:
The Paradox of Withdrawal

In his December 28, 1983 letter to UNESCO Director-General Amadou Mahtar M'Bow announcing the U.S. government's intent to withdraw, Secretary of State George Shultz expressed concern that "trends in the management, policy, and budget of UNESCO were detracting from the organization's effectiveness." He continued, "We believed these trends to be leading UNESCO away from the original principles of its constitution" (Shultz, 1983:2). In response, the U.S. government would formally terminate its membership in UNESCO on December 31, 1984.[1]

Department of State (DOS) officials leveled exceedingly serious charges at UNESCO. They claimed the organization's programs and personnel were "heavily freighted with an irresponsible political content," and that UNESCO answered to an agenda that was "consistently inimical to U.S. interests." The budget for educational programs (UNESCO's largest program area) was claimed to place "heavy emphasis on Soviet-inspired 'peace and disarmament' initiatives" (U.S. Department of State, October 31, 1984:2). Also, The DOS charged UNESCO with promoting "an endemic hostility toward the basic institutions of a free society . . . coupled with the promotion of statist theories of development" (U.S. Department of State, October 31, 1984). Functionaries of the organization were accused of leading a quest to organize "Orwellian freedom" on a global scale.[2] Furthermore, U.S. officials complained that UNESCO suffered from irresponsible and unrestrained budgetary expansion. In addition, management practices in the organization were labeled "atrocious." The DOS alleged that only one dollar out of every five was allocated to UNESCO's programs (U.S. Department of State, 1984). Although not stated publicly, administration officials accused the Director-General of using "deplorable" budget and personnel practices for personal gain and to support his personal rule over the organization.[3]

9

The charges were succinctly summarized into three primary concerns: (1) excessive politicization of UNESCO's programs and personnel; (2) promotion by UNESCO of statist theories; and (3) unrestrained budgetary expansion and poor management practices. These three concerns quickly became transformed into a litany used for justifying withdrawal.

The Reagan Administration's indictment was elaborated in a State Department document entitled *U.S./UNESCO Policy Review* (*Policy Review*), released on February 27, 1984. This report reviewed concerns in the context of each of the organization's principal sectors and in selected program areas: education; natural sciences, social sciences, culture, communications, human rights, copyright, status of women, and development. Also, the *Policy Review* briefly discussed UNESCO's management and budget and the institutional and political functioning of the organization.

The "Executive Summary" of this report charged that extraneous political debate on contentious issues and other forms of politicization dominated UNESCO's activities. Statist theories were said to supersede Western ideals in the organization's activities in science, education, and culture. Communications programs and activities were claimed to be governed by the concept of state control over free flows of information. Also, the review charged that concepts of collectivist rights (that is, "rights of peoples") prevailed over Western notions of individual rights that had been sanctioned in the Universal Declaration of Human Rights. In short, UNESCO was beyond salvation.

According to this "official explanation," then, the U.S. withdrawal action represented a rational response to a situation that had become wholly untenable. Indeed, as we will explore in subsequent chapters, the U.S./ UNESCO relationship had long been a troubled one. As was the case in many international governmental organizations (IGOs), troubled conditions had been mounting for some time in UNESCO. However, the nature and timing of U.S. withdrawal represented something of a paradox in U.S./UNESCO relations. The decision to withdraw came at a time when conditions in UNESCO had been improving markedly from a U.S. perspective. Moreover, the characterization of the situation provided by Assistant Secretary Gregory Newell and various other administration officials appears to have been quite misleading, especially when viewed in the context of the State Department's own documentation regarding the matter.

THE OFFICIAL RECORD:
THE 1983 DOS *REPORTS TO CONGRESS*

An analysis of the February 1983 State Department *Reports to Congress Required in Sections 108 and 109 of Public Law 97-241* challenges the claim that the situation in UNESCO was so serious as to warrant withdrawal.

These reports concluded that UNESCO's programs for the most part contributed to U.S. foreign policy goals and particular U.S. educational, scientific and cultural interests; vigorous continued U.S. participation was essential to protect U.S. interests; and UNESCO was not implementing any policy or procedure that would justify withholding funds under the law.

With respect to the three major concerns identified in the official explanation these reports provided fairly unambiguous assessments. For example, the main problem related to anti-Israeli activities was said to have basically been resolved a decade earlier. At that time three General Conference resolutions condemning Israel or limiting its participation had resulted in Congress voting a temporary prohibition on U.S. contributions. The actual crisis was short-lived, however, and in 1975 President Ford certified that the situation had been sufficiently rectified so as to allow funding to resume. The Israeli issue within UNESCO was further resolved in 1976 with the admission of Israel into the European regional program group.

According to the reports, the anti-Western bias in UNESCO's communications debates, a major concern of the U.S. government, had ebbed since 1981. The more pragmatic developing countries, the reports stated, had been re-defining their communications objectives away from exclusively ideological and political concerns and were concentrating more on developmental activities for bridging communications gaps. UNESCO's International Program for the Development of Communications (IPDC) had functioned since its founding in 1980 with U.S. support. The reports highlighted the IPDC as an example of the political distance UNESCO had traveled since the start of the 1970's. Secretariat officials were said to have been increasingly supportive of the new, more pragmatic approach (U.S. Department of State, 1983: p. 7).

Specifically, the discussion of UNESCO's Communications Sector focused on the activities of the unit's two main divisions: Development of Communications Systems and Free Flow of Information. The reports characterized the work of the first as largely unexceptionable. The work of the second, the Division of Free Flow of Information, was termed more sensitive and was said to have been influenced until recently by the anti-Western bias in UNESCO's communications debates. "This anti-Western bias has ebbed over the past two-years [1981–1982], however, and much of the most controversial work of the Division has been discarded or deemphasized." The ongoing activities of the Division were said to be carried out in a "more objective, even-handed manner" (U.S. Department of State, 1983:10). The Second-Medium Term Plan, which guides UNESCO activities until the end of the decade, "eliminated some of the most controversial matters" (U.S. Department of State, 1983:10). Also, this plan "provides a basis for programs which reflect U.S. and Western values" (U.S. Department of State, 1983:10).

The reports also discussed UNESCO's human rights programs. Acknowledging the minority status of the United States in the debate on established versus new human rights, the IO bureau concluded that "UNESCO can be expected to spawn numerous studies in these fields [new human rights], and the United States must be present at every stage of the debate to ensure that the programs stay within acceptable parameters" (U.S. Department of State, 1983:25). As was the case with respect to communications issues, the reports concluded that *continued U.S. leadership was essential*, not that the U.S. government should withdraw from UNESCO.

Moreover, excessive budgetary growth and mismanagement were not identified as being major problems from a U.S. perspective. While mentioning a perceived disregard of U.S. calls for greater budget stringency, the reports did not identify this condition as a major problem; nor were UNESCO's management practices targeted as an item of major concern.

Finally, the reports identified various direct and indirect economic benefits to the United States from its membership. UNESCO expenditures that directly benefited the United States amounted to about 40 percent of the value of the U.S. contribution. The expenditures included fellowships, procurement of U.S. equipment, consultants' fees, and payments to UNESCO staff members who are U.S. citizens. Also, U.S. prominence in UNESCO's sciences and education sectors was said to create markets for U.S. scientific and educational products and materials. Thus, when viewed together with the seven other ways listed in the February 1983 reports in which UNESCO membership served U.S. national interests, we are again led to question why the withdrawal decision was made when it was.

Ten months had elapsed between the publication of these reports and the announcement of withdrawal. Perhaps during that period either new information had surfaced regarding U.S./UNESCO relations or conditions in UNESCO had deteriorated from a U.S. perspective. Indeed, the latter reasoning would accord with the claims made by Assistant Secretary Newell when he transmitted his withdrawal recommendation request to the secretary of state and, ultimately, to the president. Newell had declared that his conclusion (that is, that continued U.S. participation in UNESCO did not serve U.S. interests) had been reached following a two-pronged effort during the summer and fall of 1983 to get UNESCO to respond constructively to U.S. concerns.[4] More specifically, he had commissioned an in-depth interagency review of U.S. participation in UNESCO and had ordered that a special effort be made at the 22nd General Conference of UNESCO in November 1983 to get UNESCO to respond favorably to U.S. expectations and concerns.[5]

THE U.S./UNESCO POLICY REVIEW

According to Department of State (DOS) officials, the interagency policy review of U.S. participation in UNESCO was not an isolated activity.

Beginning in 1981, the DOS conducted an eighteen-month review of ninety-six multilateral organizations in which the U.S. government participated and to which it contributed funding. Thus, the initial DOS review of UNESCO was undertaken with the same basic set of objectives as the reviews of numerous other multilateral organizations. These objectives were as follows:

1. To reassert American leadership in multilateral affairs
2. To implement a budgetary policy of zero-net program growth and significant absorption of nondiscretionary cost revenues for the first half of the decade
3. To obtain adequate U.S. representation with the secretariats of multilateral agencies
4. To reduce the financial burden imposed on all participants by an excessive number of lengthy international conferences
5. To advocate a role for the private sector in international organizational affairs

At the conclusion of this review process in May 1983 three general problems in multilateral agencies were identified: (1) undue politicization in United Nations specialized agencies; (2) promotion of statist theories especially with regard to the New International Economic Order (NIEO) and the New World Information and Communications Order (NWICO); and (3) excessive program and budgetary growth.[6]

The decision to conduct a special, more in-depth review of UNESCO was claimed to have been an outgrowth of this process. Six international organizations, including UNESCO, were said to have been identified as being problematic. However, according to the assistant secretary of state for International Organization Affairs, Gregory Newell (1983), in all organizations but UNESCO there had been significant, measurable improvements. Newell declared in his withdrawal recommendation that UNESCO, alone, had not responded constructively to U.S. initiatives for change.[7]

The UNESCO-specific interagency review was begun in mid-1983 following a meeting of senior-level officials of thirteen major agencies at which the formal mandate for the review was worked out.[8] These officials established two primary terms of reference: (1) an assessment of the management of U.S. relations with UNESCO; and (2) an assessment of the extent to which the organization served U.S. interests.[9] The State Department requested thirteen separate governmental departments and agencies with UNESCO-related mandates, eighty-three U.S. embassies and consulates, the U.S. National Commission for UNESCO, and numerous nongovernmental organizations to provide contributions to this study.[10]

The review had *not* yet terminated on December 16, when the withdrawal recommendation from Assistant Secretary Newell was sent to Secretary Shultz.[11] However, the IO Bureau had prepared a preliminary "Executive

Summary of [the] U.S./UNESCO Policy Review".[12] In part this document concluded the following:

> The main trends that emerge from the review—at this stage of its preparation—indicate that while the U.S. benefits in many tangible and intangible ways from its membership in UNESCO, the Organization is not absolutely vital to U.S. interests. . . . The results of the review, however, at this stage do not provide a clear, unequivocal answer to the question of whether the U.S. will be better served by remaining in UNESCO or by withdrawing.[13]

It would seem that a decisive determination was premature at that stage of the review process.[14]

The State Department's main statement justifying withdrawal, the *U.S./UNESCO Policy Review* (U.S. Department of State, February 27, 1984), which claimed to have been the product of this review process, was not produced until two months after the decision was announced. Moreover, analysis of the interagency contributions and other background materials upon which the *Policy Review* was said to have been based again provides a challenge to the official explanation. These materials indicate that undue politicization, promotion of statist theories, and excessive budgetary expansion and mismanagement in UNESCO were not generally perceived by the relevant governmental and nongovernmental experts and agencies to pose serious threats to important U.S. interests. Furthermore, the conclusions presented in the *U.S./UNESCO Policy Review* itself in many cases bore only marginal resemblance to the recommendations from these various bodies. In fact, none of the reports from any contributing body viewed the situation in UNESCO as being so problematical as to warrant withdrawal.

The recommendation of the interagency working group on science headed by the National Science Foundation (NSF) stated that "the scientific benefits the United States derives from participation in UNESCO clearly warrant our continued participation."[15] While identifying certain organizational shortcomings in UNESCO as raising problems from a U.S. perspective, the NSF report focused much more extensively and critically on problems of funding, coordinating, and managing U.S. participation in the organization.

The Department of Education's report on UNESCO's education sector stated that, when the U.S. is well represented, it usually prevails in negotiations that are considered to be fundamental to U.S. interests.[16] Most of UNESCO's education agenda was said not to be ideological, political, or contentious. The most troublesome area, standard-setting, was said to represent only a small percentage of what UNESCO does. Moreover, UNESCO was viewed as a stabilizing institutional influence clearly serving U.S. interests. The report claimed that "UNESCO virtually alone maintains the effort to develop effective methodologies for eradicating illiteracy."[17]

However, in the *Policy Review* a number of alterations had been made that changed in important ways the tenor of the Department of Education's report. First, a strong statement about U.S. policy having been successful when and where it counts had been eliminated. Second, a general statement about most of UNESCO's General Conference agenda in education not being politicized was greatly understated. Referring only to UNESCO's activities in illiteracy eradication and its clearinghouse and information network functions, the *Policy Review* stated that "much of UNESCO's educational activities in these areas are not ideological, political, or contentious."[18]

Similarly, throughout the report, findings that portray UNESCO in a favorable light have either been omitted or restated. For example, reference to a recent State Department survey of U.S. overseas posts had been dropped from a section on economic and human development that had been included. That survey had found that UNESCO field programs were highly praised and that some ministries of education tended to trust UNESCO more than other international organizations or bilateral agencies.

In that same section the phrase "UNESCO constitutes a stabilizing institutional influence clearly in the United States interests" had been reinterpreted to read: "the building of educational infrastructures contributes to international peace and stability."[19] Also, the phrase "UNESCO virtually alone maintains the effort to develop effective methodologies for eradicating illiteracy" had been transformed to "UNESCO leads the international effort to eradicate illiteracy."[20] In fact, if one goes back to the original USAID (1983a:2) report from which the data used in this section were taken, even stronger support for remaining in UNESCO had been articulated: "UNESCO serves several functions in educational development unique to all other development agencies. . . . No other bilateral or multilateral development agency is equipped or willing to serve in these capacities. For those purposes alone, the U.S. should not cut off funding to UNESCO completely."

The story is the same with respect to culture and communication. The Smithsonian Institution (1983:2) argued that it was "essential that United States access to UNESCO be maintained and that UNESCO's essential programs not be crippled for want of U.S. financial support and leadership." With respect to UNESCO's Communication Sector the USAID report (1983b:2) concluded, "In sum, basic U.S. interests in communications are reasonably well served. U.S. withdrawal would not enhance the achievement of those U.S. objectives." Of course, none of these omissions or changes by itself would be overly problematical. However, when multiplied throughout the entire *Policy Review*, the effect becomes significant.

Thus, while such charges as are made in the *U.S./UNESCO Policy Review* might appear to have been damning, many indicate either a basic lack of knowledge about UNESCO and multilateral institutions in general or a distorted representation of the data upon which such charges were claimed to have been based.[21] In this regard it should be noted that politicization discussed in the *Policy Review* relates primarily to debates among member states in the governing bodies, not to UNESCO itself. Unfortunately, however, Mr. Newell and various other high-level officials consistently failed to make such a distinction. Also, the approach taken in UNESCO's programs toward matters related to peace and disarmament has generally not been that of the Soviet Union. Several State Department experts on UNESCO have acknowledged that an American staff member of UNESCO had been the chief architect of the organization's approach to disarmament.

In conclusion, if one is searching for support for withdrawal in these interagency assessments of UNESCO, it is hard to find. Materials from the U.S. National Commission for UNESCO, including the views of a multitude of nongovernmental organizations (NGOs), display a similar lack of support. In fact, these materials enumerate the case for staying in. The National Commission had conducted several reviews of U.S.-UNESCO relations in recent years, including an intensive conference in June 1982 devoted exclusively to undertaking a "Critical Assessment of Relations with UNESCO." The five working groups at this conference concluded that U.S. neglect toward the organization had been an important factor contributing to UNESCO's problems. These groups also concluded unanimously that the U.S. should stay in UNESCO and increase its participation and exert a strong leadership role.[22]

Another review, conducted by the commission as part of the 1983 interagency review, came to similar conclusions. After considering the assessments of the Department of State and the U.S. delegation to the then recently concluded 22nd General Conference of UNESCO, as well as those it had previously conducted, the National Commission debated the issue at its annual meeting on December 16, 1983 and overwhelmingly adopted a resolution calling for continued U.S. membership. While the resolution criticized various aspects of UNESCO, it concluded that it was in the national interest for the U.S. government to remain in the organization and to seek change from within.[23]

Moreover, a U.S. House of Representatives staff report (1984a:31) called various of Mr. Newell's conclusions into question.

> In sum, the Department's conclusion that UNESCO is 'politicized' and acts against U.S. interests because it spends $1 million on disarmament studies, entertains discussions and adopts resolutions on peoples' rights, and provides minimal support for refugee education seems to be an attempt to denigrate the Organization's performance on extraordinarily weak grounds. . . . [I]t is difficult to sustain the argument that 'politicization' should serve as a basis for immediate, unilateral withdrawal.

Similarly, while statist theories, such as those identified with the concept of a New World Information and Communications Order (NWICO), have been debated in UNESCO's governing bodies, "it is dubious whether NWICO issues should have provided a major justification for U.S. withdrawal" (U.S. House of Representative, 1984a:32). Again, there seems to have been some confusion between the positions promoted by certain member states and the actual activities of the organization.

Finally, the data presented in the *Policy Review* raise serious questions regarding the extent to which excessive and uncontrolled budgetary expansion might have served as a reason for withdrawal. In keeping with a policy of promoting budget stringency in all IOs, the U.S. delegation to the 22nd General Conference had demanded a zero-growth budget for the 1983–1984 biennium. When only eleven other delegations supported such a resolution, the Nordic Group (Sweden, Finland, Denmark, Norway, and Iceland) proposed a compromise between zero-growth and the Director-General's proposed $384.8 million.[24] This proposal called for a $10.4 million cut to $374.4 million. The U.S. delegation was the only one to vote against this compromise.

Furthermore, the moderating actions of UNESCO's Director-General (DG) in this regard were clearly acknowledged in the *Policy Review*:

> The Secretariat's unexpected move at the General Conference to $374.4 million . . . can be viewed as a significant conciliatory step in our direction. There was a genuine sense of disappointed surprise and outright betrayal at the Secretariat's action on the part of many Third World delegations. In the end, they did as they were asked and supported the Secretariat, realizing that they had the votes to do otherwise (U.S. Department of State, February 27, 1984:165).

Certainly such an action should not be viewed as a tyrannical move by the majority to impose its will on the states of the Western Group; nor does the outcome appear to represent uncontrolled budgetary growth. In this regard, it should be noted that decisionmaking in the General Conference on such matters is based on a consensual concurrent majority system.

It could, of course, be hypothesized that each of the individual agencies that had contributed to the *Policy Review* saw only a small piece of the UNESCO problem. When the IO bureau in the State Department put all of these pieces together, it is possible that a very different overall picture emerged. However, given the uniform nature of the numerous agencies' contributions in support of continued and enhanced U.S. participation, it is difficult to imagine that such a scenario could have occurred. Moreover, an internal 1983 State Department draft document, which was based on the findings of these numerous agency contributions, concluded the following:

> Unquestionably, the more active the participation, the greater will be our visibility, credibility and influence. The broad domestic constituencies concerned (educators, physical scientists, social scientists, cultural interest groups, communication and information

specialists, and the various business and industrial interests affected by UNESCO activities) have all indicated that there is a substantial 'pay off' in such a leadership role. This is dramatically illustrated by the success of U.S. efforts in recent years to combat efforts to undermine free press values and the concept of a free flow of information.[25]

The overall picture was not one that seemed to lend strong support to such an immediate and drastic unilateral action. What else, then, could have happened after February 1983 which could have potentially negated such positive assessments?

UNESCO 22ND GENERAL CONFERENCE

In addition to the in-depth review, a second major event did occur later in the year. The 22nd General Conference of UNESCO was held in fall 1983 and had concluded just one month before the U.S. withdrawal announcement. As mentioned above, the results of this conference, along with those of the interagency reviews just considered, were claimed by Assistant Secretary Newell to have been important considerations in his withdrawal decision.

Yet, the outcome of this General Conference also had been relatively positive from a U.S. perspective. In his report to the U.S. National Commission in December 1983 the head of the U.S. delegation to the conference, Ambassador Designate Edmund Hennelly, concluded that his personal balance sheet showed that the conference had been a "clear plus for the U.S."[26] Appearing before a congressional subcommittee hearing in April 1984, Hennelly was much more specific in this regard. He testified that the instructions given the U.S. delegation were as follows:

1. To ensure to the extent possible that the conference was non-politicized
2. To eliminate from UNESCO's communications sector programs that limited press freedom or the free flow of information throughout the world. Additionally, if possible, to introduce into UNESCO programs Western free press concepts and values
3. To bring the proposed budget down to acceptable levels
4. To make a clear distinction in UNESCO programs between traditional human rights and emerging peoples' rights concepts that need additional definition and study
5. To deflect the Soviet drive to increase the number of UNESCO programs centered on peace and disarmament
6. To steer the organization towards a more Western orientation in a number of activities, including the elections of individuals to leadership positions and elections of member states to the organization's various boards and committees[27]

In reviewing the conference results in the context of these objectives he again noted that the "pluses outnumbered the losses."[28]

Hennelly then briefly summarized the positive results.

1. The conference had been the least politicized in recent memory.
2. The communications sector had been improved: "Programs which could have hampered the workings of a free press were deleted or substantially modified, and several Western concepts were added, e.g., the concept that censorship, including state censorship, is an important impediment to the free flow of information, and the idea that the press has a critical role to play in exposing abuses of power."[29]
3. An appropriate distinction was made between traditional human rights and people's rights.
4. The proposed biennial UNESCO budget had been reduced by $10 million dollars, from $384 million to $374 million. This reduction corresponded to a proposal by a subgroup of Western countries (Nordic states). While the compromise figure did not represent zero real growth, Hennelly argued that it was significant in that "some on the [U.S.] delegation, including myself, believe the Director-General might have made further reductions, but was prevented from doing so because the Nordic compromise constituted a 'political floor' below which he could not go."[30]
5. Hennelly described what he termed a victory over a proposal by a group of Third World delegates to get UNESCO to establish a code of conduct over transnational corporations.
6. The United States had been elected to all five of the major committees for which U.S. participants had sought election. Also, the U.S.-supported candidate for the chairmanship of the Executive Board won election.
7. The atmosphere of the conference was a congenial one from a U.S. perspective. "The debate in most cases was largely free of polemics. U.S. views were listened to with respect, our positions were recognized as legitimate, and our concerns were taken into account to a very large degree."[31]

On the negative side Hennelly identified four concerns:

1. The zero real growth budget desired by the U.S. was not achieved.
2. The conference had accepted an invitation from the government of Bulgaria to hold the 23rd General Conference in Sophia. The U.S. and a number of Western European delegations had opposed the decision, largely on financial grounds.
3. U.S. proposals that would have placed greater reliance on the role of the private sector in UNESCO's spheres of activities did not triumph. "Most UNESCO member states believe that the state is the most

important agent for advancing international cooperation in science, for combatting illiteracy, and so forth. This view continued to prevail during the conference."[32]

4. Soviet-inspired peace and disarmament initiatives had not been eliminated in a number of program areas.

Such an overall positive assessment of the conference was compatible with the comments of the U.S. Permanent Delegate to UNESCO, Ambassador Jean Gerard, who told the members of the U.S. National Commission, "We can take pride in the work and in many of the accomplishments of this General Conference. It has been marked, in many instances, by agreement on issues about which such agreement has not always been easy. Most importantly, I believe—I hope—that we have laid the groundwork here for greater efficiency and effectiveness in UNESCO's programs."[33] These remarks were consistent with the general tone of her speech before the National Commission the preceding year.[34]

Curiously then, a review of the results of the two main activities that Assistant Secretary Newell had claimed led him to his conclusion (that is, that further U.S. participation in UNESCO did not serve the interests of the United States) belies such a conclusion. UNESCO appears to have been responding constructively to U.S. concerns. It would appear as though the primary basis for the withdrawal action was not that officially stated in justification of the action. But how, then, can the withdrawal action be explained?

NOTES

1. According to the UNESCO *Constitution* (Article II.6), "Any Member State or Associate Member of the Organization may withdraw from the Organization by notice addressed to the Director-General. Such notice shall take effect on 31 December of the year following that during which the notice was given." Thus, the withdrawal process is not an immediate one.

2. This claim was made by Assistant Secretary Newell in transmitting his withdrawal recommendation to the secretary of state; personal interviews, summer 1984.

3. Personal interviews, summer 1984.

4. Ibid.

5. Ibid.

6. The relationship between the basic set of policy priorities and two of the three general findings (such as, undue politicization and promotion of statist theories) is not clear. Also, it is interesting to note that one of the five main criteria seems to have been largely disregarded in the UNESCO case. In fact, Assistant Secretary Newell and various other administration officials went out of their way to emasculate the one statutory (PL 79-565) private sector body, the U.S. National Commission for UNESCO, charged with advisory responsibility. As will be discussed later, the commission was zero funded and its administrative support was split between bureaucratic offices. Furthermore, the assistant secretary failed even to seek this private sector body's advice

before finalizing his plan to withdraw the U.S. government from UNESCO (U.S. House of Representatives, 1984a:25–26).

7. Personal interviews, summer 1984.

8. Note that Assistant Secretary Newell did not attend this meeting in person but was represented by subordinates.

9. However, note that the *U.N./UNESCO Policy Review* addressed only the second of these two basic terms of reference. Furthermore, as we shall see, it appears as though the assessment of how the U.S. government has managed its participation in UNESCO was basically ignored by Reagan administration officials in making the withdrawal decision.

10. The thirteen agencies included: Library of Congress, National Academy of Sciences, National Endowment for the Arts, National Endowment for the Humanities, National Science Foundation (NSF), Smithsonian Institution, Agency for International Development (USAID), U.S. Commission for Library and Information Sciences, Department of Education, Department of the Interior, Department of State, U.S. Geological Survey, and the U.S. Information Agency. The Department of Education was responsible for organizing the contributions related to UNESCO's education mandate. The National Science Foundation coordinated the contributions of a large sub-group focusing on the natural sciences. The Smithsonian Institution organized the contributions related to cultural programs.

11. It is interesting to note that on that same day Assistant Secretary Newell, speaking before the annual meeting of the U.S. National Commission for UNESCO, told the commissioners that no one had made a recommendation to the secretary of state.

12. Note that the "Executive Summary," which was produced at the time Assistant Secretary Newell made his withdrawal recommendation to the secretary of state, bears little resemblance to the "Executive Summary" issued in February 1984. Curiously, the December 1983 version reflected much more accurately the content of the numerous agencies' contributions and recommendations. It did not seem to provide support for the claims being made by the assistant secretary.

13. U.S. Department of State, "Executive Summary of U.S./UNESCO Policy Review," no date.

14. Much ambiguity existed with regard to potential financial and other impacts of U.S. withdrawal. For example, under UNESCO-sponsored marketing agreements, seventy governments had lifted barriers to the importation and circulation of books, magazines, works of art, and scientific, cultural, and communications instruments, equipment, and materials. It has been estimated that the loss of sales of audiovisual equipment alone might total $130 million —an amount two and a half times larger than the annual assessed contribution to UNESCO (U.S. House of Representatives, March 1, 1985:14, 32). Regardless of the accuracy of such estimates, what is important to note is that the ambiguity remained at the time the decision was taken.

15. U.S. National Science Foundation, "Natural Sciences in UNESCO: A U.S. Interagency Perspective," Washington, D.C., 1983.

16. U.S. Department of Education, "U.S. Policy Review of UNESCO and U.S. Participation in UNESCO: Education Sector," Washington, D.C., 1983.

17. Ibid., pp. 6–7.

18. U.S. Department of State, *U.S./UNESCO Policy Review*, February 27, 1984, p. 8.

19. Ibid., p. 5.

20. Ibid.

21. Mr. Newell's action memorandum to Secretary of State Shultz, proposing withdrawal, was characterized by misstatements and innuendos about UNESCO. Several Department of State officials have confided that in that document Newell's representation of the findings of the policy review was emotionally charged, slanted, and in some places even inaccurate. As I discussed earlier, for example, at one point he charged that UNESCO was organizing "Orwellian freedom" and that only 20 percent of UNESCO's budget goes to its programs. Neither of these statements was true. Furthermore, Newell's memorandum provided no options or objective information for a reasoned and independent decision.

A proposed withdrawal strategy accompanied Newell's withdrawal recommendation. This document outlined a strategy for state manipulation of the press coverage of withdrawal. For example, the memorandum read, "Day 3: Press and public. Letters to Editors. Articles—Washington Post, New York Times, etc. Day 4: Press and public. Articles of support by private sector individuals" (*The Guardian*, Monday, January 23, 1984). It is noteworthy that such activities were being proposed by those same individuals who decried statist orientations in the communications activities of UNESCO. Furthermore, when confronted at the 119th Executive Board with claims that the U.S. government had orchestrated a press campaign, Ambassador Gerard countered that those who made such claims were simply falling victim to the manner in which they, themselves, viewed such things (for example, press/state relations).

22. U.S. National Commission for UNESCO, *Critical Assessment of Relations with UNESCO*, June 1982.

23. "Transcript" of the 47th Annual Meeting of the U.S. National Commission for UNESCO, December 16, 1983.

24. The DG's original proposed budget would have represented 9.7 percent real program growth.

25. "Management of U.S. Participation in UNESCO." Internal working document, Bureau of International Organization Affairs, U.S. Department of State, 1983

26. Edmund Hennelly was an executive officer of Mobil Oil and a presidential appointee to the U.S. National Commission for UNESCO. He had been a strong Reagan supporter during the presidential election campaign. The U.S. permanent representative to UNESCO, Jean Gerard, served as the deputy head of the delegation. U.S. National Commission for UNESCO: *What Are the Issues Concerning the Decision of the United States to Withdraw from UNESCO?* Washington, D.C., 1984.

27. U.S. House of Representatives, April 25, 26, and May 2, 1984: 21–22.

28. Ibid.

29. Ibid.

30. Ibid.

31. Ibid.

32. Ibid.

33. U.S. National Commission for UNESCO, *What Are the Issues*, 1984:5.

34. U.S. National Commission for UNESCO, *Critical Assessment*, 1982.

CHAPTER THREE

U.S./UNESCO Relations in Retrospect

Reagan administration officials continued to profess the litany of politicization, statist theories, and uncontrollable budgetary growth and mismanagement throughout 1984 and beyond in justification of withdrawal from UNESCO. However, in mid-1984 Assistant Secretary Newell suddenly shifted these concerns to a subordinate status. While still listed as problems, they were apparently no longer of fundamental importance; their exact status, however, was unclear.

Mr. Newell presented a revised set of main concerns in a July 13, 1984 letter to the UNESCO Director-General.[1] The administration's new official position specified three reforms that were said to be of "fundamental importance":

1. Creating mechanisms to ensure that important UNESCO decisions and programs enjoy the support of all major groups, including the Western Group
2. A return by UNESCO to concentration upon its original purposes
3. The assumption by member states of their rightful authority in the organization, through strengthening of the General Conference, and in particular, the Executive Board

This statement of fundamental concerns was accompanied by a number of proposed organizational changes. Yet, time and again in the months that followed, Mr. Newell made it clear that such recommendations should not be viewed as the list of reforms necessary to keep the United States in UNESCO. He consistently and quite adamantly refused to provide such a "laundry list," as he called it.[2]

This revised set of fundamental concerns had not been mentioned in Newell's December 1983 memorandum to Secretary of State Shultz recommending withdrawal. Yet, these concerns point to several general frustrations that appear to have underlain the administration's approach to UNESCO.

DEEPER FRUSTRATIONS UNDERLYING WITHDRAWAL

Substantial frustration seems to have been associated with a perceived inability to use UNESCO effectively as an instrument of foreign policy. In the words of one IO Bureau official,

> there was a deep frustration, not just by Administration officials but also by careerists who had grown weary from the struggle to persevere. U.S. officialdom is accustomed to seeing short-term wins or gains when, in point of fact, we are engaged in a long-term struggle for the minds of men in the UNESCO context. This is something this administration (ironically, given its ideological orientation) could never understand.[3]

While attempts to beat back Soviet and Third World challenges to the concept of free flow of information had been rather successful over the years, the perception among many high-level administration officials was to the contrary. UNESCO was seen as being controlled by an anti-Western/Third World majority that ran roughshod over minority interests. Also, there seems to have existed considerable frustration over the inability to control outcomes, generally speaking. Those member states who, in combination, contribute the overwhelming majority of UNESCO's budget were perceived not to have sufficient control over how the money was spent (that is, over the program and budget). To overcome such a condition, administration officials proposed several sweeping actions:

- A strengthened drafting and negotiating group at the General Conference, directed to consider contentious issues, which issues would be decided only upon the basis of full agreement among all the geographic groups represented
- The introduction of a similar mechanism for the Executive Board
- A procedure for voting on the budget that would ensure that no budget would pass without the affirmative support of members who together contribute at least 51 percent of the organization's funds

These measures in combination would effectively give a handful of member states, including the United States, extensive control over UNESCO's program and budget.[4]

Administration officials also seemed to be frustrated with the expansion of UNESCO's programs and activities to incorporate concerns they thought to be inappropriate. These officials wished to purge from UNESCO all political debates that questioned the legitimacy of the established global economic and information orders. Thus, they called for a return to UNESCO's original principles. As we shall later explore, however, the very nature of these calls revealed that these officials knew very little about UNESCO or the history of U.S./UNESCO relations.

In addition, officials lamented the perceived loss of effective authority of UNESCO's delegate bodies to the Director-General. Administration officials viewed the resulting imbalance of authority as having worked against U.S. interests, as well as having led to flagrant management abuses.

These concerns point to conditions that were not particular to UNESCO. Yet, as pointed out earlier, administration officials argued that UNESCO had been an especially troublesome case. While other international government organizations (IGOs) were said to have demonstrated improvement from a U.S. perspective, UNESCO was said to have continued down a wayward anti-Western path. The improvements of recent years they saw as having been mainly cosmetic and temporary. With respect to fundamental U.S. concerns, they argued, UNESCO persisted primarily to promote and to serve anti-U.S. ends.[5] Thus, they saw withdrawal as both a rational and responsible action.

Again, however, the official explanation is problematic. An analysis of the evolution of U.S./UNESCO relations challenges the claim that UNESCO has promoted anti-U.S. ends or that U.S. officials cannot exert effective influence in the organization when the quality of U.S. participation is high and U.S. desires are reasonable and clearly articulated. After briefly discussing the origins of UNESCO and U.S. participation in the organization, the remainder of this chapter analyzes the evolution of U.S./UNESCO relations with respect to the revised statement of U.S. concerns.

AMERICAN INFLUENCE IN UNESCO

The Origins of U.S. Participation

Unlike many other post-war universal IGOs, UNESCO was largely European in origin.[6] Active U.S. involvement in the planning of UNESCO came relatively late and was begun only after it had become clear to U.S. observers that an intergovernmental organization in education would likely be established with or without U.S. participation.

Roots of UNESCO can be traced to both the Paris-based Institut International de Cooperation Intellectuelle (IICI), which was associated with the League of Nations, and the Geneva-based International Bureau of Education (IBE). Within these bodies a tradition of transnational intellectual cooperation in education, science, and culture had evolved over two decades.[7]

However, the more immediate stimulus to establish such an agency at the close of World War II was an outgrowth of British initiatives. A call for the United Nations to establish an "International Organization for Education" was heard in London as early as 1941. At that time the joint commission of the British Board of Education and the British Council made a recommendation to the unofficial representatives of the allied United Nations in the London International Assembly. In turn, the assembly unanimously adopted a resolution echoing the recommendation in January 1943.

This call set the stage for the second meeting of the Conference of Allied Ministers of Education (CAME), which met in London shortly thereafter. This body, which had been established at the invitation of the chairman of the British Council, was initially comprised of the eight ministers of education of United Nations governments located in London plus British representatives. The main focus of this body was post-war educational reconstruction. Before the end of 1943 representatives in CAME, many of whom were also members of the London International Assembly, expressed the need for creating a permanent international organization for education.

Similar interests were being expressed around this same time in the United States both inside and outside the national government. For example, Under Secretary of State Sumner Wells authorized the department's General Advisory Committee to consider "possible establishment and operation of an international cultural organization" (Sewell, 1975:56). The committee proposed the creation of an international agency for educational relations and cooperation. However, little immediate action ensued. The creation of an international security organization was viewed as being a first order of business that took precedence (Ninkovich, 1981:78–79).

Representatives of the U.S. government did eventually join the discussions in CAME as observer participants. And soon, external pressures began to mount for more extensive U.S. involvement. Representatives of the British Board of Education and the British Council approached State Department officials concerning the upgrading of U.S. participation. Again, however, U.S. officials did not respond immediately.

Pressures also began to mount within the U.S. government as it became apparent to U.S. observers in London that the representatives in CAME were rapidly moving toward the establishment of a more permanent arrangement. In November 1943 the U.S. observer in London, Ralph Turner, cabled the State Department that "we should enter the conference as quickly as possible if we are to affiliate with it at all, because the longer we stay out the less fluid it will become and the more difficult it will be to secure modifications in its organization or objectives."[8]

The U.S. response was a vigorous one: "Americans, wanting an originating role, tried the gambit of starting afresh. In April 1944, a U.S. delegation was sent to London for the announced purpose of opening up CAME and making of it ' an entirely new organization'" (Sewell, 1975:63).[9] The U.S. delegation brought before the conference a draft constitution, entitled "Suggestions for the Development of the Conference of Allied

Ministers of Education into the United Nations Organization for Educational and Cultural Reconstruction."

The nature of this U.S. government initiative stood in marked contrast to the British Government's more incrementalist approach. However, most of the CAME participants, including those from the United Kingdom, readily accommodated the U.S. suggestions (Sewell, 1975:64). In fact, a small drafting committee, headed by the leader of the U.S. delegation, J. William Fulbright, soon drew up and circulated a modified draft constitution.

Meanwhile, officials of the French government were attempting to recapture a more prominent role. Thus, the French representative to the United Nations Conference on International Organization in San Francisco called for a general conference to establish an Organisation International de Cooperation Intellectuelle. Both French and Dutch authorities desired to host such a conference. However, the British government moved quickly to announce that it would host a conference for such a purpose beginning November 1, 1945. Not only did this displease French authorities but also those from the United States, who had not been consulted about such an action. However, holding the conference in London did assure that the CAME draft constitution (hereafter, "CAME/U.S. draft") with its substantial U.S. input would serve as the basic working document.[10]

When the representatives of forty-four governments met on November 1, 1945, the negotiations centered primarily around two alternative draft constitutions: the CAME/U.S. draft and a French version. As we will explore below, the resulting organizational charter represented a compromise between these two competing drafts.

At U.S. insistence UNESCO's mandate had been expanded to encompass communications. Thus, Article I, Section 2 of the constitution called on the organization to "Collaborate in the work of advancing the mutual knowledge and understanding of peoples through all means of mass communication and to that end, recommend such international agreements as may be necessary to promote the free flow of ideas by word or image." Mass communication, as well as mass education, were to be basic pillars of this new world order. Indeed, from the beginning the communications work of UNESCO was a predominant concern of U.S. policy-makers.

In brief summary then, the U.S. Government did not push vigorously for the creation of such an organization; only after it became apparent to U.S. observers that an organization would emerge did State Department officials undertake a strong initiative to influence the nature of the emerging entity. They endeavored to make certain that UNESCO would be consistent with a U.S. vision of an acceptable world order and that the organization would be open to U.S. influence. As the analysis in the following section reveals, for the most part such efforts appear to have been successful.

The Best of Times, the Worst of Times

Although a constitution for this new organization had been agreed upon and brought into force when the delegates met in Paris in 1946 for the first General Conference, a number of important concerns regarding UNESCO's future had yet to be confronted. Not the least of these was the selection of the first Director-General (DG). The constitution placed substantial authority and responsibility in this position. Furthermore, from a U.S. perspective the selection of a DG took on added significance. It was assumed that the Directorship-General would go to a U.S. citizen.[11] After the London Conference in November, 1945, U.S. delegate William Benton wrote Secretary of State Byrnes, "The United States has asked for nothing thus far. The Preparatory Commission is located in London. The executive secretary is an Englishman. The headquarters of UNESCO are to be in Paris. It is generally understood that the United States Government can nominate the permanent secretary-general if it so desires (quoted in Sewell, 1975:105–106). From all indications State Department officials did desire to do so.

However, President Truman's choice for the position, Francis Biddle, received little strong support, even from within the State Department, where resentment apparently existed over what was seen as an overt act of patronage (Ninkovich, 1981:97–98). When all was done, it was Julian Huxley from the United Kingdom who was elected as UNESCO's first Director-General, not a U.S. citizen.[12]

Huxley's appointment was a matter of considerable concern to many U.S. officials. Not only was he perceived to be a weak administrator but, in addition, an atheist and left-wing sympathizer.[13] The U.S. delegates were able, however, to negotiate two concessions regarding Huxley's selection. First, his term of office was to be self-limited to two years. Second, he was to appoint a U.S. citizen as Deputy Director-General who would be responsible for administration, personnel and finance. While not tremendously significant, this early skirmish foretold much about the future of U.S./UNESCO relations.

While U.S. participation in UNESCO was not a major component of U.S. foreign policy during this period, U.S. officials did attempt to use the organization as a policy instrument. UNESCO was to serve as a mechanism for projecting a U.S. vision of a preferred world order. The creation of a global liberal democratic order was viewed as the raison d'être of the organization's communications mandate. Beginning in 1946 an attempt was launched to assign UNESCO the legitimizing role in establishing a world-wide radio network (Sewell, 1973:162). In making the plea for the network, U.S. representative William Benton argued that mass communications was UNESCO's most important area of work (Sathyamurthy, 1964:160).

However, after 1946 the proposal slowly faded into obscurity. "About 1950 . . . similar proposals appeared. These in turn were dropped before the end of the Korean War, at a time when vocal segments of the American public were turning against UNESCO because of what were frequently termed its communist tendencies" (Sewell, 1973:162). Policy frustrations and the circumstances surrounding them were indeed symptomatic of larger concerns related to the U.S. government's participation in UNESCO. "Despite the interest taken by the [State] Department in 1947, its approach to UNESCO through 1949 was largely reactive and negative, more to assure the failure of Communist penetration than American dominance" (Ninkovich, 1981:154).

As the decade of the 1950s opened, officials in Washington still voiced high hopes for UNESCO. Speaking to a meeting of the U.S. National Commission, President Truman pledged strong support for UNESCO, whose work he termed "vitally important." While predicting that UNESCO could be successful in time, he cautioned against expecting success too quickly. "In organizations like [UNESCO] . . . , if over a generation or two generations we come close to accomplishing our purpose, we have made great progress."[14] Perhaps Truman personally had reason for optimism. Explicitly building on the development theme in the president's Point Four Doctrine of 1949 and at the urging of the U.S. delegation, UNESCO had decided to participate actively in the United Nations' Expanded Programme of Technical Assistance (EPTA).

At the same time, however, other important actors in the U.S. government, including William Benton, were becoming upset at UNESCO's perceived unwillingness to face up to the "political issues of war and peace."[15] The first half of the decade of the 1950s brought numerous strains to U.S./UNESCO relations. The Korean War, McCarthyism, and the admission of the Soviet Union as a member all had important impacts on U.S. participation in this organization.

Apparently with little reluctance the U.S. State Department set out to mobilize UNESCO and its facilities as propaganda instruments in what became known as the Korean Campaign of Truth. One might have assumed that without the presence of the Soviet Union or its Eastern European allies,[16] U.S. representatives would have had little trouble mobilizing support for what was in name a United Nations action.

However, when the special meeting of the Executive Board convened in August 1950 at the request of the United States, the going was not as smooth as U.S. representatives might have assumed or hoped. The second Director-General, Jaime Torres-Bodet of Mexico, moved quickly to have his own four-point proposal accepted in place of the more highly politicized U.S. proposals. The Director-General's proposal "suggested assistance for the civilian populace and in particular the education of refugee children, a program of instruction about the United Nations for use by all peoples, a campaign to educate the public in member states upon United Nations action in Korean, and UNESCO participation in the reconstruction of Korea after the end of hostilities" (Sewell, 1975:149). The Director-General's proposal prevailed. In addition, the Executive Board agreed to produce and distribute educational materials on the Korean action and to work with the U.N. secretariat in compiling relevant information and documentation.

The DG's proposal was not fundamentally different from that put forth by the U.S. delegation. Yet, the refusal by the Executive Board members to adopt the exact U.S. plan of action had far-reaching impacts.

> In the United States there was a growth of public frustration with this U.N. agency which failed to act effectively on a problem with such an obvious solution: that of exposing Communist aggression to all the world. . . . As institution and man proved less and less tractable in cold-war undertakings . . . the U.S. government, subgovernmental officials, and a public attentive to foreign affairs grew more and more resistant to Torres–Bodet's pleas for increased UNESCO budgets. United States leaders had advanced their institutional engagement rather convulsively with an intention of controlling important UNESCO policies; now having failed, they disengaged discernibly if not convulsively on grounds that UNESCO had refused to make itself relevant to the ' real' world (Sewell, 1975:150–151).

The U.S. posture toward UNESCO was not to be short-lived; nor was it to be reversed with the passing of Torres-Bodet as Director-General.

By the time the Soviet Union was ready to seek membership in 1954, U.S. government interest in UNESCO had, in general, begun to wane. As stated above, many U.S. officials perceived UNESCO to be an unwilling and undependable instrument through which to conduct important foreign policy initiatives. The organization had failed to act as the political body many of its U.S. supporters had perceived and/or desired it to be. With the admission of the Soviet Union, U.S. officials began to desire UNESCO to be more of a technical agency rather than a political body. Indeed, the East-West conflict was not destined to orient UNESCO's programs and activities in the coming decades.

Global Change and U.S. Influence

Changes that affected most other universal IGOs during the 1960s also impacted upon UNESCO. In this regard, several interrelated factors need to be considered. First, the membership structure in UNESCO changed dramatically. The rapid increase in member states from underdeveloped regions fueled the emergent division within the organization along North-South lines. As elsewhere in the UN system, organizational agendas came more and more to reflect Third World concerns, especially development. Second, member states in UNESCO, like those in most other universal IGOs, became caught up in debates over new world orders. The polycentric character of the UN system created a situation in which similar political debates and posturings were repeated in almost every forum.[17] The call for a new international order was one such phenomenon. In addition, polycentrism resulted in considerable extraneous political debate being injected into the deliberations of the governing bodies of most specialized agencies (Lengyel, 1986:7–8). UNESCO, whose roles included that of being a world conscience, was no exception.

Third, UNESCO was experiencing an acceleration in a growing identity problem. The identity problem centered on a long-standing dispute over whether the organization's activities should be oriented predominantly toward intellectual cooperation or toward more practical action. This dispute rapidly began to be decided in favor of the more practical orientation with an increasing involvement in development activities.

Fourth, and perhaps foremost among these factors, was the change in the geographical composition of UNESCO membership. While membership growth during the 1950s had, in general, been primarily concentrated in developing regions, a new spurt in growth was even more narrowly concentrated in this regard. In 1960 alone, seventeen new African states joined UNESCO. In 1962 seven more states from Africa entered the organization. By the late 1960s the United States and the other advanced Western governments had lost what has been termed their automatic majority. By 1974 the number of member states stood at 136, the vast majority of which came from developing regions. Ten years later membership totaled 161 and the distribution was even more skewed toward less advanced nations.

With the above changes, of course, came alterations in the composition of UNESCO's governing bodies. For example, the Executive Board, which consisted of eighteen individuals in 1946, nearly tripled in size over the next four decades. A more relevant statistic, however, relates to the change in the composition of the board. Half of the original board members were from North America and Western Europe. In addition, an Australian, Sir Ronald Walker, was on that first board. Thus, ten of the eighteen Board seats were held by individuals from rich Western societies. Only one third of the original board represented member states from Latin America, Africa, and Asia.

By 1984, the Executive Board numbered fifty-one members. While board members from Group I (primarily Western Europe and North America) still numbered ten, they now comprised only 20 percent of the total membership; African and Middle Eastern members (Group V) alone made up 40 percent of the board.[18] Thus even in those cases where the rules of procedure require a two-thirds majority (for example, Rule 46), the Western members alone cannot constitutionally block the vote. Yet, when the quality of its representation is high, the Western Group is not without effective influence; consensus decisionmaking is the norm. It must be pointed out, though, that decisionmaking procedures do contain important constraints; "the voting rules, and the beliefs as to outcomes if there were votes, cast their shadows on the content of what can be agreed on by consensus" (Finkelstein, 1986:19).

Viewing demographic changes in the context of UNESCO's budgetary arrangements, the frustration inherent in Assistant Secretary Newell's July 13, 1984, statement is brought more clearly into focus. For example, in 1984 twenty-four member states of the Western Group contributed over 72 percent of the organization's budget. Those thirteen Western Information Group (WIG) members, who contributed individually 1 percent or more of the total assessed budget (that is, the Geneva Group), accounted for over two-thirds (68.6 percent) of the total. The concern that financial support was not adequately translated into effective influence over outcomes was implicit in Newell's letter.

The frustration over financial support versus effective influence was not particular to UNESCO. However, in UNESCO the Director-General and the governing bodies had made a serious effort since the mid-1970s to militate against the Third World majority running roughshod over Western interests. Also, since 1974 a form of consensus decisionmaking has prevailed with respect to contentious political issues in the organization's main governing body, the General Conference, and as discussed above, to a lesser extent in the board. A main mechanism for implementing the process of consensus decisionmaking has been the establishment of drafting and negotiating groups (DNGs) at each General Conference session. Various highly contentious and ideological issues (for example, Soviet-inspired resolutions on colonialism and racism, disarmament, and the new international economic order) are referred to the DNG, which must reach a consensus before it may return the item to the conference plenary body.

This form of consensus politics, however, does not mean that every dissenting member has to be satisfied before an issue can be returned. UNESCO's consensus mechanism operates on the basis of concurrence among regional groupings. Thus, the system is in a loose manner of speaking similar to the concurrent majority system advocated by John Calhoun in his nineteenth–century states' rights arguments in the U.S. Congress (Faulkner and Gunter, 1986). Intra-group cohesion is an important element in this process. Cohesive regional groups, including the Western Group, can effectively block action.

This is not to say that any one member state or handful of members can exercise a veto over decisions and actions. As will be discussed later in regard to the 1984–1985 biennial budget issue at the 22nd General Conference, the lack of veto control greatly frustrated Reagan administration officials. The assistant secretary echoed the same frustration in various of the specific reform recommendations he proposed in his letter of July 13, 1984.

Focusing on formal institutional arrangements, however, obscures a very important point. U.S. positions and preferences in UNESCO on matters that have been articulated by U.S. officials as being of vital importance to U.S.

interest have, in fact, generally been sustained; the U.S. has been relatively successful. UNESCO programs and activities in the area of human rights represent a case in point. Despite the rhetoric during debates in the delegate bodies about peoples' rights, the basic approach taken in UNESCO has consistently been compatible with that promoted by the United States. UNESCO has given priority to promoting traditional individual human rights; the notion of peoples' rights has never attained the status of a program. The UNESCO program on international human rights was largely U.S. built over a period of several years. It even included machinery to expose Soviet violations of human rights (Buergenthal and Torney, 1976). An examination of the impact of international change on the communications issue in UNESCO serves to illustrate this point.

The Call for a New World Order

Throughout the 1960s a fundamental element of U.S. government interest in UNESCO remained the propagation of the concept of a free flow of information through mass communication. In general, UNESCO's work in communications reflected U.S. interests. Technical assistance efforts in this area focused largely on building communications infrastructures in developing societies. The situation began to change, however, in the late 1960s and early 1970s. Beginning at a UNESCO-sponsored international meeting of specialists on mass communication and society in Montreal in 1969, communications debates in UNESCO's political bodies started to focus on Third World complaints about dependence on communications and information infrastructures centered in advanced industrial societies. Third World delegates charged that a huge imbalance existed in the global distribution and control over communications resources. They also charged that major Western wire services monopolized world news coverage, creating a one-way flow of information. To redress perceived asymmetries, Third World delegates introduced the notion of a new international information order to the UNESCO debates.

It is important at this point to recall that calls to correct imbalances were not particular to UNESCO but were heard generally throughout the UN system. The rise of a Third World voting coalition, which had become manifest in the Group of 77, brought with it a set of demands for restructuring global agendas and ultimately global relations.

The fledgling coalition of Third World states within international institutions rapidly took on the trappings of a political movement. At the apex of this new political movement was the demand for new international orders. The call for the establishment of a New International Economic Order (NIEO) at the Sixth Special Session of the UN General Assembly in May 1974 gave formal expression to such demands.

The proposals that emerged over the next few years as part of the NIEO "package" were quite diverse. However, four general concerns tended to dominate the NIEO agenda: lack of economic sovereignty; the structure of global trade relations and allocation processes; insufficient economic and technical assistance; and asymmetries with respect to participation in international institutions (Jordan, 1982). Underlying each of these concerns were perceptions of dependency and lack of decisionmaking autonomy by national governments in developing regions. Although each of these general concerns occupied an important place on the NIEO agenda, participation "more than any other, [lay] . . . at the heart of the developing states' demands for a new international order" (Jordan, 1982:22). The concern with participation focused on equality, mutual respect, and reciprocal relations based thereon, pertaining to global decisionmaking, as well as control at home.

The general demands for restructuring international relations gave rise in issue–specific contexts to calls for specific international orders, like the call for a New World Information and Communications Order, which evolved in UNESCO. Underlying all calls for particular orders, however, were much the same concerns as those expressed at the more general level: lack of economic sovereignty; gross structural imbalances in international trade relations and allocational processes; need for financial and technical assistance; and, again, asymmetries in participation in international organization.

In addition to Third World demands on UNESCO, Soviet delegates had begun an overt assault on the concept of free flow of information. Beginning in 1972, delegates to the UNESCO General Conference held discussions on a declaration on mass media. Although UNESCO did not adopt the Soviet resolutions in this regard, they posed serious challenges for U.S. officials that were soon to become the primary preoccupation of American participation in UNESCO. Moreover, Soviet proposals tended to become confused in the United States with the Third World calls for a new order.

The U.S.-based press and most U.S. government officials viewed the call for a new order as an attempt to exert state control over the press and to restrict the free flow of information. In response, U.S. officials, along with other Western delegates, became more alert and in 1974 began to engage actively in UNESCO communications debates. Contrary to popular perceptions in the United States, these endeavors were generally successful in defending free-press interests and UNESCO programs remained oriented toward Western free-press concepts. Moreover, as discussed earlier, in the years immediately preceding U.S. withdrawal the information situation in UNESCO had improved markedly from a U.S. perspective. However, the U.S. successes seem to have become blurred in the United States, even in many official circles.

At UNESCO's 18th General Conference in 1974 a Soviet-initiated declaration on media that included articles that would have sanctioned the supremacy of the state over the press, was hotly debated and sent back for redrafting. Of course, the proposal was totally unacceptable to the U.S. and other Western members. Also that year, the Director-General was authorized to undertake cooperative measures to facilitate the free and balanced flow of information between industrially advanced and developing societies.

Two years later, the 19th General Conference again debated a Soviet-initiated draft declaration on the media that was unacceptable to the United States. This proposal was defeated. However, it did serve to structure the conference debate over the new international information order around the topic of free press versus state sovereignty. Given the tendency of many U.S. officials to view the world primarily through East-West lenses, the debate seemed to reinforce an image that Soviet initiatives were one in the same as the Third World calls for a new order.

The conference concluded on a somewhat more consensual note and, with the strong support of the U.S., the Director-General was instructed to undertake a review of all of the problems of communications in contemporary society. This he did by appointing a commission, the International Commission for the Study of Communications—the MacBride Commission. This U.S. initiative was designed to move future communications debates away from ideological rhetoric. It gave structure to the international debate and set a framework for a later program of action—the International Program for Development and Communications (IPDC). This program was another U.S. initiative.[19]

However, in the minds of many American reporters and U.S. officials, the call for a new information order quickly became characterized as a Soviet-inspired Third World attack on the free press. To the contrary, as late as 1978 Soviet officials were arguing that there was no need for a new order; the current one based on state sovereignty was sufficient. Although UNESCO, including its Director-General, was actively involved in defeating Soviet initiatives, the U.S.-based press has tended misleadingly to credit UNESCO with proposing such ideas. Moreover, representatives of thirty-three media organizations in the United States, Western Europe, Latin America, and Asia joined together to form the World Press Freedom Committee (WPFC). The main purpose of this new body was to work and speak out against advocates of state-controlled media and other opponents of a private enterprise (that is, "free") press. This group became especially active in monitoring activities in UNESCO and in working to shape U.S. communications policy toward the organization.

At the 20th General Conference in 1978 Soviet delegates again tried to get UNESCO to adopt a highly restrictive declaration on fundamental principles governing the use of the mass media. In fact, a Mass Media Declaration was adopted that year. However, this one called for the free flow and better balanced dissemination of information, not for increased state controls. To the Soviet delegation's chagrin this declaration was a free-press oriented statement, calling for the exercise of freedom of opinion, expression, and information recognized as an integral part of human rights and fundamental freedoms. The statement argued that journalists must have access and freedom to report information. Yet, this free-press oriented statement would later be lambasted by Reagan administration officials as having been a Soviet-initiated declaration.

The debate continued at the 21st General Conference in 1980. This time the focus was on the report of the MacBride Commission, concerning which a resolution was adopted unanimously. In addition, however, some member states had endorsed a draft proposal to establish a Commission for the Protection of Journalists. While the proposal did not even result in a formal resolution, the debate again sent shock waves through the U.S. government and press. Moves for the "protection" of journalists were seen as largely being covers for state "licensing," a totally unacceptable concept to proponents of U.S. first amendment freedoms. The debate surrounding this one issue became the exclusive focus of Western news reports about the General Conference (Sussman, 1984b:2).

In an attempt to turn the communications issue around and refocus it toward a more Western orientation, the United States government, along with other Western free-press supporters, initiated the International Program for the Development of Communications. The purpose of the IPDC was to reorient UNESCO discussions and actions over communications away from ideological debate over new orders and toward the technical development of communications infrastructures in developing societies. Western financing and technology was to be used to create regional and local news agencies and other communication capabilities.

The IPDC was approved and a thirty-five-member intergovernmental board to supervise the program was established. While much of the funding pledged by the United States and other members has not materialized, the program has generally been hailed as a success (Sussman, 1984d:6). For example, the IPDC has been instrumental in assisting with the creation of the Pan African News Agency (PANA), which served as the continent's first interregional communications system.

As discussed in Chapter 2, by the end of the 22nd General Conference in 1983 the situation in UNESCO had become even more favorable for the United States. Several significant gains had been made by U.S. and other free-press advocates. These included a decision to treat the NWICO as merely an evolving process, not as a series of imposed regulations. Also, programs to study the watchdog role of the press and to examine governmental censorship were established.[20] Ironically, Western victory in this protracted debate in UNESCO occurred precisely as the main protagonists for the free-press position withdrew. Thus, Reagan administration officials gratuitously gave up the right and capability to defend and protect the gains secured in the interests of a free press and, equally important, to ensure that the communications debate remain in UNESCO and not be transferred to some less promising forum like the United Nations General Assembly.

An analysis of the communications debate indicates that U.S. officials had not lost the ability to influence effectively the policy outcomes in UNESCO. When U.S. needs and interests had been clearly articulated and U.S. officials had been actively engaged in the decision processes of the organization, policy outcomes had been largely satisfactory (for example, human rights and communications programs and activities). Of course, such a generalization must be qualified; for even in the early years of UNESCO, the policy preferences of U.S. officials did not always materialize as the officials would have them. Yet, in the 1980s Reagan administration officials desired to return UNESCO to principles and conditions of an earlier period. Again, a great deal of confusion and/or misperception seems to have existed within the administration in this regard.

IN SEARCH OF IDENTITY

As so aptly stated by Sewell (1975:135), "UNESCO was born plural." A single institution had been mandated the task of dealing with an agenda that included global relations in science, education, culture, and communications. Moreover, the functional foci were to be used in the service of humankind to promote world peace. One observer of the early years of UNESCO likened the new organization to the telescope atop Mount Palomar, whose giant reflector brought "into vision such a vast expanse of the universe, so many new nebulae, stars and constellations, that it will take the astronomers hundreds of years to chart them."[21] Notwithstanding its broad-ranging mandate, however, UNESCO began on a relatively small scale.

As the analysis below reveals, the uneasy and fudged compromises struck between the U.S. and European officials at the birth of UNESCO left a permanent mark. Newell's call for a return to original principles was hollow and confusing in light of the fact that it was never clarified at the outset what these original principles were. Moreover, during the early years, U.S. officials pushed hard to get UNESCO to be precisely what Mr. Newell four decades later berated it for being—a political organization in the service of ideological ends.

Original Principles

When the representatives of forty-four national governments met in London in November of 1945 to establish UNESCO, the ravages of war were still fresh in their minds, as was clearly reflected in the constitution they adopted. In the language formulated by U.S. Ambassador Archibald MacLeish and U.K. Prime Minister Clement Attlee, the preamble of the UNESCO Constitution proclaimed that "since wars begin in the minds of men, it is in the minds of men that the defences of peace must be constructed."

This new organization was to contribute to global peace and security by "promoting collaboration among the nations through education, science and culture in order to further universal respect for justice, for the rule of law and for the human rights and fundamental freedoms which are affirmed for the peoples of the world, without distinction of race, sex, language or religion, by the Charter of the United Nations."[22] It was in this light that UNESCO was founded as an organization of ideals.

When viewed in the broader context of that historical period, it appears clear that from the perspectives of the major founders UNESCO was to serve as the conscience of a new post-war world order. The constitution's preamble declared the following:

> . . . the wide differences of culture, and the education of humanity for justice and liberty and peace are indispensable to the dignity of man and constitute a sacred duty which all the nations must fulfill in a spirit of mutual assistance and concern; . . . a peace based exclusively upon the political and economic arrangements of governments would not be a peace which could secure the unanimous, lasting and sincere support of the peoples of the world . . . the peace must therefore be founded, if it is not to fail, upon the intellectual and moral solidarity of mankind.

In this regard the organization was symbolic of the renewed internationalist sentiments that then influenced U.S. foreign policy (Hughes, 1985).

By no means was this new world order to be ideologically neutral. The three major founding governments—the United States, the United Kingdom, and France—attempted to design a multilateral institution that would protect and promote Western ideals and values. Again, the preamble to the UNESCO Constitution was quite specific in this regard: ". . . the great and terrible war which has now ended was a war made possible by the denial of the democratic principles of the dignity, equality and mutual respect of men." As discussed earlier, such ends were to be attained by promoting liberal values and principles, such as mass education and mass communication.

Thus, UNESCO was at the same time a functional agency mandated to promote collaboration in education, science, culture, and communications and a political body devoted to serving as a kind of world conscience. As Lengyel (1986:6) has astutely pointed out, this hybridization of technical and ideologically normative roles has from the beginning created important difficulties in the organization. "UNESCO itself was, from the start, a sort of ideal type bound to run into trouble in a real world riven by ideological cleavages" (Lengyel, 1986:99).

Identity Problems Intensify

The tensions created in attempting to balance two roles intensified as the membership composition of UNESCO expanded and diversified. The liberal and rationalistic assumptions underlying the ideology expressed in the constitution were not universally shared (Lengyel, 1986:98–99). With the admission of the Soviet Union in 1954 it became clear to many participants, including those from the United States, that UNESCO could not function effectively with a diverse focus. Thus, U.S. officials began to desire the organization to be a primarily technical agency. To be sure, however, the ideologically normative role as world conscience did not die; it remained firmly embedded in the UNESCO constitutional foundation.

In general, UNESCO rapidly took on a more technical orientation. Early experiments with technical assistance activities expanded in scope as membership composition shifted toward the Third World. According to John Fobes (1972:113), a former Deputy-Director General, "more self-examination of UNESCO's role in development took place in the years 1960–1962 than in all the years after 1946."

President Kennedy's call for the establishment of a United Nations Development Decade had repercussions far beyond the halls of the General Assembly. Soon the UNESCO Secretariat officials were actively engaged with other multilateral agencies in an attempt to provide support to member states for operational activities related to educational and scientific development. With cooperative efforts came substantial extra-budgetary funding. By the early 1970s approximately half of the overall program resources in UNESCO were being channeled to development activities.

Thus, a shift in the dominant task orientation of UNESCO occurred; functionalism (that is, intellectual cooperation for peace) rapidly gave way to a focus on social and economic development (developmentalism) (Cox and Jacobson, 1973:425).[23] The shift, in turn, gave rise to problems of legitimacy both within and without the organization.

> A change in function of this kind cannot be done on an entirely value-free basis. The praxis of science, education and culture in advanced societies incorporates, reflects and is meant to perpetuate their value hierarchies; the transfer of these models, even in somewhat adapted forms, must therefore be accompanied by a transfer of values. That, in turn, means that conflicting ideologies or traditions cannot be avoided by a flight into technicity (Lengyel, 1986:7).

Again, however, legitimacy concerns were not particular to UNESCO.

A comparative study of UN agencies, directed by Cox and Jacobson in the early 1970s, found the phenomenon to be widespread among IGOs. "Developmentalism has weakened the justification of these sectoral structures, particularly as regards . . . the legitimacy of their appeals for support from special interests. . . . This ideological weakness . . . seems most important . . . for the future of those agencies—notably ILO and UNESCO—that defend their independence with functionalist ideology but have come to depend most heavily upon UNDP funds" (Cox and Jacobson, 1973:424). Furthermore, as the political debate over development shifted in the 1970s away from an exclusive focus on national economic development to concentrate more generally on questions about global inequality as a factor in underdevelopment, legitimacy problems intensified.

In UNESCO political debates greatly aggravated identity problems. The essence of the liberal ideological foundations of the organization were being brought into question. In this regard Lengyel (1986:103) has argued that the resulting Western counter charges that UNESCO was becoming increasingly politicized through excessive statism should be viewed in context for what they represent, a defense of private enterprise and the established liberal economic order.

UNESCO officials and governing bodies attempted to rationalize the continuing conflict between functionalism and developmentalism by saying that UNESCO would utilize knowledge gained by its traditional intellectual role (that is, research and exchange) "to inform" the planning of developing countries. Also, an emerging force in the program was that of the major programs in science (and to a lesser extent in education and culture), which focused on dealing with global issues. A global focus mainly represented neither functionalism nor developmentalism. However, the conflict between these two competing foci has persisted and the identity problems within UNESCO have not subsided.[24] Furthermore, as the analysis in the following section reveals, this shift in task focus appears to have been interrelated with another of the Reagan administration's "fundamental" concerns with UNESCO—the imbalance of authority between the delegate bodies and the Director-General.

THE BALANCE OF AUTHORITY IN UNESCO

As discussed earlier, the organizational charter that emerged from the London conference represented a compromise between CAME/U.S. and French drafts.[25] The CAME/U.S. proposal called for a much stronger executive head than did the French plan. French delegates envisioned a relatively stronger executive committee of members. As we have seen, the U.S. preference in this regard prevailed. However, a U.S.-sponsored amendment to free the DG from the obligation of submitting high–level staff appointments to the board for approval was left somewhat ambiguous.

The constitution laid the groundwork for a very strong Directorship-General. In practice, though, beginning with Huxley's administration, the organizational structure of UNESCO tended to be relatively decentralized. In this regard it should be noted that the second Director-General introduced an administrative style that would in later years facilitate considerable concentration of authority in the hands of the Director-General. Torres-Bodet surrounded himself with a French-style cabinet of top advisors, with which to administer the Secretariat. The bureaucratic necessities of development administration brought additional change in this regard and with René Maheu's ascendancy to the position in 1961 any trend toward decentralization was clearly reversed.[26]

Maheu's impact on the Directorship-General and the organization itself should not be understated. In the words of former Assistant Director-General Richard Hoggart, who served under Maheu:

> His [Maheu's] style was that of a little Napoleon . . . he could be a quite dreadful autocrat. At the height of his regime, bossing and bullying had become part of the normal order within UNESCO. He could fly into violent rages with senior men, threaten to send them home the moment their present contracts expired, demand immediate improvements and leave them literally shaking with the violence of his assault and fear for their own futures. (quoted by Massing, 1984:91).

As observed by Sewell (1975:267), "About Maheu no one seemed neutral."

However, in order to understand the full extent of his impact on the organization one must differentiate between perceptions and attitudes of Maheu's management style and his administrative effectiveness. This Director-General had successfully taken UNESCO in directions thought to be very positive by an overwhelming majority of the member states. The organization was rapidly becoming a more task–oriented agency, while at the same time retaining its intellectual orientation. In 1968 René Maheu was overwhelmingly reelected with the affirmative votes of 115 members (with two abstentions). Furthermore, when a staff rebellion broke out among Secretariat employees in 1970, the Executive Board gave him a symbolic vote of confidence.

From the beginning of his tenure in office Maheu demonstrated his determination to lead UNESCO as he saw fit, even in the face of opposition from the organization's major contributor. Finkelstein (1986:32) has provided an interesting anecdote in this regard: "the point is made dramatically by the puzzled and frustrated reaction of then Assistant Secretary of State Harlan Cleveland when, in the early 1960s, he emerged from his first official meeting with the newly appointed DG, René Maheu. Maheu had told Cleveland in no uncertain terms that he did not plan to follow the budget guidelines Cleveland had urged on him." Indeed, in 1962 Maheu was successful in getting the General Conference to approve a budget compromise larger than that preferred by the U.S. delegation. Also in that year, as Acting

Director-General he was able to win election as DG against strong U.S. opposition (Finkelstein, 1984:1–2).

By the end of Maheu's tenure in office in 1974 the scope of authority and effective influence of the Directorship-General had grown even more. It greatly exceeded the strong cornerstone role envisioned by those early U.S. planners who helped design UNESCO's constitution. As we will explore later in this chapter, growth of influence was accompanied by an associated reduction in vulnerability of the Director-General both vis-à-vis UNESCO's governing bodies and the organization's largest funder.

Under Amadou-Mahtar M'Bow's direction the position of Director-General became even more dominant in relation to UNESCO governing bodies. Furthermore, by the middle of his second term M'Bow had become even more controversial than his predecessor. However, he was perhaps no less effective as a political force within the organization.

From the beginning M'Bow demonstrated that he was an astute politician who understood the relative influence differentials of his multiple constituencies. For example, it was largely as a result of M'Bow's support that the DNG mechanism, which had been established by Maheu, became an effective device for killing attempts to force highly contentious ideological resolutions on an unwilling Western Group minority. Also, it was the DG's active mediating role that quickly defused the anti-Israeli debates during the mid-1970s. In addition, while deeply committed to redressing imbalances in the global information order, M'Bow was instrumental in negotiating outcomes in communications debates that were generally acceptable from a U.S. perspective. It is noteworthy in this regard that Mr. M'Bow was unanimously reelected for a second six-year term in 1981.

Although the details of individual DG strengths serve to illustrate the substantial growth of influence capabilities of the Director-General, they tell us little about why and how the capability exists. The answer to this deeper question lies in an analysis of the division of authority among the three main UNESCO organs: the General Conference, Executive Board, and Secretariat, headed by the Director-General.

The Division of Authority Within UNESCO

All member states are represented with equal votes at sessions of the General Conference, which, according to the original constitution, was to meet every year; but, since 1948, it has met only every two years. This primary governing body has been charged with determining the policies and main lines of work of UNESCO (Article IV.B.2). Also, it takes decisions on the program and budget of the organization, as submitted to it by the Director-General with such recommendations as the Executive Board might wish to make (Article V.B.5(a)).

The members of the Executive Board are elected by the General Conference from among delegates to the conference. In the original text of the constitution (Article V.1,2,12) Executive Board members were to serve in their personal capacities (not as governmental representatives), collectively exercising certain constitutional responsibilities and those powers delegated to them by the General Conference on behalf of the conference as a whole. The constitution was amended in 1954. Since that time, each board member additionally serves as a representative of the government of which she or he is a national (8 C/Resolution II-1.1). Thus, while each member is a governmental representative, she or he nominally serves as a distinct personality and is thus designated by name.

The constitution specifies numerous responsibilities and functions for the board. Perhaps foremost, the board is charged with the responsibility for the execution of the program adopted by the General Conference (Article V.5(b)). However, this function is somewhat obscured by the qualification that the board "shall take all necessary measures to ensure the effective and rational *execution of the programme by the Director-General*" (Article V.5(b); emphasis added). Also, it recommends candidates for the post of Director-General to the General Conference.

The board is to submit the DG's reports on the activities of the organization to the conference either with or without comments (Article V.9). In addition, the Executive Board has been mandated the important task of preparing the agenda of the General Conference (Article V.5(a)), a function which appears to have often been taken lightly. Also, the board can summon extraordinary sessions of the conference, as well as request the International Court of Justice to give advisory opinions between ordinary sessions of the conference, should the occasion arise (Article IV.9).

The board has also been given certain responsibilities in supervising UNESCO's financial regulations. In addition to reviewing the budget estimates presented in the program and budget (C/5) document, the board is to examine the reports of the DG on the establishment of trust funds, reserves, and special accounts. It can make recommendations concerning any voluntary contributions that might involve additional financial liability. Also, the board is to examine the External Auditor's reports and transmit them to the General Conference with whatever recommendations board members may decide collectively to make.

As discussed above, the constitutional division of authority between the board and the DG is somewhat ambiguous as related to the execution of the program. Over the years this ambiguity has been clarified by the Director-General assuming primary responsibility for the execution of the program, largely because of the periodicity and duration of the meetings of the board. The board meets in regular session twice a year and also holds an additional brief organizational session immediately following each ordinary session of the General Conference. Also, the board usually remains in session during the General Conferences, although it seldom meets during this period (UNESCO, 1984:21).

Over the last two decades (1963–1983) the average duration of the board meetings has been only 48 days, during years when the Conference did not meet, and 101 days, during General Conference years (UNESCO, 1984:24). Given such time constraints, it would be exceedingly difficult for the board to develop more than a supervisory capacity over the Secretariat, related to its program execution function. Indeed, it is over this question that much of the reform debate has centered.

The General Conference and the Executive Board, then, constitute the two main governing bodies of UNESCO. However, as is common in other major IGOs, in practice the Director-General and his staff play a very prominent role in these bodies (Finkelstein, 1986:24). In fact, the Secretariat provides the staff support for all General Conference and Executive Board operations. The Director-General has the right to participate in all meetings of these bodies without the right to vote (Article VI.3(a)). He can place items on the provisional agenda of the Conference and may make statements before this body with the approval of the presiding officer, which in practice has been granted automatically (*Rules of Procedure of the General Conference*, Rule 10[f] and Rule 50). In the board the right of the DG to make either oral or written statements is not qualified. In addition, the Director-General may formulate proposals for action by the board concerning any question under consideration (Rule 19).

Furthermore, as has been discussed, the Director-General is charged with the task of preparing for submission to the board the draft program and budget for the work of the organization (Article VI.3[a]). Given that this task represents the life blood of UNESCO, its importance for enhancing the authoritative role of the DG should not be underestimated. The Executive Board cannot amend the DG's draft C/5. It can, however, make "such recommendations as it considers desirable to the General Conference" (Article V.5[a]). Also, the Director-General is technically not at liberty to change the C/5 document once it has been approved by the General Conference (GC). However, the implementation of resulting program activities is the responsibility of the Secretariat. In drafting new biennial program and budget documents the DG is to follow the structure provided in the six-year medium-term plan, approved by the General Conference. Yet, such medium-term plans themselves are heavily influenced by the Secretariat's role in their construction and implementation.

Being the chief administrative officer of the organization, the Director-General is responsible for appointing the staff of the Secretariat. This body is to be exclusively international in character and is to be drawn from as wide a geographical basis as possible, subject to the paramount consideration of securing the highest standards of integrity, efficiency and technical competence. Both personnel recruitment and the general management of the organization fall within, what is in effect, the exclusive domain of the DG.

As implied in the discussion above, under both Maheu and M'Bow the secretariat has been organized and run in a highly centralized manner. Over the last two decades staff relations have become increasingly tense and UNESCO's personnel management practices have come under growing attack. In comparing staff relations and management within UNESCO to trends in personnel management more generally, Peter Lengyel, who served as editor of UNESCO's *International Social Science Journal* for more than twenty years, has charged the following:

> In UNESCO, the movement was in the reverse direction: from the liberalistic if corporatist regimes of Huxley, Torres–Bodet and Evans, under whom the Staff Association had a prominent function and was seriously consulted, if often overruled, to the authoritarianism of Maheu, who treated the report of a staff round table he had himself convoked with complete contempt. The M'Bow administration went one step further; it added arbitrariness to authoritarianism and invited paranoia by sponsoring a rival to the established Staff Association, membership in which was thought by many necessary to curry favor with the regime and thus to be a prerequisite for promotion (Lengyel, 1986:90).

It would seem that such conditions, to the extent that they have existed and have affected task performance, would have impacted to some degree upon the interrelationships between the governing bodies and the Secretariat. However, the exact nature of such impacts would be exceedingly difficult to measure. Given the overtly hostile attitudes toward Mr. M'Bow, expressed by a number of UNESCO employees during interviews and discussions in 1984–1985, it does seem likely that such conditions have not served to enhance the Director-General's effective influence and authority.

The DG's Effective Influence

From the above analysis, then, what can be said about the distribution of authority and effective influence within UNESCO? It appears as though three very important resources—information, personnel and financing—have been concentrated primarily in the hands of the Director-General. The DG and his Secretariat staff are responsible for providing and coordinating nearly all of the information used by the governing bodies. Information includes the DG's written reports on the work of the organization, the draft biennial program and budget, all official records of the governing bodies, and the DG's summaries of the debates on important agenda items. Given that the information flow is quite voluminous, the DG's summaries are very welcome to most delegates. As Senarclens (1985:9) has concluded, many delegates depend upon the Director-General to determine their own positions. In short, the governing bodies and perhaps most member states have become exceedingly dependent on, if not vulnerable to, the DG with respect to information. Indeed, such is the case with nearly all executive heads of IGOs; they have influence capability by reason of the flows of information that come into their organizations beyond that available to most governments.

Of course, dependence is related to the Director-General's other resource control capabilities. As discussed above, the DG and his immediate subordinates control hiring within the Secretariat quite directly, and that control has two important dimensions. One dimension relates to the general hiring of nationals from member states. Although standards of integrity, efficiency, and technical competence are to be the paramount considerations in hiring and other personnel decisions, due regard is also to be paid to geographical considerations. The DG can exercise discretion in this regard. A second dimension is much more interpersonal between the DG and the Executive Board members. High-level Secretariat appointments can and frequently have gone to former board members.[27] Thus, a member desiring to remain in Paris after her or his tenure on the board has expired might be very reluctant to oppose or otherwise antagonize the DG.

Influence over certain financial resources also serves to enhance the political role of the Director-General. Such influence is in addition to the somewhat limited flexibility that the Director-General can exercise over assessed programmatic spending. A substantial part of UNESCO financing for programs comes from outside of the regular assessed budget. Outside sums amounted to 38 percent of the total budget for the 1983-1984 biennium. A decade earlier extra-budgetary funding roughly equaled the regular budget. The main sources of these funds were from other UN agencies, funds-in-trust, and other extra-budgetary sources (Finkelstein, 1986:34). UNESCO's focus on development has played an important role in the Secretariat's ability to attract funds. The sources of outside funds generally specify clear guidelines for their use. However, in seeking and acquiring funds, members of the Secretariat can significantly influence the nature and scope of the UNESCO program of work.

In a more direct sense, Participation Programme funds provide the Director-General with considerable influence capability. This program, established in 1955, permits the DG to disperse small fixed cash sums to member states. "The DG has authority under broad guidelines approved by the GC to make direct cash appropriations of up to $25 thousand per project. In the 1981-1983 triennium, one member received between $140 and $150 thousand under the programme, two received between $130 and $140 thousand, eight received between $110 and $120 thousand, 16 received between $100 and $110 thousand, and 136 received less than $100 thousand" (Finkelstein, 1986:35). When linked to funding for UNESCO's regular program activities, it is not surprising that to a degree a pattern of pork barrel politics exists in UNESCO's governing bodies, similar to the U.S. Congress (Ripley and Franklin, 1980). The great bulk of this funding is highly subject to disaggregation and the related program activities generally involve tangible stakes. Indeed, the DG's central role in steering and mediating such processes provides him with a high level of influence capability.

A related, smaller fund, which the DG administers, also provides an important basis for influence. This Special Account for Increased Aid to Developing Countries, created in the mid-1970s, amounted to $8.5 million as of December 31, 1983 (Finkelstein, 1986:36). While this fund is treated as being a supplement to the Participation Programme, "it is altogether extra-budgetary and full authority is vested in the DG, with no supervision by the governing bodies, under a decision of the Executive Board in 1979" (Finkelstein, 1986:36). Such lack of supervision in general was a complaint of many of the Western members. However, the important consideration for the present discussion is that this unilateral authority further enhances the Director-General's position vis-à-vis members and groups of members, especially those from developing regions, for whom these funds were to be allocated.

On the other hand, with respect to at least two of these three resources—information and financing—the DG has proven also to be somewhat vulnerable. Although the Secretariat has controlled access to information internally within UNESCO, major wire services and other news agencies have largely controlled access to and dissemination of information about UNESCO externally. External control of information has been especially problematical for the DG in relation to the United States in recent years. As discussed in a later chapter, the way in which the American press has reported about UNESCO, when linked to a failure of the UNESCO Office of Public Information to put forth the UNESCO side of the story effectively, has left the organization and its Director-General quite vulnerable with respect to maintaining a viable domestic support base in the United States.

The weakness in information control appears to have intensified the DG's vulnerability with respect to its largest funder. A growing problem of legitimacy in U.S./UNESCO relations created a situation in which little reciprocal vulnerability existed between the two. While UNESCO was dependent on the United States for 25 percent of its annual assessed budget, the United States was not heavily dependent financially on UNESCO.

In summary, a substantial imbalance of authority, then, had evolved in UNESCO. All three main organs—General Conference, Executive Board, and Secretariat—were very vulnerable to the office of Director-General, if not to the personality of the DG. Yet, in the case of U.S. withdrawal it is not clear to what extent the imbalance of authority can be directly linked as a primary causal variable. In other IGOs the executive heads are also very powerful vis-à-vis the delegate bodies. In addition, the authority and effective influence of the DG in UNESCO have more often than not been used to appease or otherwise satisfy U.S. demands, when U.S. officials have made it clear that the disposition of a certain outcome was important to the United States.

At least part of the frustration that Reagan administration officials voiced about UNESCO appears to have resulted from confusion and/or misinformation about conditions in UNESCO and U.S./UNESCO relations. An important element of the confusion was the tendency to equate what member states do and say in debates of the delegate bodies and what UNESCO, the organization, actually does. The delegate bodies are political forums in which a wide array of ideological forces and competing interests clash. Various delegates, especially those from the Soviet Union, have attempted time and again to use UNESCO and other IGO delegate bodies to promote their particular ideological objectives. As the outcomes of the communications and human rights debates in UNESCO demonstrate, however, the Soviets have generally not been successful. The statist challenges to the established information and communications order, as well as those against traditional (that is, individual) human rights, have consistently been turned back. UNESCO's programs and activities continue to embrace the liberal democratic ideals upon which the organization was founded.

The Reagan administration also seems to have experienced substantial confusion with regard to the call for UNESCO to return to its original principles. From the beginning the exact nature of these principles has been considerably ambiguous. Furthermore, in the earliest years of the organization, U.S. officials chided UNESCO for not being willing to confront the major political issues of the day; yet, four decades later Reagan administration officials attacked the organization as being overly politicized. Administration officials wanted UNESCO to be largely a technical development agency, not a functional agency promoting intellectual cooperation in the service of world peace and security as described in the UNESCO constitution.[28]

When placed in historical context, then, the administration's statements about a lack of effective Western influence, a need to return to original principles, and the implications of an imbalance of authority appear to have either misstated or dramatically overstated the nature of conditions in UNESCO. As discussed in the following chapter, no other member, not even from the Western Group, was willing in 1984 to support U.S. proposals for major structural change. Yet, representatives of most of these other Western governments did feel that numerous problems existed in the organization.[29]

How then can we explain U.S. withdrawal? Were Reagan administration officials simply determined from the outset, for whatever reasons, to terminate U.S. membership in UNESCO? When one fabricated justification (that is, politicization, statism, uncontrollable budgetary expansion, and mismanagement) failed, had they simply invented another with little or no intention of seeking constructive change within the organization? Or can withdrawal be meaningfully explained as a strategy for reforming UNESCO, even though the official justification may have been subject to much confusion and/or misinformation? Answers to these questions can be found in an analysis of U.S. participation in the reform process within UNESCO during 1984–1985.

NOTES

1. Although numerous of the more specific proposals associated with these fundamental reforms had appeared in the list of thirteen points circulated by U.S. delegates within WIG, that list was non-attributed and was not made public.

2. If such a list were provided, it was argued, UNESCO and its member states might move to satisfy the demands in a minimally acceptable way. Then, if administration officials did not reverse the decision to withdraw, other member states, who had negotiated in good faith, might become angry. Thus, no such list was to be provided. Personal interviews, summer and fall 1984.

3. Personal interviews, summer 1987.

4. Given the contribution formula used to assess dues in UNESCO, four governments theoretically (for example, United States [25%], Soviet Union [10.41%], Japan [10.19%] and FRG [8.44%]) and five governments practically (for example, United States, Japan, FRG, France, and any one of several other Western member states) could in combination exercise an effective veto under such a plan.

5. Personal interviews, summer and fall 1984.

6. The historical material discussed in this chapter draws heavily on Laves and Thompson (1957) and Sewell (1973 and 1975), as well as on comments by John Fobes.

7. The IICI was technically an autonomous body under the League of Nations. Its membership included some of the most eminent intellectuals of the time (that is, Madame Curie, Albert Einstein, Paul Valéry). However, the work of the institute was limited primarily to intellectual cooperation. The IBE was founded in Geneva in 1925 and was converted two years later to serve as a quasi-governmental body to provide technical support for ministries of education. In 1969 this organization was integrated with UNESCO. The IBE serves as the information component of the UNESCO program for improving educational systems.

8. Quoted in Sewell (1975:6). This group included representatives of the education ministries of the governments of Belgium, Czechoslovakia, France, Greece, the Netherlands, Norway, Poland, and Yugoslavia.

9. This U.S. delegation included: J. William Fulbright (delegation head);

Grayson Kefauver; Archibald MacLeish; John Studebaker; C. Mildred Thompson; and Ralph Turner. An excellent discussion of the decisionmaking processes within the State Department with respect to this issue is provided in Ninkovich (1981:76–86).

10. Important as these skirmishes were, one should not overlook the fact that UNESCO was launched amid noble and highflown aspirations for a post war era in which cultural, educational and intellectual cooperation would eliminate the prospect of a future conflagration. It was an important pillar—to some like Archibald MacLeish the most important plank—of a new world order of cooperation among the civilized to permanently eradicate the scourge of world war. I wish to thank Jonathan Davidson for reminding me of the need to clarify this point.

11. An informal agreement had been concluded in CAME in which, in exchange for locating the headquarters of the new organization in Paris, the DG would be an English-speaking person. While such a qualification did not narrow the field exclusively to U.S. nationals, the U.S. representatives had assumed that a U.S. national should and, indeed, would be selected for the post.

12. Ninkovich (1981:97–98) presents an excellent discussion of the politics behind the selection of Huxley as the first Director-General.

13. Ibid.

14. Quoted in Sewell (1973:162–163).

15. Quoted in Sewell (1975:140–141).

16. Although the governments of Czechoslovakia, Hungary, and Poland had all previously been members of the organization, each had withdrawn prior to this point in time. Subsequent to the admission of the Soviet government, they rejoined UNESCO.

17. Polycentrism in the UN system refers to the absence of a central system-wide coordinating and control center (Lengyel, 1986:7).

18. In 1968 the Rules of Procedure of the General Conference were amended to provide for a system of electoral groups for the purpose of electing members of the board. Five groups were created. While not solely based on geographical criteria, the groups do approximate such a distribution. In 1984 seats on the board were divided as follows: Group I (Western), 10; Group II (Eastern Europe), 4; Group III (Latin America), 9; Group IV (Asia-Pacific), 8; and Group V (Africa-Middle East), 20.

19. Personal interviews, summer 1987.

20. Further crucial U.S. victories were scored in the 23rd General Conference of UNESCO in 1985.

21. Calder (1946), quoted in Sewell (1975:135).

22. UNESCO, Constitution, Article 1, paragraph 1.

23. In keeping with Cox and Jacobson's (1973:22) definition, organizational ideology refers to (1) an interpretation of the environment as it relates to action by the organization, (2) specification of goals to be attained in the environment, and (3) a strategy of action for attaining these goals.

24. I would like to thank Jack Fobes for clarifying this point for me.

25. As we will explore, the Constitution defined three main organs: a General Conference, Executive Board, and Secretariat. While membership was reserved to national states [CAME/U.S.], Article VII called on each member to "make such arrangements as suit its particular conditions for the purpose of associating its principal [private and governmental] bodies . . . preferably by the formation of a National Commission. . . ." [French]. Also, individuals were to be elected to the Executive Board in their individual capacities and not

as representatives of their respective governments [French]. Yet, board members were to be elected from among the national state representatives to the General Conference.

26. I am grateful to Larry Finkelstein for the many insights provided in his excellent paper, "The Political Role of the Director-General of UNESCO." Paper presented at the 1984 Annual Meeting of the International Studies Association/West, Denver, Colorado, revised August 18, 1986.

27. As we shall see in Chapter 6, hiring practices had been a concern to both U.S. and British officials.

28. Personal interviews, summer and fall 1984.

29. The views of these and other Western governments were in general similar to those expressed by the U.S. National Commission for UNESCO and many of the thirteen federal agencies that had contributed to the 1983 interagency policy review discussed in Chapter 2. If Western support for UNESCO was to remain firm, certain changes would be required in how the organization and its member states conducted business.

CHAPTER FOUR

U.S. Participation
in the Reform Process

Following the December 1983 U.S. withdrawal announcement, the issue of reform quickly captured center stage at UNESCO headquarters in Paris. High level officials of the Secretariat generally expressed surprise and frustration. Within the Western Group the response was varied. The British announced that they had been undertaking their own review of British relations with the agency. Other delegates expressed great shock that the U.S. government would undertake withdrawal without close consultation with their Western Group partners.[1] Many organized groups of "Third World" states expressed official regret.

Regardless of their governments' official policy positions, however, a variety of delegates from every geographical region confided privately in interviews in 1984 that they believed the withdrawal announcement had an overall beneficial effect on the organization. Although no Executive Board representative outside of the U.S. delegation supported all of the demands being made by the U.S. government, a great many desired some form of change in UNESCO.[2] The U.S. initiative was perceived to have opened the door for the consideration of change.

Thus, the withdrawal announcement served as a catalyst in bringing the issue of organizational change (that is, "reform") to the forefront of the agenda in UNESCO. During 1984 the Belgian, British, Canadian, Danish, Dutch, Finnish, Icelandic, Italian, Japanese, Norwegian, Swedish, and Swiss governments all submitted letters to the Director-General concerning the need for organizational change. A reform agenda rapidly took form as the British and Dutch letters, along with that from the United States, were placed before the UNESCO's Executive Board for formal consideration.

These various calls for organizational change were quickly met by resolutions and declarations from numerous other groups of member states.

Forty-two governments meeting in a summit conference of the Organization of the Islamic Conference in Casablanca (January 16–19, 1984), expressed their continuing support for UNESCO and appealed to the U.S. government to reconsider its decision. The Ministers of Information of 101 Non-Aligned Countries meeting in Jakarta in late January issued a resolution reaffirming their support for UNESCO and its Director-General (NAMI/Conf.1/Res.5/ Rev.2, January 28, 1984). A similar declaration was issued on March 15 by the group of Non-Aligned Countries in UNESCO. The chairmen of the chapters of the Group of 77 in New York, Geneva, Rome, Vienna, Nairobi and Paris (February), the Council of Ministers of the Organization of African Unity (March 6), and the Arab League (March 31) also issued similar declarations. In addition, various geographical groups in UNESCO issued declarations: African Group (December 29), Arab Group (January 6), and Asia and Pacific Group (March 6).

It would be a mistake, however, to assume that the debate over the reform issue became rigidly polarized along either North-South or East-West lines. Various governments from developing regions also expressed the need for change in UNESCO. Notable in this regard, the Philippines' permanent delegate issued a paper on April 27, proposing a fourteen-point agenda for UNESCO self-appraisal. Among other things this Philippine paper addressed the needs to restore the balance of power among the UNESCO main organs, to improve consultation with member states, and to decentralize authority, functions, and responsibilities within the organization.

In the twenty-four months following the U.S. announcement, the issue of organizational reform played a dominant role in focusing the debate and work of the organization. During the first year of this period a dominating concern was whether sufficient change could be negotiated in order to convince the U.S. government to reconsider its withdrawal decision.

Reagan administration officials had hinted that such reconsideration might be possible. Moreover, on two occasions U.S. National Security Advisor McFarlane, acting for the president, had requested the State Department to develop a clear plan of action and to launch a major campaign to mobilize international support to turn UNESCO around. The plan of action was to have clearly stated goals and "precise milestones to measure . . . accomplishments" (McFarlane, February 11, 1984). In addition, U.S. participation was to have been strengthened. But did such an overall coherent strategy to force organizational change in UNESCO ever materialize and, if so, in what form?

BOYCOTT DIPLOMACY AND THE ILO MODEL

A strategic approach would not have been without precedent in recent U.S. multilateral relations. The nature of U.S. participation in the International

Labor Organization (ILO) during the late 1970s has been described as representing a style of "boycott diplomacy" (Jordan, 1984). Furthermore, certain similarities between the ILO and UNESCO cases in this regard have been discussed by several writers (Jordan, 1984; McHugh, 1984).

While not assuming that the ILO case should serve as the model for all such strategies, a brief examination of the U.S. withdrawal actions and outcomes in that case might be instructive. After having officially withdrawn from the ILO on November 5, 1977, the U.S. government reestablished its membership in February 1980, based on its assessment that sufficient reform had been achieved within the organization. An examination of that case should provide at least a partial understanding of kinds of U.S. policy actions that might be associated with inducing organizational change in multilateral institutions.[3] Furthermore, the withdrawal from the ILO did serve as a point of reference in Washington during 1984 for attempting to establish criteria for monitoring reform in UNESCO. In one of the first meetings of the Monitoring Panel on Reform, which was attended by the leadership of the IO bureau, representatives of the Department of Labor presented a detailed briefing on the ILO case.

Also, Lois McHugh (1984) of the Foreign Affairs and National Defense Division of the Congressional Research Service made available to the panel, as well as the IO bureau, copies of an in-depth analysis of similarities and differences of each case and of U.S. participation in the ILO during the withdrawal period. Her analysis addressed three main questions, based on a series of interviews with U.S. officials and delegates to the organization. First, had the ILO altered its behavior and incorporated changes to meet U.S. demands after withdrawal? Second, were changes the result of U.S. withdrawal or other factors? And finally, could the U.S. withdrawal from the ILO serve as a precedent for withdrawal from UNESCO?

Although inconclusive with regard to the latter question, McHugh's findings are quite helpful in identifying the nature of U.S. actions and U.S. officials' retrospective assessments of the resulting impacts. For example, the study concluded the following:

> Many, but not all, of the authorities interviewed . . . have seen an improvement in the ILO since the late 1970s. No one has called the change a dramatic improvement, but it was described in interviews as a reversal of a downward trend. There was, however, also no consensus on the significance of the changes or their cause. Many saw the changes as merely minor evolutionary developments in the organization caused either by changes in the international political situation or the passage of time. Others suggested that the changes were more dramatic and significant and the result of two U.S. actions: withdrawal from the ILO and improvements in participation in the ILO. *None of those interviewed indicated that withdrawal alone was responsible for the improvements in the ILO* (McHugh, 1984:vii; emphasis added).

According to McHugh (1984:viii), there existed a "consensus among those interviewed that any improvement . . . was at least partly caused by changes in U.S. participation in the ILO." Improved participation included better staffing, improved delegate preparation and coordination, established coherent policy goals, and more careful examination of the organization's program and budget.

Those interviewed who supported the idea that withdrawal had been the key to inducing change identified three main positive effects of the withdrawal action (McHugh, 1984:23—24). First, the interviewees reported that the withdrawal had a shock value. It jolted the other participants in the ILO to confront and respond to U.S. concerns. Second, the withdrawal was said to have improved U.S. credibility: withdrawal had been used as a last resort; a list of problems and proposed solutions had been clearly identified; and when they were not dealt with in a satisfactory manner, the U.S. had followed through on its threat to withdraw. After a serious and at least partially effective attempt had been made to respond to U.S. concerns, the government rejoined the organization. Third, the rapid loss of funds forced the DG to make personnel and administrative changes.

While not totally disagreeing that some positive changes had been undertaken in the ILO, critics of the withdrawal claimed that the action had not been the reason for the changes; these officials argued that the changes resulted from improved U.S. participation. From this perspective the U.S. "lack of leadership" had been a contributing factor to the problems in the organization (McHugh, 1984:25).

> A series of major improvements in U.S. participation were undertaken. At the time of the U.S. announcement of our intention to withdraw in 1975, the President established a Cabinet Level Committee (CLC) to monitor the progress of any ILO improvements, and to coordinate U.S. efforts to reform the agency. After our withdrawal, the CLC continued to function as a coordinating body and to monitor improvements in the ILO in preparation for the day when the United States would return to the agency (McHugh, 1984:26).

In addition, long-term goals were established in each of the agencies dealing with ILO affairs. The Department of Labor was designated as the agency that would maintain expertise in ILO affairs and staff support was increased to do so effectively (McHugh, 1984:27). Also, delegate preparations were improved, as was the official performance of the delegates at ILO meetings.

It would appear from the ILO case that the effectiveness of any strategy of "boycott diplomacy" would depend heavily on effective follow-through and enhanced participation (Richardson, 1984), a finding that would seem to be compatible with National Security Advisor McFarlane's call in the name of the president for a major campaign to turn UNESCO around in 1984. As discussed earlier, such a campaign would have entailed specifying a clear plan of action, identifying what was to be accomplished and how; the plan would include precise goals and criteria with which to assess goal attainment. A major campaign to mobilize international support for reform would also be launched. And U.S. representation to UNESCO would be strengthened.

McFarlane's strategy, if carried out, would seem to support the hypothesis that the U.S. withdrawal from UNESCO was an important component of a more general strategy of boycott diplomacy aimed at promoting constructive change in UNESCO. The remainder of this chapter and the next will examine U.S. involvement in the politics of reform in UNESCO in an attempt to determine to what extent the boycott strategy was indeed carried out.

CATALYST FOR CHANGE

As discussed earlier, in announcing withdrawal U.S. officials gave three main reasons to justify the action: (1) excessive politicization of UNESCO's programs and personnel, (2) the promotion of statist theories, and (3) unrestrained budgetary expansion and poor management practices. During the first half of 1984 these three broadly stated concerns served to define the official U.S. position. However, concrete solutions to these problems were not clearly and openly proposed; nor was a specific list of desired reforms articulated by UNESCO.

The Reagan administration's action, as we have seen, induced activity elsewhere in the U.S. government, and throughout the year numerous U.S. officials could be seen in Paris busily "observing" UNESCO. The investigation team of the General Accounting Office (GAO), the staff of the U.S. Mission, and members and staff of the Monitoring Panel were joined by members of the Executive Committee of the U.S. National Commission for UNESCO, staff of the State Department's Bureau of International Organization Affairs, staff study missions from congressional committees, and staff members from the White House and National Security Council. Also, numerous other U.S. nationals representing various governmental and nongovernmental bodies or in some cases simply themselves, travelled to UNESCO headquarters on reform-related matters. Indeed, during times when the Executive Board was in session, it was difficult to walk around UNESCO headquarters without running into such individuals from the United States.

Yet, the presence of so many different groups and individuals from the U.S. in Paris did not serve to clarify the ambiguity inherent in the official position on the reform issue. If anything, the large number of such individuals might well have served to create even greater confusion. Because neither the U.S. Mission nor the Bureau of IO Affairs would state clearly what reforms, if any, might lead to a reversal of the withdrawal decision, many UNESCO officials and permanent delegates would frequently seek such clarification from these other U.S. nationals. With respect to the "bottom lines," Assistant Secretary Newell also kept these individuals very much in the dark.

Restated in brief, the U.S. government's withdrawal announcement served as a catalyst for reinvigorating the reform issue and bringing it to the top of UNESCO's agenda. Yet, because U.S. officials would not articulate specific proposals for reform, it was up to the other national delegations within the Western Group to do so. Indeed, in large measure it was through the efforts of delegates in the Western Information Group (WIG), including the greatly constrained and oftentimes frustrated U.S. Mission staff in Paris, that a degree of clarity and direction was imposed on the agenda formation process.[4]

Reform Initiatives of the Western Information Group

The U.S. withdrawal sparked substantial debate over reform among the representatives of the member states of the Western Group. Beginning on January 10, 1984, these representatives engaged in what was to become an almost continuous dialogue on reform. In order to facilitate the work of the WIG in this regard a working group on reform was established. This group was chaired by Ambassador Maarten Mourik of the Netherlands.

By mid-February the chairman of the working group had produced a draft working paper on reform, the Mourik Paper. After further debate and revision a final text of this Western Information Group paper was released on March 12, as reflecting the views of a large majority of the group. Three basic categories of problems were identified: (1) structural/institutional, (2) political, and (3) program/administrative problems.

The discussion of structural/institutional problems focused mainly on two general concerns. One was a perceived imbalance in authority between the Secretariat and the delegate bodies (that is, General Conference and Executive Board) of UNESCO. The second was the decline of the Western Group from a position of dominance to a status of automatic minority. It was perceived that the views of this smaller group were not taken into consideration sufficiently, given that this group includes an overwhelming majority of UNESCO's main contributors.

According to the Mourik Paper, both of these concerns were largely by-products of the tremendous growth in membership in the organization. Such was also the case with regard to the second main category of concerns: political problems. Here, the paper's main focus was on undue politicization in the debates of UNESCO delegate bodies and with respect to a few program areas. The criticism was primarily a warning to other governments not to bring extraneous political issues (for example, Arab-Israeli conflict) into

UNESCO's debates. With respect to program areas, the paper specifically mentioned the NWICO, collective rights, and peace and disarmament. These concerns, however, the paper stated in much less strident and ambiguous terms than had been the case with U.S. claims.

With respect to the third basic category of problems, program/ administrative problems, the paper cited a number of specific concerns. Among these were problems related to program planning, lack of program concentration and prioritization, insufficient program monitoring and evaluation, and budget management. Other management concerns were grouped under two general headings: personnel and decentralization.

The proposals presented in the WIG paper have been summarized in Exhibit 4.1[5] at the end of the chapter. This exhibit also notes those proposals which had been explicitly mentioned by the U.S. and/or British Governments in written communications with the Director-General during the agenda formation period. These WIG proposals are important with respect to understanding the politics of reform in UNESCO during 1984. Not only did the paper represent the views of a large majority of the Western Group, but, in addition, it represented the first detailed enumeration of proposals for reform. Thus, the WIG paper played an important role in structuring both the agenda and direction of the subsequent reform debates within UNESCO.

In order to deal with these problems the working group was divided into seven subgroups. These groups focused on planning and management, communications, programs, peace and disarmament, human rights, structures and institutions, and the budget. Each subgroup was chaired, respectively, by Swiss Ambassador Hummel (planning and management); FRG Ambassador Vestring (communications); Swedish Permanent Delegate Watz (programs); British Second Secretary French (peace and disarmament); Austrian Ambassador Pein (human rights); Dutch Ambassador Mourik (structures and institutions); and U.S. Ambassador Gerard (budget).[6]

The work of various of these subgroups, and the WIG Working Group as a whole, played an important role in the process of building a reform agenda and negotiating change during the subsequent two years. By late April 1984 a WIG reform strategy had begun to take concrete form. It was agreed that a number of coordinated initiatives would be taken at the 119th Executive Board. For example, the British delegation would concentrate on drafting a resolution focusing on the need for reform. The Japanese delegation was to place formally before the board an agenda item on personnel questions. In a related move Ambassador Mourik would request the Director-General to provide specific personnel data. The Belgian permanent delegate was to introduce a draft resolution on evaluation. A U.S. draft resolution would call for concentrating the organization's program of work on "core" concerns, as identified in the UNESCO Constitution. Finally, the French delegate would propose the formation of a committee of the board to consider the issue of

60   ROGER A. COATE

reform and to come up with specific proposals for the 120th Executive Board.[7]

During the Western Group negotiations the U.S. Mission had become somewhat more specific regarding its position with respect to reforms. U.S. representatives in WIG circulated an unattributed list of thirteen proposed reforms. It should be noted, however, that this list (reproduced in Appendix 1) was not meant to be interpreted as an enumeration of what it would take to satisfy the U.S. government. As discussed above, Assistant Secretary Newell consistently refused to provide a detailed listing—or what he referred to as a laundry list—of the reforms required to keep the U.S. government in the organization.[8]

Newell's stance produced a great deal of frustration and anxiety among most members of the Executive Board, including those from the Western Group. U.S. officials, having raised the issue of reform, could or would not be drawn into forthright discussion of a program of action to identify reform proposals. Despite a competent U.S. Mission staff in Paris, the official U.S. policy position inhibited that staff from fulfilling its full leadership potential within WIG. During the first half of 1984 most of the non-WIG members were forced to operate on the assumption that the concerns of the U.S. government were represented in the positions articulated by the Western Group as a whole.[9] Thus, it fell to the British government to produce a detailed listing of desired reforms and assume a leadership role abdicated by the United States.

The British Government's Reform Proposals

On April 2, 1984, the British Minister of Overseas Development, Timothy Raison, transmitted a formal letter of concern regarding the situation at UNESCO to Director-General M'Bow. He expressed concern "about the political aspects of certain programmes, about the way in which UNESCO fora seem to be used increasingly by some to attack values and ideals set out in the constitution and about the growing size of the UNESCO budget. Above all we have increasingly questioned whether many of UNESCO's programmes represent good value for the money" (Raison, 1984). Mr. Raison also endeavored to make it clear that his government's review of UNESCO "was a national initiative and was not influenced by the actions or attitudes of others." This review of UNESCO's role and effectiveness was begun in mid-1983, well before the 22nd General Conference and the subsequent U.S. withdrawal announcement.

Raison attached to the letter a paper detailing those areas in which the British government felt that reform was necessary. That paper offered a number of specific recommendations with respect to program prioritization. Also, the paper addressed concerns related to the strengthening of the governing bodies, budgetary questions, program concentration and evaluation, decentralization and other management concerns, and preparation of the Third Medium Term Plan.

In this context the letter was relatively clear regarding the expectations of the British government for reform during 1984: "we expect to see significant indications of change during 1984 particularly in the context of management action and the Executive Board's consideration of the Director-General's preliminary proposals for the programme and budget for 1986/87. . . . We shall review our position before the end of this year" (Raison, 1984). Thus, while the British proposals did not call for constitutional change or any major structural reforms, the British government made a clear statement that some important changes were expected in other areas during 1984.

On July 4 Mr. Raison sent a second letter to the Director-General in response to a request from the DG for clarification of the British position on a number of points. Raison attached a two-page statement enumerating "further points on UK proposals" and addressed four general concerns therein. First, the British position on UNESCO's human rights program (XIII.2) was clarified. Program XIII.2 (education for peace and human rights) "should contain nothing which would have the effect of downgrading or diminishing the universally recognized human rights. . . ." Second, Major Program (MP) XIII ("Peace, International Understanding, Human Rights and the Rights of Peoples"), as a whole, should be revised to remove those elements over which considerable political tension exists. The statement reiterated the position that research on the arms race and disarmament is not a proper topic for UNESCO. Third, while expressing satisfaction with progress in the area of budgetary reform, Mr. Raison expressed the belief that further improvements were needed with regard to budget presentation. Finally, the question of organizational efficiency and effectiveness was addressed. On this topic Mr. Raison (1984) concluded by saying,

> It is important when programmes are being planned, that the resource inputs required should be carefully weighted against the potential benefits. If this examination indicates that the activity concerned represents poor value for money, the proposed project should be dropped, however intrinsically worthwhile the activity may be in itself. The importance of UNESCO being able to demonstrate that every dollar it receives is put to good use cannot be over-emphasised.

A summary of these and the various other British proposals (in addition to those noted in Exhibit 4.1) have been summarized in Exhibit 4.2.

By mid-May a reform agenda was for the most part in place. The WIG and British proposals discussed above constituted the main components of the agenda.[10] However, nearly half of the year was gone. From the perspectives of most delegates seriously concerned about reform in 1984 the time for agenda formation had passed. The time for serious negotiation was at hand.

NEGOTIATING REFORM

At times various of the U.S. observers, who knew little about the dynamics of decisionmaking in multilateral organizations, could be heard to bemoan the "business as usual" atmosphere they perceived in the formal proceedings at UNESCO headquarters. Yet, behind-the-scene business was anything but usual. Of course, the routine work of the organization did have to be done. However, even routine activities in UNESCO during 1984–1985 were significantly touched by the exigencies of the reform agenda. As discussed above, the preparation of a "Draft Program and Budget for 1986–1987" represented a case in point. Given that 1984 was the first year of a program biennium, planning and drafting of the next biennial budget (1986–1987) was an important order of business for the Secretariat. This process itself became entwined with the reform effort. In his letter (CL-2989) requesting suggestions for the new biennial program and budget, the Director-General asked for member states' opinions on several specific matters. For example, which program actions should be increased or decreased? Which should be regrouped and how? What should be done to increase program effectiveness?

Thus, from the beginning of 1984 the issue of reform was a dominant concern in Paris. Almost every aspect of UNESCO work was affected. However, the arenas within which substantive and procedural action could be taken to respond to demands for reform were relatively limited. As outlined earlier, the General Conference is the primary governing body of UNESCO. However, this body meets in ordinary session only once every two years. The U.S. notice of withdrawal came just a month after the end of the 22nd General Conference. The 23rd General Conference met only at the end of 1985, ten months after the U.S. government had terminated its membership.

Throughout most of this two-year period the main institutional arena for negotiating reform was the Executive Board.[11] The first meeting of this body after the U.S. announcement was the 119th Session, which met in Paris on May 9–23, 1984. Thus, the 119th Executive Board represented the first opportunity during 1984 for representatives of member states and the Director-General to clarify their positions and to interact in an organization-wide discussion of reform issues.

The 119th Executive Board

The issue of reform dominated the deliberations of the 119th Executive Board. Early in the session the Director-General moved to identify himself with the movement for organizational change. His "Oral Report to the Board on the Activities of the Organization Since the 118th Session" enumerated steps that had been or would be taken to improve the functioning of UNESCO. The general debate that followed was joined by an overwhelming majority (43 of 51) of the board's members. Most speakers praised the DG's report and the work of the organization. Yet, most also expressed the opinion that change was needed.

However, notions of what was to be done varied substantially. Numerous Asian delegates seemed to be primarily concerned about decentralization. Various members of WIG discussed the need for changes in numerous areas, including personnel, budget, and management practices, as well as institutional reforms. Some speakers, especially those from Eastern Europe, stated that although certain changes (for example, decentralization) were needed, care should be taken not to upset existing machinery.

Subsequent agenda items induced even more discussion of reform. The U.S. and British letters to the Director-General were introduced as separate items (items 5.1 and 5.11, respectively) and served as focal points in the reform debate. With respect to the discussion of the communication from the U.S. government (Item 5.1) most speakers expressed regret over the withdrawal and urged President Reagan to reconsider. Debate on Item 5.1 also provided delegates with an opportunity to elaborate certain concerns related to the issue of reform. For example, the U.S. and British delegates stressed the need to return UNESCO to its "original principles." The Japanese ambassador stated that the organization's program must be concentrated on "core areas" and prioritized accordingly. The delegate from Iceland, speaking on behalf of the Nordic Group (Denmark, Finland, Iceland, Norway, and Sweden), outlined ten main themes to guide the discussion of reform.[12] For the most part, however, the statements were very general in nature, as was the communication from the United States, which was the focus of the debate.

The debate on agenda item 5.11 was rather more specific. In large part this seemed to reflect the more specific nature of the communication from the government of the United Kingdom. Indeed, the specificity of the British letter even afforded U.S. Ambassador Gerard the opportunity to specify more explicitly various reform proposals that her government supported. In doing so, however, she carefully specified in each case that she was endorsing a proposal made previously by some other member of the board or, alternatively, some action promised by the Director-General.

At one point in her presentation Ambassador Gerard did begin to touch on several new points. For example, she suggested,

> she could go on—if time permitted—to raise other issues that deserved attention, such as a greater use of the secret ballot; the need for attitudinal changes between the Secretariat and Member States and

among Member States themselves; and the unfortunate and paradoxical fact that a considerable number of the major contributors to the Organization had the impression of being more and more excluded from the real process of establishing its goals, philosophy and direction (UNESCO Doc. 119 EX/SR.15 (prov):10).

However, in her subsequent comments she offered no concrete proposals for bringing about such changes.

The generally serene discussion that had characterized the debate on this agenda item was disturbed by the Director-General's oral response to the debate. In his comments he recalled that several board members (that is, Kaul of India and Pompei of Italy) had raised the issue of the U.S. government's financial obligation to the organization for 1985, should withdrawal actually occur. These board members suggested that the withdrawal of the United States might not exempt it from payment of the remainder of its assessed contribution for the 1984–1985 biennium.

The U.S. obligation was a matter of constitutional interpretation (that is, UNESCO Constitution, Article II, paragraph 6) and was one over which even Secretariat officials were divided. In his presentation the Director-General made it clear that the UNESCO chief counsel, Karol Vasak of France, had stated the opinion that no such legal obligation existed. However, the DG stated that he personally was uncertain. Apparently, another juridical study conducted within the Secretariat had reached the opposite conclusion from that of the chief counsel. Mr. M'Bow further commented that should differences of opinion continue on this matter the members of the board might wish to seek an advisory opinion from the International Court of Justice.

The U.S. ambassador's response came quickly and sharply. The U.S. government's legal experts had also studied this matter and were firm in their conviction that no such obligation existed. She also commented that she was shocked that she had not been informed that the matter would be raised by the DG. Later, in private, the Director-General apologized for having raised the issue without consulting the U.S. delegation beforehand. Also, the DG did not pursue the issue for the rest of that year. However, the incident remained clear in the minds of many U.S. officials. For a few it seemed to reinforce a privately held image that M'Bow was an "evil emperor."[13]

On the final day of the conference a deadlock arose over a Western draft resolution (DR) proposing greater program concentration in core areas. This DR, which had been co-sponsored by the representatives of nine Western states, plus Jamaica and the Philippines, was the subject of heated debate. Opponents challenged that the proposal was ambiguous and possibly unconstitutional; they argued that the resolution was the prerogative of the General Conference, not the Executive Board. Also, program implementation was the responsibility of the Director-General. Finally, after midnight of the last day of the session the Director-General broke the deadlock by suggesting that the operative paragraph of the draft resolution be referred to the newly established Temporary Committee.

At this session the board agreed upon a number of organizational changes. For example, they decided (Decision 3.3) that beginning with the 120th Executive Board, Assistant Directors-General responsible for program would meet individually with the board's Program and External Relations (PX) Commission for program hearings. These meetings were designed to strengthen the oversight function of the board.[14] The Assistant Directors-General were to be questioned on the planning, implementation, and evaluation of programs under their responsibility. Also, the board requested the Director-General to strengthen consultations with member states during the preparation of the draft program and budget documents. In order to capitalize on this action the Western Information Group agreed that the subgroup on programs would consult closely to establish a consensus on program priorities.

In addition, the Director-General consulted orally with the board in private session on the appointment of a replacement Deputy-Director General (DDG). This occurrence was noteworthy because it represented the first time that the Director-General put forward alternative candidates for the position of DDG.[15] Three candidates were put forward: Assistant Director-General (ADG) Knapp of France; ADG Tanguiane of the Soviet Union; and ADG Bolla of Switzerland. Most of the board's members favored Knapp and he was subsequently appointed DDG.

In his oral report the Director-General announced that he would establish five working groups within the Secretariat. These working groups (WGs) were to examine issues in the fields of personnel, evaluation, budget, programs, and public relations. Each of the groups, except for that dealing with programs, would include outside experts. These groups were to address reform issues that fell within the DG's realm of responsibility. Each was to complete its work during the summer and was to report to the Director-General. He would then incorporate the findings of these groups into his recommendations to be presented to the 120th Session of the board. In Resolution 4.1(i) the board noted the initiative with satisfaction and stated that it looked forward to the subsequent reports.

Perhaps most notably with respect to reform issues, the board created a thirteen-member Temporary Committee (TC) on reform (decision 5.11). This committee was "to present to the Board recommendations and concrete measures designed to improve the functioning of the Organization" (paragraph 8). The TC was to examine all proposals raised at the 119th Executive Board, including those dealing with the program and budget for 1986–1987, personnel and management concerns, and all other issues arising from the DG's reports and the debates over agenda items 5.1 and 5.11.

The membership of the Temporary Committee was to be comprised of two representatives from each of UNESCO's geographical groups, plus a representative from the French government in its capacity as host government. At the conclusion of the board session the region groups selected their representatives. In addition to France's J.-P. Cot, the following individuals were selected:

- Western Group: J. Gordon, United Kingdom
                  A. Isaksson, Iceland
- Eastern Group: J. Ostrovsky, USSR
                 I. Margan, Yugoslavia
- Asian Group: T. Kagawa, Japan
                 T. Kaul, India
- Arab Group: A. Rahal, Algeria
                 M. Messadi, Tunisia
- African Group: M. Musa, Nigeria
                 Y. Diare, Guinea
- Latin America: J. Vargas, Brazil
                 H. Wynter, Jamaica

As is clear from the list, there was no representative of the United States. Although the U.S. ambassador was strongly urged to participate, she declined membership. Ambassador Gerard later justified this decision as follows:

> Our strategy was not to seek a place on the committee, itself, but influence it through active work within the Western Information Group, which will act as a kind of staff for Western representatives on the committee. By continuing to work in close cooperation with the Western Group, the indispensable impetus we have given the reform process acquires wider support. At the same time, we preserve complete independence to make an objective assessment of the magnitude of change effected by the end of the year, and we avoid the danger of leading others to believe that we are signing on in advance to whatever issues eventually [emerge] from the committee's deliberations (Gerard, 1984a).

Such a strategy appears to have been consistent with U.S. officials' refusals throughout this period to identify specific reform proposals. Thus, the TC was forced to organize and conduct its work with only indirect participation by the U.S. representatives.

The Work of the Temporary Committee

The Temporary Committee held its first session on May 25. At this relatively brief meeting the committee decided on its rules of procedure and established a working agenda. Also at this session, a chairman was selected. The chairman of the Special Committee of the Executive Board, Dr. Ivo Margan of Yugoslavia, was elected by acclamation to this position.

It was decided that the Secretariat should prepare a list of questions raised at the 119th Session of the board that were relevant to the mandate of the TC. Members were invited by the chairman to submit in writing additional suggestions and proposals to be included on the agenda of future meetings.

The second session of the TC was held July 2–13. The agenda for this session contained four main items: (A) working procedures and effectiveness of the General Conference, (B) working procedures and effectiveness of the Executive Board, (C) decisionmaking procedures at both the General Conference and the Executive Board, and (D) decentralization.[16] In addition, several other minor items were placed on the agenda (for example, documentation, publications, use of external advice). Out of the discussions on these issues emerged an initial listing of observations and recommendations for consideration by the full Executive Board.

The work of this session of the committee, though, did produce some incremental results. What was done was "to draw together a series of detailed minor proposals which, if properly implemented with the good will of both the majority of Member States and the Director-General, would without doubt have a major impact on the conduct of business by both the Board and by the General Conference" (Church, July 17, 1984:4). This assessment by a member of the British delegation was offered with caution, given that only part of the terms of reference of the TC had at that point been addressed.

Furthermore, the British assessment (Church, 1984:4) continued: "Of the proposals we had put forward the only one of any real significance which was rejected was the increased use of secret ballots, and that is certainly not an issue on which the UK felt particularly strongly." It was perceived that the secret ballot would be divisive. This statement is significant in that it points to a major flaw in the U.S. strategy for dealing with the TC. According to Assistant Secretary Newell's letter and other official statements this was an issue about which the U.S. government did feel strongly. However, the policy pursued in Paris apparently failed to articulate and follow through effectively on such a concern.

The mid-point of this critical year of reform activities had passed. As will be discussed in detail later, from that point on it became structurally very difficult to add new items or otherwise to modify substantially the reform agenda that had been established. Furthermore, in his letter of January 31, 1984, requesting input to the drafting of a new biennial program and budget, the Director-General had established a June 30 deadline for member state's written contributions. Mr. M'Bow made it clear that it would be problematic to incorporate responses received after that date into the proposed main lines of the "Draft Program and Budget for 1986–1987" (23 C/5), which had to be presented to the 120th Executive Board in early fall for consideration.

However, it was mid-July when Assistant Secretary Newell transmitted the U.S. response. This July 13 letter, discussed earlier, arrived in Paris on the same day that the TC concluded its deliberations of those agenda items that focused most directly on two of Mr. Newell's three new fundamental concerns. Coincidence or not, the major round of TC deliberations over decisionmaking and working procedures and effectiveness of the governing bodies had now passed. The agenda for the third and final session of the TC had already been established. Regardless, U.S. officials would not be present to press directly for reconsideration of their concerns; they had declined membership on the committee and, thus, had given up their seat at the negotiating table. Given that there was little or no support in the Western Group for many of Mr. Newell's most sweeping demands for structural change, the U.S. had lost the opportunity for having these demands seriously considered.

The work of the TC continued at its third session, which was held September 3–21. The agenda was extended to include the following items: (E) questions related to the program, (F) administrative and budgetary questions, and (G) other business. With respect to agenda item E the TC placed specific focus on program elaboration, implementation, publications and documentation, operational activities, and evaluation. On each of these concerns, as well as for the other agenda items, discussion centered around draft recommendations. Those recommendations that were adopted by the TC were incorporated with those negotiated earlier into the "Report of the Temporary Committee of the Executive Board Responsible for Reviewing the Functioning of the Organization" (UNESCO Doc. 120 EX/3, October 3, 1984). This report was then placed on the agenda of the 120th Executive Board, which was to convene in Paris in late September.

Solidification of the Reform Agenda

As this final 1984 meeting of a UNESCO governing body approached, the reform agenda solidified. While the major structural changes demanded by Newell were not part of that agenda, various other U.S. concerns were incorporated. Newell's July 13 letter had called for a concentration upon those programs that the government viewed as the core activities of the organization and were widely agreed upon by member states. The assistant secretary specified a number of examples of types of activities that he found particularly troublesome. In addition, attached to the letter was a lengthy subprogram-by-subprogram response to the DG's request for contributions to the draft program and budget. This statement enumerated subprograms that were considered to be troublesome, as well as those that U.S. officials strongly supported.

Mr. Newell noted that some positive changes had been agreed to at the 119th Executive Board meeting in May. He mentioned specifically the decision to have Assistant Directors-General appear before the board for "hearings" and the board's request for the DG to intensify consultations on the preparation of the draft program and budget. However, Newell argued that further reform was needed in this area.

In addition, the letter proposed a series of changes in the general areas of management and budget. These reforms included a call for a zero real growth budget for the 1986–87 biennium, which should be achieved, Newell suggested, by reordering program priorities. Also, he called for improvements in budget preparation. With respect to management he concentrated primarily on personnel management and recruitment concerns, as well as on evaluation and decentralization.

As is clear from Exhibit 4.3, at the end of the chapter, U.S. officials were calling for a substantial number of changes that were not represented in either the WIG or the British government's statement on reform. However, again please note that because of the official U.S. negotiating posture, U.S. fortunes in the reform negotiation processes were inextricably linked to those of the Western Group more generally.

Before concluding his July 13 letter the assistant secretary again made it clear that the U.S. government was not undertaking its reform initiative alone.

> As you know, the Western Information Group, in its informal consultations prior to the submission of individual member states' recommendations on the 1986-87 program and budget, formulated a rank-order list of major sub-programs, according to their worth and value in the estimation of those member states. We believe that this rank-ordering is worth your consideration, not only for its expression of views about the programs themselves, but because the technique seems to us especially valuable. . . . A genuine rank-order listing of programs would, it seems to us, be an invaluable intellectual and management tool (Newell, July 13, 1984).

Thus, the U.S. government's commitment to use WIG as the primary mechanism for bringing about organizational reform was once again reiterated. However, the congruence between the U.S. government's reform proposals and those of other Western governments, as well as the Western Information Group as a whole, was by no means unambiguous.

In addition to the U.S. letter, two other member states—the Netherlands and the Soviet Union—asked to have separate items related to reform inscribed on the agenda of the 120th Executive Board.[17] Also, numerous other suggested changes were incorporated in various governments' responses to the Director-General's January 31 request (CL/2989) for recommendations regarding the drafting of the program and budget for 1986–1987 (23 C/5).

The letters from the Netherlands government and the Soviet government represented quite different approaches to the issue of reform. The Dutch letter stressed agreement with the main points made in the WIG paper, which had been drafted largely by the Dutch ambassador to UNESCO. Furthermore, this letter highlighted a number of those concerns about which Dutch officials felt particularly strongly, including undue politicization in the deliberations of UNESCO's governing bodies and in certain program areas (for example, Major Programs I [world problems and future studies], III [communications], VIII [development], and XIII [peace and human rights]); budgetary growth, transparency, and monitoring; personnel management practices; and decentralization of authority away from headquarters. The letter concluded with a diplomatic warning, hinting at the possibility of eventual withdrawal, though falling short of a formal notice: "If reforms which are generally agreed to be necessary are not carried out, or are not carried out sufficiently, and in particular if this should lead to the withdrawal of one or more of the Member States, the Netherlands Government will again have to review its position vis-à-vis the Organization" (Newell, 1984).

The letter from the deputy minister of foreign affairs of the Soviet Union had a quite different tone. It was highly critical of most of the Western states' demands for change in UNESCO, especially the major structural changes proposed by the U.S. government. A number of the major programs under attack were considered important by Soviet officials. Furthermore, the letter (page 14) charged that "the growing attacks in UNESCO are, in effect, directed at the whole United Nations System. . . ."[18]

However, the Soviet government also expressed the desirability of bringing about some organizational changes, including improvements in administrative efficiency, reductions in administrative costs, and improvements in personnel recruitment and management policies. Being the second-largest assessed contributor, Soviet officials attached importance to sound management and budgetary practices.

These two letters do not represent the most extreme positions in the reform debate. However, they do illustrate that the debate was not unidimensional.[19] While these governments were in opposition to one another with regard to one aspect of reform (for example, program prioritization and the related question of politicization), they expressed compatible positions with respect to other aspects (for example, personnel, management, budget administration). In general, however, the reform agenda that emerged primarily reflected the concerns of the Western Group.

While at an abstract level there appeared to be a consensus within WIG regarding major reforms, important differences did exist. Thus, arriving at a common policy position on specific reform items was in certain areas difficult to achieve. Such was the case even in the area of management reform, where there did appear to be relative agreement. To a few WIG participants, Director-General M'Bow represented the essence of the problem. Thus, management concerns were not universally perceived as involving exclusively tangible stakes. These delegates saw M'Bow as a despotic and incompetent administrator who frequently injected favoritism into personnel and administrative decisionmaking. As long as M'Bow remained, the management problems would remain.[20]

A great many other WIG delegates, however, attempted to confront management problems without personalizing them to the current Director-General. They viewed the stakes as being basically tangible. The Secretariat, as manifested in the person of the Director-General, was seen as being the most powerful organ in the organization. M'Bow's support was needed if reform was to be achieved; not only with regard to management reform but for almost all of the changes being proposed by the Western Information Group. Thus, not only were reforms possible under M'Bow's directorship, he could and should be used to attain such changes. Through cooperation, they believed, everyone could benefit.

With respect to other reform concerns, like program prioritization or redressing perceived structural/institutional imbalances, consensus was generally even more elusive. As we have seen with respect to the United States, some participants viewed the stakes in highly ideological terms. Other participants in WIG perceived the stakes to be basically tangible and subject to disaggregation. The extent of consensus in the various reform areas and the implications thereof for negotiating change in UNESCO during 1984 and 1985 will be explored in detail in a later chapter. Consensus or not, however, a reform agenda, modeled primarily along the lines outlined in the WIG paper, had been set firmly in place.

A substantial portion of that reform agenda had already been the focus of negotiations in the Temporary Committee. The 120th Session of the board not only would be asked to affirm officially the results of the negotiations, but represented the last opportunity for U.S. officials to work constructively for change within UNESCO.

THE 120TH EXECUTIVE BOARD

When the 120th Session of the Executive Board convened in Paris on September 26, 1984, reform once again dominated the agenda. The formal discussions on reform centered primarily around six agenda items:

3.1 Report by the Temporary Committee

4.1 Preliminary report by the Director-General concerning the draft program and budget for 1986–1987

5.1.1 The DG's oral report on the activities of the organization since the 119th Session

5.1.2   Report by the Director-General on the initiatives he has taken to improve the functioning of the organization

6.7   Communication from the Netherlands' minister of education and science to the DG concerning the Netherlands' policy on UNESCO

6.8   Communication from the deputy minister of foreign affairs of the USSR to the DG concerning the position of the USSR on the reform issue

The first four items mainly focused on the status of reform activities going into the 120th session: those recommendations for change negotiated in the TC and those initiated by the Director-General. As discussed above, the last two agenda items represented conflicting statements by member states regarding the need for and nature of reform.

The reform debate opened with consideration of the two reports by the Director-General under items 5.1.1 and 5.1.2. These reports contained among other things the DG's syntheses of the recommendations of his working groups. In this regard, Mr. M'Bow enumerated the decisions that he had already taken or intended to take. On numerous other matters he requested guidance from the board in the form of recommendations.

The debate continued with consideration of the communications from the governments of the Netherlands and the Soviet Union. In presenting his government's communication (item 6.7), the Dutch ambassador challenged the board to "agree to disagree" on those issues where fundamental differences existed. Thus, such issues would not be allowed to enter into UNESCO's program of work. Also, Ambassador Mourik announced that, should one or more other member states withdraw from UNESCO, his government would review its position regarding its continued membership. The discussion that ensued generally reflected a broad range of positions regarding organizational change.

The Report of the Temporary Committee was introduced for debate on October 8 by TC Chairman Margan. After interventions by nearly every member, the board adopted a resolution (Resolution 1) that endorsed all of the recommendations of the TC. In addition, the board acted upon several other resolutions related to the work of the Temporary Committee, including a decision (Resolution 5) to extend the operation of the committee until the 122nd Executive Board with a mandate to oversee the implementation of the TC's recommendations within an appropriate timeframe.[21]

In her intervention before the board on this item the U.S. ambassador stated that her government accepted the recommendations of the TC, although it regretted the limited nature of the decisions. Ambassador Gerard also let it be known that she would be introducing various additional recommendations in the form of draft resolutions. Specifically, she proposed that a majority of 85 percent of the members present and voting be required for the approval of the program and budget (UNESCO Doc.120 EX/DR. 24). Also, she proposed a mechanism by which any five members of the board could request that any matter related to the execution of the program or to relations with member states be "entrusted" to the Special Committee. Furthermore, unless the committee could come to "full agreement" on a recommendation to the board, the agenda item in question would be postponed to the next session of the board (UNESCO Doc.120 EX/DR. 16).

The Director-General's presentation of the possible main lines of the draft program and budget for 1986–1987 (Draft 23 C/5) was the final main agenda item dealing with reform to be taken up by the board. This presentation was made in four parts, which reflected the structure of the proposed draft 23 C/5. Part 1 of the DG's four-part report presented an analytical summary of the replies by member states and various international organizations to the Director-General's request for comments regarding the program and budget for the next biennium.[22] Respondents' comments had been grouped in such a way so as to highlight proposals for discontinuing or scaling down program activities, maintaining or reinforcing program activities, and/or regrouping activities.

Part 2 presented the DG's suggestions regarding the program for 1986–1987. An innovative feature of this part was that the DG specified options on contentious issues. He asked the members of the board to define their positions with regard to the options and to provide him with clear direction. The third part discussed budgeting techniques and proposed a budget base for the biennium. The budget base was set at $391,168,000, which represented a proposed budget freeze for the 1986–1987 biennium.

The structure of debate over this item followed the lines of the member states' positions as outlined in Part 1 of the document. Delegates from the Western Group once again stressed the need for further program concentration and prioritization. Also, they called on the Director-General and the other board members to reduce or eliminate programs over which there was contention. Again, various aspects of major programs I, III, VIII, and XIII were the main focus of concern.

The statement delivered by the U.S. ambassador added a new and very controversial element to the deliberations. Although the U.S. mission staff had prepared an extensive speech for Ambassador Gerard to deliver on the draft program and budget, about which UNESCO experts in the IO bureau felt quite favorable, she discarded that text in favor of her own more politicized version. The last half of her speech did not even focus on the draft program and budget but, instead, on the GAO's yet to be released draft report, titled "Review of UNESCO's Management, Budgeting and Personnel Practices."

The ambassador proposed that the Executive Board formally consider the report and, furthermore, that an extraordinary session of the board be convened in November to do so.

Ambassador Gerard had attempted earlier in the session to get the chairman of the Executive Board to circulate the GAO draft report as an information document. Chairman Seddoh had refused to do so, indicating that such an action posed a number of procedural legal problems. At the time the report was only in draft form. According to the formally established procedure of the GAO itself, the Director-General was to examine and comment on the study before it was to be put in final form. However, having just received the draft text, he had not yet been able to do so. Nor had the report been translated into the working languages of the organization. In addition, the document had no official character in UNESCO, given that it had been prepared by an internal agency of one member state. It had been commissioned by members of Congress not by the State Department or any other agency of the administration from which Ambassador Gerard was supposed to take her instructions. When the issue came up in the bureau of the board, it was the Belgian and Italian members who led the argument for rejection; they saw the U.S. delegate's move as a threat to the entire reform package, which was still being negotiated.

This new action by the U.S. ambassador on October 15 caused confusion and resentment both in Washington and in Paris. Ambassador Gerard had evidently not consulted with Assistant Secretary Newell beforehand, nor with members of her own mission, who were taken by surprise. Newell was not pleased by the action.[23] In Paris the reception was equally cold. The ambassador had also surprised the members of WIG, which met privately each day during the Executive Board and was the appropriate forum for launching such initiatives. Moreover, she had not followed UNESCO procedures for calling for an extraordinary session, even though only six signatures of board members are needed to do so. However, after considering the matter, the Director-General said that he would have no objection, should the board wish to consider the GAO report (UNESCO/2464, 19 October 1984).

Whatever the intent of the action, it had more the appearance of introducing a wrecking ball into the proceedings rather than a constructive step.[24] The proposal did not appear to contribute positively to the reform negotiation underway. The incident came to a close with the board member from Belgium indignantly declaring that there was no point in discussing a report that did not yet exist or a request for an extraordinary session that had not yet been made (UNESCO/2464, 19 October 1984). A general consensus had emerged among the members of WIG, excluding the U.S. representatives, that the reform package was a good start and was probably all that could be expected, given the constraints within which the reform process had had to operate. In the end Ambassador Gerard decided not to pursue the matter further.

In order to consider resolutions on all of the items before the Executive Board a drafting group was established. This group was comprised of two members from each regional group. Unlike the position taken with regard to membership on the Temporary Committee, the U.S. ambassador agreed to serve on this body.

In this regard the U.S. delegation put forth several draft resolutions (DRs). Two of these draft resolutions presented proposals for major structural reforms for which the U.S. representatives could find no other support, even within WIG. These were DR 16 and DR 24 mentioned above. In fact, the other members of WIG made a unanimous appeal to the U.S. delegate for her to drop DR 24 (that is, the 85 percent majority proposal). Another draft resolution (DR 17), which was co-sponsored by French, British, Icelandic, and West German board members, requested the General Conference to amend the financial regulations so as to allow the board to request the external auditor to carry out specific examinations.

Five other draft resolutions (DRs 18–22) focused generally on management concerns. The U.S. ambassador was joined varyingly by representatives of a few other governments in sponsorship of these proposals. The British representative cosponsored all but one, DR 22, which called for the establishment of "an advisory group of experts to assist the Finance and Administrative Commission in reviewing and formulating recommendations on the 1986–1987 budget proposal for consideration by the General Conference." The West German ambassador was the only cosponsor of this draft resolution. Only the U.S. and British representatives cosponsored DR 18 on the matter of requesting the Joint Inspection Unit to undertake a study on decentralization within UNESCO.[25] On the remaining three draft resolutions on personnel (DRs 19 and 21) and program evaluation (DR 20) the British, West German and French board members joined the U.S. ambassador, with the addition of Ambassador Isaksson of Iceland who also cosponsored DR 21.

The two U.S. draft resolutions on structural reform (DRs 16 and 24) caused a great deal of controversy within the Western Information Group. During a caucus meeting of the group a strong unanimous appeal was made to the U.S. ambassador not to push to have these resolutions brought before the board, especially DR 24 (85 percent majority). It was argued that such an action might destroy the delicate framework upon which the reform package, which had been negotiated over the year, was based. One Western permanent delegate confided that one important reason for the lack of support was that a formal voting requirement was not necessary. He argued that the Western Group already had effective control over the budget through the mechanism of the Geneva Group, should the members of this group choose to exercise such control.[26] Also, it was feared that DR 24 might have negative ramifications elsewhere in the UN system.

The five management resolutions (DRs 18-22) gained little support from the other members of the board, especially with members of the Group of 77. Numerous members of the board expressed the feeling that if these resolutions were brought to a vote they would be overwhelmingly voted down, perhaps setting back the momentum of the reform movement that had been established. Thus, to avoid such an eventuality the senior African ambassador and head of the Group of 77 at UNESCO, Mohammed Musa of Nigeria, suggested a compromise in which these DRs would be deferred until the 121st Executive Board session. Richard Aherne, deputy chief of the U.S. mission, stated that his government was willing to do so, even though U.S. representatives might not be present at that time.

An Icelandic proposal (DR 25) to prioritize programs within the draft program and budget for 1986–1987 also was withdrawn for lack of support. In general, this proposal would have given higher priority to practical programs for which there exists a high degree of support. Programs over which contention exists would receive lower priority. Of course, the United States and other Western delegations supported the idea. However, there did not appear to be overall agreement with respect to the specific prioritization of subprograms enumerated in the resolution.

On the final day of the 120th session the drafting group produced an omnibus resolution, DR 28. This resolution focused on the draft program and budget for 1986–1987 and made suggestions to the Director-General for revising the draft C/5 document. The nature of this document can perhaps best be summarized by quoting from the U.S. ambassador's comments on this item:

> Much progress is apparent in this DR. Program guidelines which are based on concentration, and a good sense of priorities, are given, and we support those trends with the conviction that, if followed over a period of years, they could produce a vibrant and responsive program for the organization. Our specific comments should be understood in the context of this generally positive view of the first part of the text—especially in comparison with analogous past resolutions on the program.[27]

The first part of the draft resolution to which she was referring focused on program. The remaining part of DR 28 addressed budgetary matters.

With respect to the budget the ambassador confined her comments to the question of the budgetary growth level. In the draft resolution the board was asked to choose between two budget base levels. Option 1 would allow a two percent growth rate. The second option would freeze the budget at the

1984–1985 level. The first option was favored by the representatives from the Group of 77.

On this question Ambassador Gerard stated a position quite clearly:

> If one calculates the amount of money involved in a two percent per year growth rate, one sees clearly that the sums are not particularly large. They do not compare, in fact, with the symbolic value that their forfeiture, by a decision of this Board in the interests of responsible financial behavior, would have in the eyes of my Government and other governments. *The passage of option two of paragraph 113 would be a truly significant sign of change in UNESCO* (emphasis added).[28]

The final language of the adopted resolution indeed gave the U.S. the zero-growth budget they demanded. A face-saving compromise was worked out that permitted the representatives from the Group of 77 to support the decision. Under the new wording the Director-General was invited to submit separately to the 121st Session of the board a list of additional proposals "outlining possible projects with costing amounting to up to 2 per cent of the 1984–1985 budget base for action programmes for developing countries, especially the least developed among them, preferably through arrangements within the framework of Technical Co-operation between Developing Countries (TCDC)." It was understood that funding for such projects was neither guaranteed nor even, if desired, necessarily to come from the regular program funds.

The 120th Session of the board, thus, concluded on a somewhat positive note. Yet, the future of U.S. membership in UNESCO did not look bright. Although it was clear to most close observers in the United States and in Paris that the U.S. government would soon be departing the organization, the future policy direction of the British government was less certain. The focus of this study is on U.S. participation in and relations with UNESCO; yet, the dynamics of the U.S. and British withdrawal processes were such that a full understanding of the U.S. action can be gained only by analyzing the interrelationships between the two.

Exhibit 4.1 Western Information Group Proposals

Management	UK	US
Secretariat should be made more efficient.	x	
Evaluation techniques, including self-evaluation, should be implemented and utilized fully.	x	
A separate Central Evaluation Unit should be set up and should report directly to the DG.		
Targets and progress indicators should be specified for each subprogram in the Draft C/5.		
All evaluation reports should be made available to member states and board members on request.		
Increased use should be made of outside experts in program planning, implementation, and evaluation and in seeking management improvements.		x
More intersectoral cooperation is needed.		x
More attention should be paid to quality as opposed to geographical origins in filling staff positions.	x	x
Member states should be encouraged to and assisted in completing consultation replies through simpler and more straightforward drafting.	x	x
Fewer documents should be produced.	x	x
Collaboration with other UN bodies should be improved to increase effectiveness of UN system.	x	x
A review should be carried out identifying the major areas of collaboration with other UN bodies.	x	x
Number and grading of proposed meetings ought to be studied carefully. Better preparation of meetings with particular reference to questions of agenda and the reduction of documentation.	x	x
A study, drawing on outside experience, ought to be carried out on management of fellowship programs for presentation at the 122nd Executive Board.	x	x
A review of the Office of Public Information should be made with goal of increasing its effectiveness.	x	
Administrative and personnel costs should be reduced and so reported in the C/5 document.		

Budget	UK	US
Method of calculating and presenting budget needs to be improved.	x	x
If U.S. withdraws, proportional cuts should be made in budget so as not to increase others' burden.	x	
The DG should make prompt return of all 1981–1983 Part VIII currency fluctuation gains in the form of credits to assessments of member states.	x	
The Executive Board should consider setting up a committee of experts on budgetary matters.		

Programs		
A shift of resources is needed from reflection to action (fewer studies).	x	x
Studies should be better planned and more relevant to both the urgent needs of member states and the action oriented elements of the programs.	x	x
Program priority should be given to activities aimed at assisting member states, particularly the developing countries, to find solutions to their urgent problems through international collaboration.	x	x
The Media Declaration of 1978 should not be enlarged.	x	x
Account should be taken of all views expressed by member states in the program commissions of the General Conference when implementing the program.	x	x
Clear criteria should be drawn up by the Secretariat for the selection of the most appropriate forms of action.		
Resource inputs should be weighed carefully against potential benefits for all proposed activities, and those which are ineffective should be rejected.	x	x
A reduction is needed in program spending in the biennium (1984–85) by the elimination of obsolete programs, programs that are really underfunded.		x
Activities for which UNESCO spends less than $100,000 excluding staff and indirect cost should be examined for their viability.	x	
A Secretariat paper should be prepared or an in-depth study should be carried out by the Special Committee, to enable the 121st session of the board to consider whether adjustments are needed in the major programs.	x	

UK   US

	UK	US
Draft programs for 1986–1987 should give greater priority to the core programs in education, science and culture; lower priority to: MP I, Programs III.1 and XIII.1, as currently constituted.	x	x
Programs need to be highly concentrated into a few core elements in education, science, culture, and communications where a "true consensus" exists.	x	x
UNESCO programs need to be streamlined.	x	x
Reduce program support for the NWICO.		x
The Draft 23 C/5 should include a rank-order list of subprograms, according to their priority.		x

Structural/Institutional

	UK	US
The Special Committee of the board should be charged formally with the oversight of all evaluation and related activities.	x	
Full use should be made of the presence in Paris of permanent delegations as representative of the governments of other member states.	x	x
Endorse practice of Director-General undertaking a full scale consultation of member states and NGOs in the first six months of the biennium.	x	x
Basic decisions about the method of preparation and timetable for the next medium term plan should be taken at the 23rd General Conference and should include a major exercise of consultation.		
Special committee of the board to be informed of and invited to comment on methods used within the Secretariat for monitoring progress of program implementation throughout the biennium.	x	x
Consultations between the DG and member states should continue and be intensified while the C/5 documents are being prepared (especially with regard to the elaboration of "main themes").	x	x
Stress importance of in-depth study, to be carried out by the Special Committee, on dissemination of results of studies and research.	x	x
Full consultation is needed between the Secretariat and member states during the preparatory stage of the medium term plan and discussion needs to be enlarged regarding possibilities for amendments.	x	

	UK	US
A more effective role should be established for and by the Executive Board in monitoring and evaluation of each major program.	x	
The existing practice of informative sessions with the DG and his closest collaborators on the eve of meetings of the Executive Board and General Conference should be extended to informal consultative sessions in the preparatory stage, including matters of substance.		x
Permanent delegations should strengthen their informal contacts on short term and longer term issues of a general interest to the organization.		x
Decentralization is needed to achieve the most effective distribution of responsibilities between headquarters and staff.	x	x
UNESCO debate should be kept focused on program and budget issues rather than on political issues.		x
Endorse practice of the DG undertaking a full scale consultation of member states and NGOs in the first six months of the biennium.	x	x
A review of the formal consultation practices of other UN bodies should be undertaken by the DG.		

Sources: The *Final Western Group Paper on UNESCO's Problems* (March 12, 1984); British letter to the Director-General of April 2, 1984 and various other statements by British officials; U.S. letter to the Director-General of July 13, 1984, the unattributed list of 13 points circulated by the U.S. Mission, and various other statements by U.S. officials.

Exhibit 4.2 British Proposals in Addition to Those Articulated as Concerns of the Western Information Group

Management	US
Recruitment standards need to be tightened and procedures should be improved and speeded up.	x
The external auditor should devote more attention to the "value of money" aspects of his work.	

Programs	
A recommitment to the fundamental importance of individual human rights is needed, maintaining an open mind about the development of new concepts that might further strengthen respect for them.	x
A review of provisions of the Second Medium Term Plan with regard to MP XIII (peace and disarmament and human rights) is needed.	

Structural/Institutional	
There should be fewer meetings.	x
The Executive Board should be given the opportunity to discuss in-depth the work of the Inspectorate General in monitoring Secretariat activities.	
Particular means should be found of ensuring that the General Conference benefits to a greater extent than hitherto from the policy guidance produced by the Executive Board and by the various specialist intergovernmental bodies.	
UNESCO periodical publications should, so far as possible, be self-financing.	
The board should reaffirm the decision of the 113th Session of the board that UNESCO standard-setting activities should concentrate on areas in which consensus appears possible and in which the need for universal norms is widely felt.	

Sources: Official letters as indicated in the text and interviews with officials from the governments of the United Kingdom and the United States.

Exhibit 4.3 U.S. Reform Proposals in Addition to Those Articulated by WIG or the United Kingdom

Budget and Management

Fixed term appointments should be just that, fixed term, and should not be rolled over year after year indefinitely.

Competence and experience should be given more weight in the promotion process.

Establishment of a policy forbidding employment by the Secretariat of Executive Board members until "x" number of years after they have ceased their function as Executive Board members.

The Secretariat should increase and expand its consultations with member states during the process of drafting the program and budget.

Unbiased implementation of personnel regulations and proper delegation of decisionmaking powers are needed, with due attention to the concerns of employee unions and associations.

Consultants should not be employed for tasks that can be done within UNESCO itself by its employees.

More U.S. citizens need to be appointed to UNESCO positions, especially at senior levels.

Contracts of high-level personnel should contain clear and specific provisions, regarding the degree and nature of the authority and responsibilities.

Budget

More accessibility is needed to budgetary data.

Programs

Zero real-growth budget should be achieved through a reordering of program priorities as outlined in U.S. program recommendations.

Emphasis in communication should be directed toward the basic objectives of UNESCO (e.g., IPDC).

Clarification is needed regarding the degree of responsiveness of UNESCO to program suggestions coming from the UNO.

A clear distinction between traditional human rights and peoples' rights should be articulated.

Structural/Institutional

A subcommittee of the Executive Board should be created to focus on budget and program matters before they become locked in.

A voting procedure is needed to ensure that no budget would pass without the affirmative support of members who together contribute at least 51% of UNESCO funds.

A broadened mandate for the external auditor should authorize and require the auditor to receive and respond to inquiries from geographic groups.

There should be more frequent and longer private sessions of the board to cover numerous subjects.

The Assistant DGs should appear before the program commission on a periodic basis for question and answer sessions on their respective programs.

A drafting and negotiating group (DNG) of the board should be created to review proposals and resolutions that have political overtones. The DNG would operate under a strict rule of unanimous consent. It could block contentious resolutions.

The DNG of the conference should be strengthened.

Increased use of secret ballots needs to be made in the Executive Board where possible.

Establishment of some mechanism of procedures to insure that individual member states are given appropriate influence, and are accorded due respect and consideration by the organization's Secretariat.

Mechanisms are needed through which member states are given real decisionmaking power, including the ability to change or eliminate programs presented in the Draft C/5.

Consideration, at or before the autumn Board session, of means by which the effectiveness of the board's subunits might be increased.

Reservations expressed at the time of the adoption of a consensus decision should be attached to text.

The board should more clearly define the roles, authority, and responsibilities of senior officials.

The role of the General Conference in determining general policy and in considering and approving the program should be reinforced.

Sources: Assistant Secretary of State Newell's July 13, 1984 letter to Director General M'Bow; the 13-point U.S. nonpaper submitted to the Western Information Group; U.S. interventions at the 119th and 120th Executive Board sessions; and summaries of U.S. reform proposals prepared by the Secretariat of the U.S./UNESCO Monitoring Panel; the *Final Western Group Paper on UNESCO's Problems*.

NOTES

1. Consultations with representatives of a number of governments from the Western Group, including Canada, France, and Israel, were reported to have taken place in Washington prior to the announcement of the decision (U.S. House of Representatives, 1984:26). State Department officials who were interviewed reported that the Israeli government had officially expressed concern that U.S. withdrawal would seriously affect their interests within UNESCO.

2. Actually, most delegates interviewed, even those from WIG as late as October 1984, expressed bewilderment and frustration regarding exactly what changes it would take to satisfy the Reagan administration.

3. However, we must be cautious in drawing conclusions in this regard. While the two cases appear to be very comparable in certain ways, in other regards they are somewhat different. Both institutions have very broad mandates, which range from rather narrow applied development projects to much broader and more ideologically based issues, like human rights. Both are what Cox and Jacobson (1973) have termed participant subsystem dominant organizations: decision processes and outcomes are heavily influenced by factors internal to the institutions themselves. Also, the main concerns of the U.S. government in both cases were initially linked to the promotion of statist theories and politicization (McHugh, 1984).

The fundamental concerns in UNESCO, however, as reformulated in July 1984, were different from those in the ILO case. For example, even though increased use of the secret ballot was being called for in both cases, the nature of the stakes involved was defined quite differently. In UNESCO the secret ballot proposal was linked to much broader notions of protecting minority states' rights, redressing a perceived imbalance between the governing bodies and the DG, and restoring authority to member states. In the ILO case the proposal was directed to more specific and tangible concerns: protecting labor and employer representatives in the ILO from recrimination for their specific voting behaviors from the officials of the states of which they were nationals.

4. The Western Information Group is a caucus within UNESCO established to provide a forum for Western delegates to debate issues and develop a coherent policy toward the organization. In 1984 there were twenty-four members of the group:

1.	Australia	13.	Italy
2.	Austria	14.	Japan
3.	Belgium	15.	Luxembourg
4.	Canada	16.	Norway
5.	Denmark	17.	The Netherlands
6.	Finland	18.	New Zealand
7.	France	19.	Portugal
8.	Federal Republic of Germany	20.	Spain
9.	Great Britain	21.	Switzerland
10.	Greece	22.	Sweden
11.	Iceland	23.	The Republic of Turkey
12.	Ireland	24.	United States of America

5. It should be noted that the table also specifies those reform proposals specifically mentioned in the British letter of 2 April and in the U.S. letter of July 13, as well as the Dutch letter of 17 July, 1984.

6. The work of the budget subgroup was in effect carried out through the mechanism of the Geneva Group. This body is comprised of those WIG members that contribute 1 percent or more of the assessed contributions to the UNESCO budget. The structure of the Geneva Group transcends UNESCO and cuts across the United Nations system.

7. On April 24, 1984, the French foreign minister had sent a letter to the Director-General proposing the creation of such a body.

8. The U.S. ambassador to UNESCO also refused to provide details. At the 119th Executive Board she argued that the U.S. government was not a defendant on trial. "Nor was it attempting to define terms of negotiation, for it was not negotiating" (Ambassador Gerard's intervention on agenda item 5.1).

9. The existence of the assumption became apparent during interviews with numerous non-Western Executive Board members in Paris in July 1984.

10. It should be recalled that the U.S. State Department's strategy was to work through WIG and not to undertake an independent initiative.

11. Of course, numerous reform proposals (for example, management reforms) fell under the exclusive authority of the Director-General.

12. These themes included (1) program concentration, (2) administration, (3) personnel recruitment and management, (4) budgetary questions, (5) operational programs and activities, (6) decentralization, (7) communication, (8) political problems, (9) UNESCO style, image, and credibility, and (10) the role of the organization's constitutional bodies (UNESCO Doc. 119 EX/SR.10 [prov.]).

13. Personal interviews and discussions, July 1984.

14. This item was originally initiated by U.S. representatives within the WIG and was advanced at the Executive Board meeting by the chairman of the PX Commission, Ambassador Dumont of Belgium.

15. This action was a marked departure from the Director-General's previous practice of putting forward only one candidate and then consulting the board only by letter. This practice had been opposed by a majority of the members of WIG. Furthermore, the WIG had proposed such changes as the DG adopted.

16. These agenda items covered many of the U.S. government's deepest concerns, as identified in Assistant Secretary Newell's July 13 letter to the Director-General.

17. Such requests were made in separate letters to the Director-General from the Dutch minister of education and science on July 17 and the deputy minister of foreign affairs of the Soviet Union on September 17.

18. It is interesting to note in this regard that Western delegates frequently made similar charges in private, when referring to U.S. proposals for major structural reform in UNESCO.

19. Perhaps the extremes are best captured in the positions of the U.S. and Indian governments. The U.S. officials were calling for major structural change, program concentration, and a budget freeze. The Indian ambassador countered that the UNESCO budget was too small and that the organization's governing bodies should continue to operate according to democratic principles (for example, one government, one vote). Also, there were perceived imbalances and inequities in the current world information and communications order that needed to be addressed; UNESCO was the institutional setting viewed to be appropriate for such a task.

20. Personal interviews, summer and fall 1984.

21. The Temporary Committee met and established such a timetable, which was to include three meetings in 1985.

22. Replies were received from 75 member states, 14 UN agencies, three IGOs, and 47 NGOs.

23. Personal interviews, October-November 1984.

24. I am indebted to Jonathan Davidson, former executive secretary of the U.S. National Commission for UNESCO, for the numerous insights that he has provided me in this regard.

25. It should be noted that by the time of the 120th Executive Board the State Department had reconsidered its position on decentralization. No longer were U.S. officials strongly demanding such action. Instead, the new U.S. position was that decentralization was a complex question that needed further study. According to U.S. officials, such action, if not handled properly, could raise administrative costs and make local offices susceptible to "undesirable influences" (for example, the Soviet Union).

26. The Geneva Group is an institutionalized mechanism throughout the United Nations system by which those Western governments that contribute 1 percent or more of the budget caucus with respect to budgetary concerns.

27. Jean Gerard, statement on DR 28, 120th Executive Board of UNESCO, Paris, October 15, 1984.

28. Ibid.

CHAPTER FIVE

Reform Successes and Policy Failures

Any uncertainty regarding the official U.S. or British responses, however, was short-lived. Exactly one month after the close of the 120th Executive Board the British foreign secretary, Sir Geoffrey Howe, announced his government's intent to withdraw from UNESCO at the end of 1985. A formal notice to this effect followed in a letter to the Director-General on December 5, 1984. The letter stated that this action was being taken to "safeguard" the British position should desired reforms not materialize at the 23rd General Conference.

The letter enumerated nine areas in which the British government desired additional reforms: (1) further program concentration and prioritization; (2) more action-oriented projects and fewer studies; (3) lower priority given to specified areas of concern in MP III (communications); (4) further reform of MP XIII (peace and human rights), including the rapid implementation of actions already agreed upon by the Executive Board; (5) assuring that nothing in program XIII.2 would downgrade universally recognized human rights; (6) the immediate return of surplus funds and agreement on how to reduce the program and budget to compensate for any change in membership (that is, U.S. withdrawal); (7) avoiding overlap with other UN bodies; (8) appointment of outside experts to advise on efficiency, economy, management and coordination; and (9) implementation of decentralization away from headquarters. The letter made it clear that the British government would conduct a further review of British participation in UNESCO at the end of 1985 to assess progress with respect to these various concerns.

The British decision surprised and angered many observers, including various Western Group delegations in Paris.[1] Representatives of the Commonwealth governments made a joint protest to the British foreign secretary. Gough Whitlam, former Australian prime minister and ambassador to UNESCO, went further to accuse Prime Minister Thatcher of basing her decision on a "disinformation campaign by an American right-wing research institute" (that is, the Heritage Foundation), which had been aided and abetted by the U.S. ambassador to UNESCO.[2] As we will explore later, these claims do appear to have had foundation.

Unlike the British case, however, the U.S. government's action surprised few observers close to UNESCO and/or the U.S. State Department.[3] In the words confided by a leading Western envoy to UNESCO, "the Americans gave too many signals that withdrawal was inevitable." Also, while the main text of the *Report of the Monitoring Panel on UNESCO for the Secretary of State* enumerated the various changes initiated in UNESCO during 1984, the "Executive Summary and Conclusions" of the report stated that "while there was considerable discussion and some incremental movement in the direction of . . . *fundamental* concerns of the U.S., there was no concrete change" (emphasis added). Here the report was referring to Newell's three "fundamental concerns." It should be noted, however, that most observers question whether this report had any real impact on the decision to withdraw. Indeed, even some State Department officials have confided that they believed the final decision had been made twelve months earlier.

As we shall explore later, close observation of the State Department's handling of the reform issue during 1984 leads one to question whether the reform of UNESCO was ever a serious primary objective of the Bureau of International Organization Affairs. Yet, in his official statement in mid-December 1984, confirming the U.S. withdrawal, Assistant Secretary Newell reiterated that U.S. officials remained "committed to the belief that genuine reform of UNESCO is a desired goal" (Newell, 1984c).

In announcing the policy decision, Newell outlined a three-pronged approach toward UNESCO:

- To promote UNESCO's reform—from the outside—the U.S. will designate a Reform Observation Panel of independent experts. It will be charged to assess and report on events within UNESCO, and to advance our continuing interest in reform.
- We will work with those—countries, individuals and private organizations—who seek improvement in UNESCO.
- We will establish an observer mission in Paris to protect American interests at UNESCO and to work with like-minded member states on reform measures, particularly between now and the 23rd General Conference in 1985. (Newell, 1984c)

The statement concluded, "When UNESCO returns to its original purposes and principles, the United States would be in a position to return to UNESCO." Indeed, U.S. officials initiated various of these actions outlined above. However, as 1985 wore on the U.S. government's capacity to participate effectively in the UNESCO reform process rapidly diminished.

FURTHER REFORM ACTIVITIES

Actual U.S. withdrawal threw UNESCO into yet another crisis. This time the problem was that of completing the second half of the 1984–1985 program and budget biennium without one quarter of the second year's assessed budget. The chairman of the Executive Board moved quickly to deal with this crisis. He called a special session of the board to be devoted exclusively to considering the consequences of the U.S. withdrawal. This Fourth Special Session of the Executive Board was set for February 12–16, 1985, at UNESCO headquarters in Paris.

As the opening of the session neared, the anxiety level among WIG delegates seemed to rise. Suspicions abounded regarding how the DG would attempt to cover the $43 million deficit. In general, Western diplomats wanted Mr. M'Bow to make up for the loss by cutting back those program activities which they viewed as being problematical. However, many of these same delegates feared that the DG was planning to make up the loss by withholding member states' shares of a $79.5 million surplus in a special reserve fund of the 1981–1983 program and budget. This fund had been established to protect against a decline in the value of the U.S. dollar.

The Director-General's *Report on the Consequences of the Withdrawal of a Member State from UNESCO* did little to relieve tensions, especially in the way it dealt with U.S./UNESCO relations.[4] Of specific concern was the final section of the report, which focused on the budgetary and financial consequences of the withdrawal. Mr. M'Bow took this opportunity to resurface the question of the liability of the United States for paying its originally assessed contribution for the entire 1984–1985 biennium. He stressed the following point:

> It has become clear that the provision of the Constitution concerning
> the withdrawal of a Member State . . . can give rise to divergent
> interpretations as to whether the contribution of a State which
> withdraws is or is not claimable. . . . The divergence of
> interpretations of the constitutional texts and regulations relating to
> this question raises a problem of international law that . . . the
> Executive Board has the power, under the Constitution, to have
> elucidated (UNESCO Doc. 4 X/EX/INF.4[prov]).

While worded diplomatically, the inclusion of statements like the above provided a foundation for individual board members to call for further action in this regard. Indeed, during the subsequent debate ambassadors Kaul (India) and Rahal (Algeria) again suggested that the International Court of Justice be requested to give an advisory opinion on this matter. Other board members, however, argued that calling on the ICJ would not be appropriate until all possibilities of direct negotiation between UNESCO and the United States had been exhausted.

In his reply to the general debate on the consequences of the withdrawal of a member state the DG reviewed the various interventions on this matter. Furthermore, Mr. M'Bow ended his remarks addressing what he referred to as the philosophical and political questions underlying the U.S. withdrawal. The DG's frustrations clearly surfaced as he queried, "What are these people hoping to gain? What are their real motives? What do the accusations of politicization and ineffectiveness conceal? Why these relentless efforts to travesty the truth? To condition public opinion in many countries? Why this apparent coordinated pressure and these persistent threats?" (UNESCO Doc. 4 X/EX/INF.6[prov], p. 11). Stating that he intended to conduct a study in this regard in the coming months, M'Bow added:

> For the time being I shall quote from only one text, that distributed by the former representative of the United States of America to the Executive Board on 15 October 1984, in which she wrote: 'But, our interests go beyond the functioning of the Organization. If all the management and personnel and budgetary reforms were agreed to, if UNESCO quite suddenly became the perfect model of administrative efficiency, management effectiveness, and staff productivity, that still would not, by itself, be enough. It must do things well, but it must do the right things. We have no interest in simply improving the machinery; were we to do so, we might just produce a machine which more efficiently did the wrong things.' The stakes are, it is clear, essentially political. And we should have the honesty to recognize this and the courage to say so (4 X/EX/INF.6(prov), p. 11).

While targeted against U.S. officials' seemingly one-sided conceptualization of politicization, the DG's comments served to draw attention to an important element of contemporary multilateral relations.

> Everything seems to point to a wish in some circles to call into question the basis of the entire international system created after the Second World War. . . . To understand the situation properly, it must be placed in its proper context. The public debate which has gone on for over a year has made it clear that the events centering on UNESCO are simply a reflection of the deep-seated political, economic, ideological and philosophical contradictions which characterize today's world (UNESCO Doc. 4 X/EX/INF.6[prov], p. 11).

Such analytical reflection might well be essential for problem solving in UNESCO in the long run. Yet, the attention of the board quickly returned to the more immediate exigencies of coping with the 1985 budget shortfall.

Indeed, a ten-hour continuous session climaxed and concluded this short special session. A composite resolution incorporating numerous decisions emerged at the end (UNESCO Doc. 4 X/EX/Decisions(prov), February 18, 1985). The Executive Board decided to invite the U.S. government to resume its relations with UNESCO and to authorize the Director-General to provide facilities to the U.S. Observer Mission.[5] The Director-General was asked to prepare a supplementary report for the 121st Session, examining adjustments that might be made to the 1986–1987 program and budget to allow for the budget shortfall. In this regard the board recommended to the General Conference that such a shortfall should not result in any increase in the assessed contributions of any of the member states.

Delegates of the special session invited the Director-General to undertake any appropriate adjustments, financial or structural, to reduce the organization's expenditures. Also, he was asked to explore other possibilities for fund raising and to create a special account for all voluntary contributions received. In this regard member states were urged to pay any assessed contributions that might be in arrears. Several members had already agreed to forego voluntarily their shares of surpluses that had accrued as a result of the appreciation of the U.S. dollar in Part VIII of the 1981–1983 budget. Other members were urged to consider similar sacrifices. In addition, Mr. M'Bow was to provide the 121st Board with an annex to the 23 C/5 in which the problem of adjustments and priorities is examined, so that the board could make recommendations to the 23rd General Conference regarding appropriate changes in the program and budget.

The board approved economy measures that the DG had already taken, amounting to about $15 million. Also, the DG had set up two working groups to consider additional measures in two specific areas. One group was undertaking a detailed study of staff needs with a view to eliminating or freezing particular posts where possible. The second group was examining the restructuring of various services in the Secretariat. The main targets of this study were the Sector for Co-operation for Development and External Relations and the Office of Public Information within the Sector for Programme Support. The main objectives of such reorganization were greater efficiency and economy.

In conclusion, the fourth special session ended with much uncertainty. A substantial budgeting shortfall still remained. Outside of the Director-General's articulated frustrations with the United States, the session was characterized by relatively little overt conflict. However, fear that the DG would continue to push to use funds from the 1981–1983 reserve fund surplus kept the tension level relatively high. Yet, although many board members appeared to have been greatly frustrated, the special session was characterized by relatively little overt conflict.

Frustrations appear to have been intensified for the members of the Temporary Committee when they met in April to establish a timetable for implementing those organizational changes that the board had agreed upon.

Various members expressed disappointment with the perceived inadequate preparation for the session by the Secretariat. In addition, some members expressed concern over the apparent delay in implementing many of the committee's recommendations.[6] Subsequent discussions with the chairman of the TC and U.S. officials seem to indicate that such conditions served to move the members of the committee into a more independent position vis-à-vis the Director-General.

In any event, the report that the TC sent to the 121st Session of the board clearly established the extent of reform that had been taken to date.[7] The TC provided concise tables showing the main measures adopted or planned to give effect to each of the recommendations on the TC's agenda. Also, a timetable was provided for implementing all relevant decisions taken by the board and by the DG.[8] Implementation activities and plans, as well as the lack of implementation, were portrayed with clarity. Thus, the format used would seem to serve as a reform score card, as well as a reform tool.

At its 121st Session the board adopted this report. Furthermore, the board also implicitly expanded the mandate of the TC to consider additional reform proposals, which was accomplished by a compromise over the management DRs that had been deferred to the 121st Session from the 120th Executive Board. When it was apparent that a forced vote would likely result in having the DRs voted down, their Western Group sponsors agreed to refer them to the TC.

Later interviews with members of the board revealed some interesting observations about this 121st Session. A general impression seems to have existed among Western Group delegates that this session was a turning point in the reform process. The session began with deep-seated feelings of frustration, which were intensified by the Secretariat's tardy submission of the 23 C/5 document. The session ended, however, on a rather consensual and positive note.

When the new draft 23 C/5 did arrive, the members found it to be a basically rewritten document. This revised version now took into account the decisions made at the 120th board session, as well as the recommendations of the DG's working group on programs. The program descriptions were clearer and more precisely costed and the General Conference was given the opportunity to select between options on controversial program activities.

This new draft, however, still contained numerous substantive problems from the perspectives of various WIG members. These concerns were directly confronted, and by the end of the session the Western members of the board had been able to achieve desired change in every major program area except major program XIII (peace and human rights). Questions about MP XIII were referred to the 122nd Session of the board. The mechanism by which the board and its WIG members reach agreement was a drafting group, created under the chairmanship of French Ambassador Gisèle Halimi. Under Halimi's strong direction, a full set of program recommendations was put together and quickly approved by consensus.

The budget crisis was also diminished in scope and magnitude. The Director-General announced that he had been able to cover much of the shortfall for 1985. Although a $10 million deficit remained, the perception of crisis had subsided. Also, the board agreed upon a method for handling the $82,575,000 budget shortfall for the 1986–1987 biennium. Cuts would be made in programs and program services by creating a new budget category called Part IX—Blocked Funds. Second priority program actions would be transferred to this account and placed in reserve,[9] and would be implemented later only if voluntary contributions were made to the organization. Thus, in effect program prioritization would be rigorously applied.

Subsequent to this session of the board the Temporary Committee completed its work and on September 24 issued its final report, *Third Report of the Temporary Committee*.[10] This four-part report contained a detailed review of the progress on implementation, based on the timetable that had been previously established. The report also included a discussion about future arrangements for monitoring the process of reform. This report was presented and approved at the 122nd Session of the board, which met in Paris in late September, just prior to the opening of the 23rd General Conference in Sophia on October 8, 1985.

The two years of reform negotiations came to a climax in Sophia. The conference served mainly to concretize the numerous changes that had already been agreed upon. Included in the more than 100 resolutions that were adopted by consensus was approval of a zero-growth budget, which reflected the loss of U.S. funding by placing 25 percent of lower priority program activities in reserve.[11] This action represented the first time that a system of priorities had been applied to UNESCO programs. As discussed above, the formal adoption of the program and budget for 1986–1987 (23C/5) brought movement toward program concentration in line with the recommendations of the internal working group's Critical Analysis of the Programme.[12] Other notable decisions were: creation of a program on intergovernmental informatics,[13] preparation of an action agenda for the elimination of illiteracy by the year 2000,[14] and establishment of a World Decade for Cultural Development.[15]

A resolution on Peace, Development and International Scientific and Cultural Co-operation was adopted unanimously on the proposal of the drafting and negotiating group[16] and the British won further concessions on major program XIII.[17] The conference reaffirmed the importance of MP XIII and redirected its focus. With respect to the maintenance of peace and international understanding, particular attention is to be placed on promoting capacities for research, training, and exchanges of information in UNESCO's spheres of competence. Also, UNESCO is to contribute to the promotion, protection, study, and teaching of human rights, as well as "to clarify the relationship between rights of peoples and human rights as they are defined in existing universal international instruments."[18]

In adopting the report by the Executive Board on its activities in 1984–1985 the conference appealed to the U.S. government to rejoin and to the British government to reconsider its position. The board decided that the U.S. should be reimbursed for its $5 million advance to the Working Capital Fund. Also, consideration of a proposal to request an advisory opinion of the ICJ on the matter of the U.S. obligation for its 1985 budget assessment was deferred. Finally, UNESCO reaffirmed its commitment to treat nationals of withdrawn member states under the prevailing laws on international civil service.

At the close of the General Conference the 123rd Executive Board convened for a brief organizational session. It made clear that reform activities would continue. Ivo Margan, chairman of the Temporary Committee, was elected as the new chairman of the board. Furthermore, the Special Committee of the board was reduced from thirty-three to eighteen members and its terms of reference were revised. The board instructed the Special Committee to monitor, assess, and report on the implementation of reforms approved by the Executive Board and/or initiated by the Director-General. The Special Committee's mandate was further broadened to enable it to suggest adjustments to reform decisions, as might be deemed necessary in the light of such results.[19] This was viewed by members of the Western Group as an important step for it further institutionalized the reform process.

As the representatives departed Sophia, press reports circulated that British delegates "were guardedly satisfied" with conference results.[20] Referring to the contents of a confidential U.S. observer mission report to Washington, British authorities were quoted as saying that they had achieved significant improvements in major program XIII, which had been identified earlier as the single most important remaining concern, and that it could be made to work if Britain remained a member. Yet, this report went on to add that the British delegation had refused to speculate on the prime minister's assessment.

Such a posture turned out to be a very prudent one. Three weeks later Mrs. Thatcher took her government out of UNESCO. Apparently, the changes that had been initiated or agreed upon during 1984–1985 were insufficient for the British, as well as for the U.S.; or were they? As the analysis of reform outcomes in the following section reveals, UNESCO and its member states had undertaken a substantial amount of constructive change in a rather short period of time.

CHANGES IN UNESCO: AN APPRAISAL OF REFORM

Reform-related activities during 1984–1985 did appear to bring about some change within UNESCO. But to what extent did such change correspond to the demands being made by these two governments? Also, which of the numerous reform proposals were addressed during the year and how?

A general caveat is in order in this regard. Change is a continuous process in all social institutions. Also, it almost always occurs incrementally and, thus, should be viewed as a matter of degree. The full magnitude of any planned organizational change may take years to materialize. In complex social systems small planned changes in one area might become enhanced or be negated by natural or planned changes in other areas. Thus, it is exceedingly difficult to assess change in any precise fashion without the wisdom of time.

This analysis of reform outcomes will follow a format similar to that used in the preceding chapter to describe the various sets of reform proposals. Thus, management, budget, program, and structural decisions and actions will be examined as distinct reform areas, each being analyzed in a separate subsection below. In addition to identifying those reforms which were initiated, those major reform proposals in each area that do not appear to have been addressed in any meaningful way will be enumerated.

Management Changes

As discussed earlier, in mid-1984 the Director-General created five working groups, four of which focused primarily on management concerns. Numerous suggestions made by these groups of experts appear to have been adopted by the DG (UNESCO Doc. 120 EX/9 and 121 EX/3). The process of adopting these suggestions was itself a novel activity within UNESCO. Furthermore, the adoptions were notable for they signaled the DG's willingness to become a party to the reform process.

Also, the Director-General appointed two Deputy-Directors General in 1984. These DDGs were delegated expanded responsibilities. The process by which the DG consulted with the Executive Board regarding these appointments was viewed by most Western delegates as marking a new willingness to involve the board more fully in such deliberations. Traditionally, and indeed constitutionally, the sole responsibility for such appointments rests with the Director-General.

Various recommendations of the Temporary Committee pertained directly to management concerns. The TC welcomed the measures that the DG took with respect to program evaluation. Emphasizing the importance of evaluation, the first TC report stressed the value of enhancing the role of the Central Evaluation Unit.[21] In this regard the importance of both internal and external evaluation was underscored, as was the need for clear targets for programs. Also, the TC recommended that the special committee examine evaluation reports annually and report its findings to the board.

In order to enhance evaluation activities the DG established a separate Central Evaluation Unit. Subsequently this unit was strengthened by the commitment of additional professional and director posts and two general service posts. Also, one officer in each program sector was given responsibility for evaluation work. In addition, an intersectoral evaluation committee was established to coordinate and direct evaluation activities.

The Temporary Committee also called for the establishment of a comprehensive personnel policy, which would be aimed at bringing new talent into the Secretariat. The DG therefore initiated various steps designed to improve the recruitment process.[22] For example, the Office of Public Information and the Bureau of Personnel were restructured, as were various personnel recruitment procedures. Two special advisory boards were established to provide advice on the appointment of interim contracts. This action was accompanied by a decision to reduce the number of temporary staff.

With respect to the matter of delegating authority, the Deputy Director-General and Assistant Director-General for Administration were charged with the responsibility of making appointments at various ranks. Also, the Assistant Director-General, director of the cabinet, was delegated the responsibility for liaison activities with regional coordinators and for implementation of the decentralization policy. In this regard an intersectoral committee was established to coordinate decentralization activities. Furthermore, all operational projects executed at headquarters were to be examined and a list was to be enumerated of projects and posts to be decentralized.

These and other management reform decisions and activities are enumerated in Appendix 2.1. These data, as well as those presented in Appendixes 2.2–2.4, represent a comprehensive assessment by substantive area of actions taken with respect to each reform proposal listed in Exhibits 4.1–4.3. In addition to listing those reform actions that were initiated, Appendix 2.1 specifies those management proposals that were not addressed in any meaningful way.

While changes in UNESCO's management procedures and practices were not fundamental concerns for the U.S. government, they were for the British government and other members of the Western Information Group. Nearly all of the WIG management proposals were acted upon; only two were not. Those which were not requested a study on the management of UNESCO's fellowship programs and the establishment of a policy whereby all evaluation reports would be made available to member states and board members on request. While in practice board members will have access to such reports, it is not clear that the same applies to officials of member states.

In addition, three other British proposals went unaddressed. The external auditor had not been instructed to devote more attention to the "value of money" aspects of his work. Also, no board action was taken with respect to limiting the use of fixed term appointments in the Secretariat. Nor was any action taken to curb the practice of hiring former Executive Board members upon their departure from the board. It should be noted, however, that the vast majority of British concerns in the area of management were addressed.

Budgetary Changes

Closely associated with management change were numerous demands for budgetary reform. And, as illustrated in in Appendix 2.2, it was the budget area in which the most dramatic reforms were achieved. Foremost, a budget freeze was instituted for the 1986–1987 biennium; the 1986–1987 program and budget was planned on the basis of the 1984–1985 budget level. An additional 25 percent reduction was absorbed in the 23 C/5 subsequent to U.S. withdrawal.

Numerous recommendations were approved that aimed at making the budget more "transparent" and at increasing comprehension. As recommended by the TC, a parallel set of budget documents was prepared to show the effect of biennial recosting. Also, as discussed below, biennial program and budget documents are to be prepared in two volumes. One volume presents the main lines of the budget. The other volume describes the proposed program with corresponding budget provisions. In addition, the budget base is to be adjusted to show inflation costs at the end of the biennium.

The board also decided that any shortfall in revenues, resulting from the withdrawal of a member state, should be offset by voluntary contributions or by internal cost-saving measures; no supplemental assessments were imposed after the U.S. withdrawal. The shortfall in the 1986–1987 biennial budget was addressed by placing second priority program actions on reserve.

Finally, with respect to budgetary reforms, the Director-General conducted a feasibility study regarding the establishment of a small group of experts to advise the board on budgetary matters. The DG's study, however, fell short of the U.S.-sponsored draft resolution (DR 22), which called for the immediate creation of a body of budget experts.

Program Changes

The preparation of the draft program and budget for 1986–1987 occupied center stage on the program reform agenda. The nature of the Director-General's report in this regard was discussed earlier, along with his various innovations (for example, providing the Executive Board with choices on programs over which contention exists and asking the board for direction in such regards).

The Executive Board at its 120th Session addressed, the subject of program changes in the form of the omnibus resolution on program and budget, draft resolution (DR) 28. As summarized by the U.S. Monitoring Panel on UNESCO (1984:5–6),

> The resolution . . . provided important policy guidelines on program planning as well as numerous decisions and recommendations on particular program issues. The resolution contained a decision reflecting U.S. concerns on core concentration. . . . This highly watered-down version of core concentration is . . . new and therefore significant since it is the first time that this principle has been adopted as an operational guideline. Beyond that, the omnibus resolution in inviting priority attention to programs which the U.S. considers to constitute the core, is a beginning step in the right direction. However, it should be noted that no progress was made in agreeing to criteria for establishing programs nor any mechanism for prioritizing existing programs.

The panel also concluded that some meaningful progress had been made in addressing the problem of the proliferation of programs. These actions were important because they represented a renewed commitment by the board to become more actively involved in the planning and execution of the organization's program of work.

With respect to extraneous politicization "the Executive Board and the Secretariat were notably more restrained in their pronouncements on the program" (U.S. Monitoring Panel, 1984:6). There was little or no reference to world orders such as the New World Information and Communications Order. Nor was there reference to certain other issues that particularly troubled the Reagan administration, such as support for national liberation movements. At the end of 1984 the U.S. Monitoring Panel concluded the following:

> While this does not mean that these activities will automatically cease, it indicates concern for U.S. sensitivities. This applies too in the case of a number of specific decisions the Board took on programs regarded by the United States as unduly anti-Western in their orientation: communications, people's rights, peace and disarmament. The Board adopted operational language *in each case* which offers the opportunity to chip away at the more offensive aspects of these programs and redirect resources and activities into more constructive and positive channels. While there was no single dramatic gesture in this regard, the cumulative shifts in attitude by the Secretariat and the Executive Board on the program add up to a helpful step—and open the way for the West to build on this progress as the program is elaborated further (U.S. Monitoring Panel, 1984:6–7, emphasis added).

The U.S. delegation had desired a much stronger action with respect to program prioritization. The Icelandic representative had proposed a draft resolution (DR 25) at the 120th board that would have established differential priorities for eighty-eight specific subprograms. Although the U.S. government's priorities, as defined by Assistant Secretary Newell in his July 13 letter, were in specific instances significantly at variance with those proposed by Mr. Isaksson, the practice of undertaking such a prioritization exercise was strongly supported by the U.S. delegation.[23]

Other specific reform recommendations that had not been acted upon by the end of 1984 included the WIG proposals for an in-depth study of the major programs by the Special Committee, the elimination of obsolete programs, the reexamination of the viability of all activities for which UNESCO spends less than $100,000, and the rejection of any proposed activities that are ineffective with regard to the relationship between costs and benefits.

Also, the U.S. and British governments had pushed for greater change in the area of human rights. Both governments had proposed a recommitment to the fundamental importance of individual rights. The U.S. government furthermore desired a clearer distinction between traditional human rights and peoples' rights. This latter concept was apparently very problematical to the Reagan administration.

Program reform continued as a major focus of reform efforts during 1985. At year's end a program and budget for the 1986–1987 biennium was approved that represented a marked improvement over previous C/5 documents from British and U.S. perspectives. Many contentious programs were given low priority and were not funded for the biennium; others were eliminated. In addition to being less contentious than in the past, the 23 C/5 spoke directly to U.S. priorities. These and other reform decisions and actions are enumerated in Appendix 2.3.

The format used by the Secretariat in preparing the *Draft Program and Budget for 1986–1987* represented a substantial improvement over past practice (Coate and Davidson, 1985). For example, the program and budget was prepared in two volumes. Volume 1 presented the DG's exposition of general policy regarding the organization's program of work and a brief overview of its main lines. Although from a U.S. perspective this volume could have been more explicit regarding the elaboration and explanation of changes that were made, the new format did clarify the presentation of the program.

Volume 2 contained a detailed and specific description of the program and corresponding budget estimates. For example, statements regarding expected results and targets were generally clear and precise. Expenditures were broken down for each subprogram by activity. The additional information in volume 2 has been helpful in assessing the 23 C/5.

In the draft 23 C/5 a significant number of options for the General Conference to choose between had been specified. In nearly every case the options provided WIG members the opportunity to make additional program changes. More elaborate information was also provided on operational activities. Additionally, much helpful information was included in the appendixes (for example, various types of activities in each subprogram, personnel by sector and location, including headquarters/field). However, more precision might have been helpful regarding the life cycles of program actions (Coate and Davidson, 1985).

It would appear as though the two volumes were an important step toward prioritizing UNESCO program activities. Program activities were classified according to two levels of priority. Those activities specified by two stars were to receive high priority and those with one star were to receive low priority. As discussed earlier, the Executive Board has already made use of this innovation in coping with the 1986–1987 budget shortfall. As a result UNESCO's program of work has been made more concentrated, reflecting Western priorities for doing so.

According to the unclassified cables sent in May 1985 from the UNESCO desk in the IO bureau (IO/UNESCO) to the U.S. Mission in Paris assessing the draft 23 C/5, IO/UNESCO officials were favorably impressed with the draft. With respect to the major programs about which the U.S. government expressed most concern (for example, MPs I, III, VIII, XIII) significant change was made. These changes are summarized in Exhibit 5.1 at the end of the chapter. In most cases the funding for contentious program activities was sharply reduced or eliminated. Also, the program was substantially depoliticized. References to new world orders were muted. Furthermore, progress was made toward a more generally acceptable definition of the concept of peoples' rights. Priority in the communications area has clearly been given to communications development. The New World Information and Communications Order is described as "an evolving and continuous process," wording designed to meet U.S. and other Western concerns. Recognition was given to Western communications concepts such as self-censorship, pluralism, and the "watch-dog role" of the media. Technical aspects of disarmament have been declared outside the mandate of UNESCO.

More specifically, the major program on reflection on world problems and future oriented studies (MP I) was modified in the direction desired by most Western countries:

- By retaining a broad endorsement: "Emphasizing the importance of Major Program I, which is consonant with the intellectual mission of the Organization and which plays an essential role in the overall planning of UNESCO's activities"
- By reducing funding by 29%, from a $2,654,100 base in 1984/85 to $1,880,000 in 1986/87

This more modest approach was welcomed by most WIG delegations.

Furthermore, the targets and expected results from this major program have been more clearly and concisely stated than in the past.

The proposed Major Program III—communication in the service of man —reverses the general past emphasis on theoretical programs. On the balance, MP III stands decidedly improved, decidedly more balanced, and decidedly more open to Western views and priorities. The changes in this major program go a long way in meeting both the British and U.S. objections.

The revised Major Program III has moved its focus from reflection to action. Fully 72 percent of the total communications budget now goes to the development of communications infrastructures in Third World countries, and to the training of communicators. The programs devoted to the development of communications have been increased by a planned 2.9 percent (1986/87 over 1984/85), while the theoretical programs, studies on communications and free flow and dissemination of information, have been reduced by 7.6 percent and 6.8 percent respectively. That represents a cut of $310,200 in theoretical programs and an increase by the same amount in development programs. The preamble to MP III furthermore stressed the special importance of the strengthening of the activities of the International Program for the Development of Communication (IPDC).

The 23 C/5 goes a long way to meet the criteria for change in UNESCO set out in Assistant Secretary of State Newell's letter to Director-General M'Bow of July 13, 1984. The draft now gives high priority to programs the U.S. government favors: training for communications development, the U.S. approach to censorship and self-censorship, diversity in the content and mode of communications, support for private media, and the crucial definition of the NWICO as "an evolving and continuing process."

The Newell letter urged the reduction or elimination of activities that excessively politicize communications issues, continue the debate over the NWICO, concentrate on theoretical studies and conferences rather than action programs, or undermine the free flow of information. The 23 C/5 moved to meet these criticisms. Programs to study theoretical questions have been reduced. Politically controversial activities have been given secondary priority. For example, programs on the impact of new technologies, and the working conditions of journalists—both highly contentious in the past— have been given secondary rating and, thus, have not been funded for 1986/87.

The revised major program on principles, methods and strategies for development (MP VIII) is also an improvement over previous versions. The activities contained therein appear to be much more oriented toward the UNESCO main mandate. Increased emphasis is placed on the elaboration of evaluation approaches and techniques and the strengthening of the UNESCO capacity for using them. Also, overall the major program is less statist oriented. However, this major program is still somewhat problematic from the U.S. government's perspective. For example, the proposed program structure seems to be moving away from concentration (an increase in the number of program actions from twenty-four to twenty-seven). In addition, various elements remain ill-defined and appear to go beyond UNESCO competence.[24] On the positive side MP VIII appears to be much less statist-oriented, although some of the language used is ambiguous in this regard.

In short, the balance between reflection and action has been improved. Also, the new MP VIII (strategy for development) should yield improved collaboration with other UN agencies and NGOs. Given that development has been a dominant concern in UNESCO for several decades, improvements such as those contained in the 23 C/5 should enhance further UNESCO's development-related activities.

Major changes have also been made in Major Program XIII (peace and human rights), both in substantive content and in emphasis. "On balance," the IO/UNESCO cable about this major program declared, "our overall impression is that Major Program XIII has undergone significant change which, if concurred in by the 121st Executive Board session and the 23rd General Conference session, could contribute to defusing the contentiousness of this program."[25] Those elements of MP XIII declared by the U.S. government to be most politicized and controversial have been removed or downgraded. Also, prioritization within this major program closely reflects those priorities outlined in Mr. Newell's letter of July 13, 1984. Highest priority has been assigned to the promotion and protection of human rights. Greater resources have been allocated to the development of public international law, actions to strengthen the application of human rights instruments, the expansion of human rights education, and the improvement of UNESCO activities in human rights supervision.

The highly contentious area of peace and disarmament has undergone substantial revision. Funding for disarmament-related issues has been reduced. Furthermore, some of the most controversial disarmament-related activities have been eliminated (for example, production of disarmament and security handbooks, studies of alternative military strategic doctrines). Technical aspects of disarmament are now acknowledged to lie outside UNESCO mandate. Finally, emphasis is now placed on the role of scholars and postgraduate students in clarifying issues related to peace, human rights, and fundamental freedoms in lieu of stressing the need for disarmament education in the schools.

Serious efforts were made to address U.S. and other Western concerns about the contentious issue of peoples' rights. Individual rights are clearly regarded as the basic element in any consideration of human rights. Peoples' rights are considered in the context of the fundamental importance of individual human rights. A clarifying statement from the Secretariat declares that "there exists no tension or opposition between the rights of man and the rights of peoples, since the rights of peoples are rights of man and their realization makes more effective the exercise of the rights of man."[26] Instead of treating peoples' rights as an existing and separate concept, the new program poses the issue mainly for consideration within the fundamental field of individual rights.

Programs on the issue of peoples' rights have been reduced. The issue is treated as an idea deserving to be studied by a variety of groups and scholars (for example, U.N. Center for Human Rights, The Hague Academy of International Law), an orientation that is more compatible with U.S. beliefs and values. Also, the new program reduces the direct involvement of UNESCO in conducting studies of human rights and issues such as the consequences of arms races. Instead, emphasis is placed on conducting literature surveys of academically responsible bodies. Finally, it should be noted that the work of the UNESCO human rights action committee—the confidential body that seeks to help individuals who claim their human rights were violated—has been enhanced. This is one of UNESCO's most useful and beneficial programs.

Overall in the 23 C/5 document, there has been a decided shift of priorities from reflection to action. Throughout the program there is greater emphasis on training activities, including workshops, technical advice, and assistance. At the same time the need has been acknowledged to keep reflection and action closely linked.

The 23 C/5 reflects numerous recommendations made by the Executive Board and various internal groups. Steps have been taken toward program concentration although much remains to be done in this direction. The number of subprograms has been reduced from 186 (22 C/5) to 149. Also, there has been a reduction in the number of individual program actions from 477 (22 C/5) to 447. A substantial part of this reduction has resulted from the reduction in support for contentious programs.

Structural Changes

The main activities in the area of structural reform focused on the work of the Temporary Committee. These and other structural reform decisions and actions are outlined in Appendix 2.4. As mentioned above, all of the recommendations of the TC were adopted by the Executive Board. However, the scope and magnitude of the changes were limited. The major structural changes proposed by the U.S. government did not materialize. Moreover, various of these proposals received no other support.

The main thrust of the Temporary Committee's recommendations was an attempt to give and/or restore to the governing bodies a greater degree of authority and control over the Secretariat and the work of the organization.

Specifically, the TC recommended reinforcement of the role of the General Conference in determining general policy and in considering and approving the organization's program of work. More careful preparation of the General Conference was called for; and specific recommendations for accomplishing such ends were put forth. Also, the TC made a number of specific recommendations for reasserting the authority of the General Conference and the Executive Board.

With respect to the role of the Executive Board the TC recommended that the number of board members not be increased for ten years. The bureau of the board was to play a greater role in discussing agenda items. Also, the bureau, not the Secretariat, should set the time and duration of Executive Board meetings. The role of consensus decisionmaking was also reaffirmed. Furthermore, as far as possible the program and budget should be approved by the consensus process.

The Temporary Committee endorsed the notion of greater decentralization and recommended that the Executive Board monitor decentralization, as well as operational activities. The Director-General was invited to submit to the board a decentralization program for the rest of the decade. Several of the DG's resulting initiatives are noteworthy. He established an intersectorial committee within the Secretariat to coordinate decentralization activities, and a working group to consider one by one all operational projects still executed at headquarters and to submit proposals for projects and posts to be decentralized. Also, the DG announced the decentralization of thirty-seven additional projects and the transfer of seven headquarters posts to the field for implementation.

Other of his noteworthy recommendations include a reduction in the number of General Conference documents and a review of publications. The precedent of establishing a body, like the TC, could be viewed as an indication of reform. It should be recalled that the mandate of the Temporary Committee was renewed for an additional year to ensure that the recommendations of the Executive Board are carried out by the Secretariat. Furthermore, the TC has been asked to make any recommendations to the board that it deemed necessary to facilitate further progress and implementation of reform.

As mentioned above, the sweeping structural reforms, which Assistant Secretary Newell termed "fundamental reforms," received virtually no support, even within the Western Group. Thus, the establishment of a drafting and negotiating group (or its functional equivalent) in the Executive Board did not occur. Similarly, the creation of a voting mechanism to assure that those governments who contribute the majority of UNESCO funds could control the organization's program and budget failed to materialize or even to be considered seriously. Also, no decision was made regarding the increased use of secret ballots or holding more frequent and longer private sessions of the board. These and most other major structural changes, even if there had been support for them, would have required either constitutional changes or changes in the rules of procedure of the General Conference, both of which lie outside the scope of authority of the Executive Board and, thus, the board was loath to treat them.

The difficulties surrounding the implementation of structural changes bring into focus a more general consideration with which an assessment of reform outcomes must be qualified. Numerous constitutional and interrelational factors served to circumscribe decisionmaking parameters in UNESCO rather narrowly, especially during 1984. Various constraints appear to have been important in shaping both the reform process and the resulting outcomes.

STRUCTURAL CONSTRAINTS TO REFORM

As we have seen, UNESCO had a particularly broad constitutional mandate and a rather imbalanced functional division of authority. The nature and scope of role relations among the main organs, as well as among the participants interacting within the organization, had evolved over four decades of practice. Thus, whether grounded in constitutional provisions or having resulted from historical practice, the decision processes in UNESCO were delimited by a highly structured set of parameters within which the reform processes had to operate. The analysis below explores the extent to which organizational characteristics impacted upon the reform process and shaped the nature and scope of the changes that we have observed.

Perhaps foremost among organizational factors was the division of authority among the main organs (that is, General Conference, Executive Board, and Secretariat). As discussed in the preceding chapter, the Executive Board's scope of authority has been rather circumscribed. Simply stated, the board has been mandated the authority and operational capability to provide only a rather general oversight function over the activities of the Director-General (and therefore the Secretariat) and to make recommendations to the General Conference with respect to a variety of concerns, including the draft program and budget. The work load of the board and the periodicity of its sessions have in practice further limited its effective authority; the board's authority has not been fully exercised.

During winter and spring of the first year of a biennium (for example, 119th Session in 1984), the Director-General normally undertakes a general consultation with all member states in regard to drafting the next biennial program and budget. At the spring session in this first year, the main activity is the adoption of decisions required to implement the decisions of the recently concluded General Conference. The autumn session of the first year focuses on the preliminary proposals of the Director-General relating to the draft program and budget for the next biennium. The board's scrutiny of the draft intensifies at its six-week spring session of the second year, the largest of the biennium. Given that the draft C/5 document is required to be transmitted to all member states ninety days prior to the opening of the General Conference, this is the session at which the board must make its recommendations about the DG's proposed program and budget.

Concrete action on most reform matters requires approval by UNESCO's principal governing body. Yet, as we have seen, there was no meeting of the General Conference during 1984. Without a session of the General Conference during that year, relatively few of the organizational changes being demanded by the U.S. government could have been effected conclusively. Significant changes in the program and budget, especially if they were to deviate from the second medium term plan, would require action by this primary governing body. Also, nearly all of the major structural reforms were matters to be dealt with by the conference. Yet, even in the face of its December 31, 1984, ultimatum, neither the U.S. delegation nor any other member called for an extraordinary conference session.[27]

In addition, by the time that Mr. Newell specified publicly the U.S. government's "fundamental" concerns (for example, on July 13, 1984), it was already too late constitutionally to make major structural changes during 1984 because such changes would have required amendments to the UNESCO Constitution (Article XIII.1). Yet, whether by plan or by policy failure, the six-month deadline required for formally communicating proposed constitutional amendments to member states precluded any such actions after the beginning of July. Thus, it was no great surprise that the U.S. Monitoring Panel on UNESCO (1984:i) concluded that "while there was considerable discussion and some incremental movement in the direction of these . . . fundamental concerns of the U.S., there was no concrete change." Given established operating procedures within UNESCO, constitutional requirements, and the way the administration implemented its withdrawal strategy, concrete change could not have been expected to occur during 1984.

This conclusion is reinforced by the failure of the IO bureau to submit its response to the DG's consultation inquiry on the 1986/87 program and budget on time. Other than rather vague statements about politicization and statism in UNESCO, which identified only a small number of specific program activities, the IO bureau made no enumeration of specific proposals for changing the substance of the organization's voluminous subprogram structure during the first six months of 1984.[28] Mr. Newell's letter, setting out such proposals, came when only three months remained before the opening of the last meeting of an executive organ prior to the deadline when withdrawal was to take effect. Thus, as Mr. Newell repeated often, UNESCO could not change enough in 1984 to satisfy the U.S. demands; it appears as though the way in which the U.S. withdrawal policy was implemented assured that would be the case. Short of the General Conference enacting "concrete" changes, the position of the Director-General assumed preeminence in the reform process.

Management reform, of course, was largely dependent on the DG's unilateral response. Even in this seemingly specific area, however, much ambiguity existed. The issue of decentralization was a case in point. To the Director-General, decentralization meant moving the execution of programs from UNESCO headquarters to the field. However, U.S. officials also requested moving authority downwards from the Director-General and his immediate staff to lower levels of the UNESCO bureaucracy in Paris and the field. As discussed earlier, since the days of Torres-Bodet, the DG has surrounded himself with a French style "cabinet" of top advisors. Centralization was an important component of the management problem, as initially stated by U.S. officials. In discussions with U.S. officials in late summer 1984, however, it appeared that they were sudddenly downplaying the decentralization issue. Apparently, a concern over who might gain effective influence over localized authority led to a reconsideration of the official U.S. position. Thus, by the time the 120th Executive Board convened in October, decentralization was not an issue the U.S. representatives aggressively pursued.

In each of the other reform areas, too, the DG's position was central. He and his staff were responsible for drafting the program and budget document. Also, the five working groups that Mr. M'Bow established in May-June 1984 played important roles in defining the nature and scope of change in their respective areas.

The Director-General's political role within the organization, especially vis-à-vis the Third World majority, meant that he could, within broad limits, effectively manage much that went on in the negotiations and even block specific changes, should he decide to do so. As U.S. officials were obliged to admit privately, however, the DG did not assume such an obstructionist role. To the contrary, by May 1984 it was clear to U.S. officials that M'Bow, perhaps unwillingly (as suggested by several U.S. officials), had become a party to the reform process.

In brief summary, then, the politics of reform were played out in a highly delimitated organizational environment. The structural constraints governing decision processes in UNESCO, when linked with the rigid time constraints inherent in the U.S. withdrawal actions, precluded any serious consideration of major institutional-structural reform. The kinds of concrete actions demanded by the U.S. government to address what its officials termed "fundamental" reforms simply could not have been attained in 1984. It should be recalled that only five and a half months remained in the calendar year following Mr. Newell's articulation of U.S. concerns. In terms of actual decisionmaking, of course, much less time remained. Also, concrete reform would have at a minimum required General Conference action. Yet, little or no effort was made to call the conference to a special session.

Structured organizational change depended mainly on the success of Western delegates operating within the context of the Executive Board. In turn, the board delegated reform negotiations primarily to its specially created Temporary Committee on Reform. It was largely in the context of this body, and in its relations with the Director-General that significant organizational reform was negotiated during 1984–1985. Indeed, the change was such that most of the articulated demands of the British government were addressed. Moreover, given the constraints within which the reform process was forced to operate, it appears that those reforms that were attained closely approached the limits of change that could reasonably have been expected.

BOYCOTT DIPLOMACY OR FAILED POLICY?

Reviewing U.S./UNESCO relations during 1984, there was little evidence that during much of 1984 the IO bureau attempted to respond to McFarlane's request in any concerted way. It took two full months after the withdrawal announcement for the IO bureau to produce a justification for the decision.[29] Throughout the year, U.S. officials consistently refused to provide a detailed listing of those reforms necessary for the U.S. government to reverse its decision. Although a panel of experts was formed to monitor reform in UNESCO, Assistant Secretary Newell would not even provide this body with the necessary list.

It was a strange coincidence that the only detailed public statement outlining proposed reforms made by the U.S. government—Assistant Secretary Newell's letter to the Director-General on July 13, 1984—was made on the very day that the Temporary Committee had been scheduled to conclude its negotiations on structural and institutional reform. The deadline for that letter, which was in reply to the DG's request (CL-2989) for member states' suggestions on the 1986–1987 program and budget, had been June 30. What is even more curious is that this letter, for the first time, publicly referred to structural and institutional reforms as being fundamental concerns of the U.S. government. Prior to this time, the main focus of U.S. statements on reform had been undue politicization, the promotion of statist theories, and excessive budgetary expansion. Only as the TC was concluding its scheduled major round of deliberations on decisionmaking in the General Conference and the Executive Board did Mr. Newell publicly link U.S. reform proposals rigidly to major structural reform in those organs of UNESCO. It should be recalled that the U.S. delegation had declined membership on the TC, following Ambassador Gerard's forceful declaration at the 119th Session of the Executive Board in May 1984 that the U.S. government would not define terms of negotiation, because it was not negotiating.

Curious as these coincidental happenings may appear, it should be noted that there was a significant bureaucratic process in operation within the IO bureau. As one careerist in IO summarized that process, ". . . Newell and his minions thought they could get by with platitudes. It then dawned on them—very late in the game and out of sync with UNESCO's processes—that they had to be more specific to be credible, thanks in large part to WIG pressures. The July 13 statement was hastily put together to respond to this contingency."[30] Again, it appears as if the long-time UNESCO experts in IO dragged their feet and kept attempting to frustrate Newell's withdrawal activities. Newell and his newly appointed IO/UNESCO director knew little about UNESCO or, for that matter, about IGOs generally; the old timers who possessed knowledge of UNESCO and IGOs refused to cooperate.

As a congressional study regarding McFarlane's request to strengthen U.S. participation in UNESCO concluded, "There is little evidence that from January–May, the Bureau [of International Organization Affairs] and the U.S. Mission responded to this request, and the U.S. policy in UNESCO did not reflect a strong commitment to reform. Instead, the United States demonstrated ambivalence about its role in UNESCO . . ." (U.S. House of Representatives, 1985:5). However, the IO bureau did take several actions. A deputy assistant secretary for the private sector was appointed. Although the responsibilities of this position appear never to have been clearly defined, she did oversee the UNESCO office in the Bureau of IO Affairs. The U.S. mission in Paris was raised from a class 4 to a class 3 ambassadorial post. The grade/rank of the political officer at the mission was upgraded from Foreign Service Officer (FSO) 3 to FSO 2. An individual (non-FSO) was hired to draft speeches for the U.S. ambassador to UNESCO. Two half-time local hires were made, one to serve as a budget officer and one to identify positions in UNESCO for U.S. nationals. Also, a budget officer was temporarily assigned to the mission in Paris (U.S. House of Representatives, 1985:21–22).

At the same time, however, an experienced director and deputy director of the IO/UNESCO office were rotated out of the bureau in early 1984. Both of these individuals were FSOs, experienced in UNESCO affairs. In addition, there was no AID/Development Officer in the U.S. Mission (U.S. House of Representatives, 1985:21–22). Thus, while some changes were made with regard to U.S. participation, a substantial upgrading did not occur.

As stated colloquially by one U.S. observer, Newell had "hit the mule between the eyes but then had walked away."[31] U.S. officials had failed to capitalize on any possible shock value that the initial action might have had.

Furthermore, in the UNESCO case, U.S. credibility within the organization had not been enhanced. Quite to the contrary, the actions of certain U.S. officials (especially Ambassador Gerard) throughout 1984 brought much consternation from other members of WIG.[32] A leading Western reform proponent on the Temporary Committee confided bluntly that more could have been achieved in the TC for the U.S. position, if U.S. officials had been willing to articulate specific reform requirements in a timely fashion.[33] There emerged a general concern in WIG, as well as in the TC more generally, that no matter what major concessions were granted to the United States, Mr. Newell would simply make additional demands for even more far-reaching change.

The U.S. actions with respect to DR 24 (the 85 percent proposal) and the GAO report proposals brought even greater consternation to members of the Western Group. It should be recalled that the Italians and Belgians had led the move in the bureau of the board to reject Ambassador Gerard's GAO report proposal in October 1984. The general perception among WIG members was that Ambassador Gerard was attempting to break apart the consensus over the package of reforms that had been negotiated. Although most members of WIG did not feel that the package in itself was sufficient, they believed that it was a good start and that much more could be accomplished later. Her forcing the issue at that point with the DG and the Group of 77 would not facilitate such longer term objectives. For similar reasons the WIG members had made a unanimous appeal to Ambassador Gerard to get her not to push DR 24 at the 120th board. In short, the actions of Assistant Secretary Newell and Ambassador Gerard—and by default the U.S. government—did little to enhance U.S. credibility in UNESCO following the withdrawal announcement.

Overall, there is little evidence to support the hypothesis that the U.S. withdrawal action was in practice part of a larger strategy to reform UNESCO. U.S. officials had called into play what is perhaps a major funder's ultimate weapon in international organization politics: threat of withdrawal and in this specific case termination of 25 percent of the organization's budget base. However, it does not appear that the United States used its policy instrument well, if at all.

> When the United States announced its decision in December 1983 to withdraw from UNESCO in December 1984, it appears to have had no clear set of goals and strategy for reforming the organization. General U.S. objectives were articulated throughout 1984. However, specific recommendations were still being developed as late as October 1984. Because U.S. objectives were not clearly laid out for UNESCO, many believed that the decision to withdraw was irreversible even though the United States has expressed willingness to reconsider its withdrawal decision if reforms were made (U.S. House of Representatives, 1985:5).

While a strategy of boycott diplomacy might well have been envisioned in the minds of National Security Advisor McFarlane and/or members of his staff, the activities of other political appointees appear to have inhibited that strategy from materializing.

We are left at this point asking a new, as well as an old, question. In the face of such feeble participation in the reform effort by Reagan administration officials, how can we account for the substantial amount of change that occurred in UNESCO? Moreover, given the change that did occur, why did the U.S. withdraw? The following chapter expands the analysis of reform politics in order to answer these questions.

Exhibit 5.1 Major Program Reform Balance Sheet

	Positive	Negative
Major Program I Reflection on World Problems and Future Oriented Studies	—limitation of MP I to areas of competence of UNESCO —substantial program reduction and concentration —targets and expected results have been clearly and concisely stated	—more program concentration required, and still less emphasis on this major program vis-à-vis areas of higher priority
Major Program III Communications in the Service of Man	—the major program is more balanced and open to Western views —high priority is given to programs that the U.S. favors (communications development) —major shift of resources to III.3 —major refocusing from reflection to action —NWICO continues to be treated as an evolving process —substantial program concentration (reduction from 47 to 34 program actions)	—certain programs opposed by the U.S. government remain —further reduction in the theoretical element of MP III (III.1) is needed —explicit reference remains to the application of the 1978 Declaration on the Mass Media
Major Program VIII Principles, Methods and Strategies of Action for Development	—reorientation of program activities to UNESCO mandate —increased emphasis on evaluation —less statist oriented —Programs VIII.2 and VIII.3 are consistent with U.S. interests —balance between reflection and action has been improved —emphasis on collaboration with UN agencies and NGOs	—increased number of program actions —Program VIII.1 is vague and ill-defined —Program VIII.1 needs to be further concentrated

	Positive	*Negative*
Major Program XIII Peace, International Understanding, Human Rights, and the Rights of Peoples	—MP XIII has been restructured to restore prominence to individual rights —peoples' rights are no longer treated as a universally accepted concept —peoples' rights activities have been reduced —prioritization reflects U.S. concerns —disarmament-related funding has been reduced —various controversial activities have been eliminated —technical aspects of disarmament are declared outside of UNESCO mandate —increased support for the UNESCO human rights action committee —emphasis on human rights education	—more program concentration is needed —activities dealing with the causes and consequences of arms races and with disarmment remain part of MP XIII

Source: Roger Coate and Jonathan Davidson (eds.), *Assessment of the Draft Programme and Budget for 1986–1987 of UNESCO*, Washington, D.C., U.S. National Commission for UNESCO, December 1985.

116   ROGER A. COATE

NOTES

1. "Anger at Britain's Unesco Threat," *The Guardian*, Tuesday, November 27, 1984.
2. Ibid. The U.S. ambassador's activities will be discussed in detail in Chapter 7.
3. Apparently, Director-General M'Bow was an important exception in this regard. In April 1985 former Deputy Director Bolla described to members of the United States UNESCO Observation Panel M'Bow's great shock when the U.S. government announced its final decision to withdraw and the British government announced its intent to do so at the end of 1985.
4. UNESCO Document, 4 X/EX/2 and corrigenda.
5. It is noteworthy that the board did not adopt a proposal that any staff reductions resulting from the U.S. withdrawal should be applied in the first place to members of the Secretariat, who are nationals of the state that has ceased to be a member. The Director-General had opposed such a move (UNESCO Doc. 4 X/EX/INF.4(prov), p. 2).
6. UNESCO Document, 121 EX/39, p. 5.
7. UNESCO Document, 121 EX/3.
8. UNESCO Documents, 120 EX/Decision 31, Sect. 1; and 120 EX/9.
9. UNESCO Document, 121 EX/INF.8(prov.), p. 25.
10. UNESCO Document, 122 EX/3, Parts 1–4.
11. UNESCO Document, 23C/Resolution 21, November 9, 1985.
12. UNESCO Document, GT/INTERNE/REP, July 19, 1984.
13. UNESCO Document, 23C/Resolution 6.2, November 8, 1985.
14. UNESCO Document, 23C/Resolution 4.6, November 5, 1985.
15. UNESCO Document, 23C/Resolution 11.10, November 8, 1985.
16. UNESCO Document, 23C/Resolution 25, November 9, 1985.
17. UNESCO Document, 23C/Resolution 13.1, November 8, 1985.
18. Ibid.
19. UNESCO Document, 123 EX/Decisions 7.1.
20. "Unesco `Satisfied' British Objections," *The Guardian*, London, November 16, 1985.
21. For references in regard to specific reforms, please consult the notes for Appendixes 2.1–2.4.
22. The reforms were enumerated in a 13-page statement, "Recent Decisions and Initiatives of the Director-General," which was prepared by the Office of the Director-General at the close of the 120th Executive Board Session. Also, see: UNESCO Doc. 120 EX/3(Part 2).
23. For example, on nine of the twenty-eight subprograms for which Mr. Isaksson proposed to give priority, the U.S. official position had been either to reduce or to eliminate them.
24. U.S. State Department, IO/UNESCO cable to U.S. Mission in Paris, May 1985.
25. Ibid.
26. Ibid.
27. The constitution does make provision for the calling of extraordinary sessions of the General Conference (Article IV.9(a)). Extraordinary sessions can be called by the conference itself or by the Executive Board or on the demand of at least one-third of the member states.
28. A qualification should be noted with respect to this point. There had been a substantial change in personnel within IO/UNESCO. There were few

people left in the IO bureau who knew anything about the intricacies of UNESCO programming and budgeting. Moreover, those few UNESCO experts who did remain appeared to have a strong dislike for the new IO/UNESCO director, who was considered by some as "Newell's stooge." As one careerist put it, "we sought to undercut him and make him look ridiculous." In short, constant personnel changes, ignorance, deliberate efforts to sabotage, and battle weariness, as well as the ideological disposition of high-level IO bureau officials, were important factors affecting the way the bureau implemented its withdrawal strategy during this period. Personal interviews, winter and summer 1987.

29. U.S. Department of State, U.S./UNESCO Policy Review, February 27, 1984.

30. Personal interview, summer 1987.

31. Personal interview, spring 1985.

32. Personal interviews, fall 1984 and fall 1985.

33. Personal interview, fall 1984.

CHAPTER SIX

When Ideology Triumphs

The United States was only one among a number of member states who had called for change of one kind or another in UNESCO. The Dutch ambassador, Maarten Mourik, attempted to place the U.S. position in a larger perspective: in his introduction to the Western Information Group paper on reform, Mourik argued eloquently that

> it would be tantamount to confounding cause and effect if one would consider the U.S. decision to withdraw from UNESCO as being at the origin of UNESCO's present crisis. The U.S. decision . . . is a symptom, to be taken very seriously, of tensions that have been building up within UNESCO over a long period of time, leading to disappointments and frustrations which wholly or in part are shared by many other Member States, irrespective of their geographical situation (Western Information Group, March 1984).

From the earliest days of 1984 the members of the Western Group came together fairly cohesively to take advantage of the reform possibilities created by the U.S. government's withdrawal announcement. Yet, WIG's cohesion was limited.

However, as we have seen, no consensus existed in WIG with regard to many major reforms being demanded by the U.S. government; for some of the U.S. demands (that is, major structural changes) there was no support at all from WIG. What difference did WIG's lack of support make with regard to negotiating change in UNESCO?

As illustrated in Table 6.1, a relatively distinct pattern can be noted in three of the four general reform areas: management, budget, and structural-institutional reform. In the management area WIG initiated or agreed upon some degree of change in all but two of the eighteen WIG paper proposals. These two proposals had called for the Director-General to carry out a study

Table 6.1
Western Information Group Consensus and Reform

	WIG Consensus	No WIG Consensus
Management Addressed	16	2
Management Not Addressed	2	7
Budget Addressed	5	0
Budget Not Addressed	0	1
Structural Addressed	12	4
Structural Not Addressed	2	15
Program Addressed	14	6
Program Not Addressed	1	2

Source: Appendixes 2.1–2.4 in this book.

on the management of UNESCO's fellowship programs and to make all evaluation reports available to member states on request. In both cases, few obstacles appear to stand in the way of making such changes subsequently.

Of the nine remaining management reform proposals for which support had not been articulated by an overwhelming majority of the members of WIG, only two were addressed in any meaningful fashion. These included a proposal to tighten recruitment standards and one dealing with limiting the use of outside consultants. It should be noted that no clear policy statement detailing limitations on use of outside consultants had been articulated by U.S. officials.

In the area of budget reform there had been relatively widespread consensus in the Western Group, especially among the members of the Genevà Group, regarding desired changes. This was the reform area in which UNESCO organizational change was most comprehensive and clearly identifiable. Only with respect to the U.S. government's call for more accessibility to budgetary data was there much uncertainty in WIG regarding changes UNESCO had implemented. That uncertainty seems to have resulted, at least in part, from the somewhat ambiguous nature of the proposal. Although WIG members appear to have been united in the assessment that the budget has been made considerably more transparent, it is not clear what this meant with respect to data accessibility.

Institutional change in UNESCO did not begin to approach the structural reforms that were demanded by the U.S. government. However, of the fourteen structural reform proposals supported by WIG all but two were addressed in some way. These two proposals requested a review by the DG of the formal consulting practices of other UN bodies and stressed the importance of an in-depth study by the Special Committee, focusing on the dissemination of the results of studies and research.

Of the nineteen proposals that had not been explicitly enumerated as WIG concerns, only four were subjects of any meaningful activity. The Temporary Committee had addressed the question of reinforcing the roles of the General Conference in determining general policy and approving the program and budget. In adopting the TC's recommendations, the board endorsed reinforcing the roles of the conference and agreed that members could attach reservations to the text of consensus resolutions. In addition, the TC had made various recommendations aimed at increasing the effectiveness of the board's subunits. Also, as early as the 119th board session, the TC had made movements in establishing the practice of having high level Secretariat staff (ADGs) appear before the board and its bodies for program hearings.

While not directly implemented, the Executive Board dealt with another proposal indirectly. The U.S. delegation had called for the establishment of a drafting and negotiating group in the Executive Board, but the group was not formally established. However, the practice of convening a "drafting group," comprised of regional representatives and charged with the task of combining the diverse resolutions before the board into one omnibus resolution, appears to have become institutionalized at sessions of the Executive Board.

In review, the data for these three general reform areas—management, budget, and structural-institutional reform—appear to indicate that Western Group consensus played a significant role in reform politics: where there was consensus in WIG there was movement toward reform; where there was no consensus in WIG, there was relatively little or no movement. However, the data concerning program reform are less clear. A main difficulty in this regard is that of the twenty-three program reform proposals identified in Appendix 2.3, UNESCO addressed twenty in some meaningful way, regardless of the existence of previous Western Group consensus. Two of the remaining three were concerns expressed in the WIG paper, and both dealt with a reduction in program spending for obsolete, underfunded, or relatively small programs. The remaining proposal was one put forth by the U.S. government: it called for clarification regarding the degree of responsiveness of UNESCO to program suggestions coming from the United Nations.

What is interesting about the program reform area in general is the extent to which UNESCO addressed nearly every articulated concern in some way. Furthermore, a vast majority of the program reform proposals (seventeen out of twenty-four) were concerns that WIG had articulated. In this regard, the program and the budget areas were quite similar. Also as was the case with the budget area, all parties had articulated program reform proposals in exceedingly clear terms (that is, the long, elaborate statements that both

U.S. and British officials had sent to the DG, detailing specific subprogram reform proposals).

In addition, a subgroup of WIG, chaired by Swedish Ambassador Watz, had undertaken a very detailed exercise of subprogram prioritization. All of the WIG members were asked to classify each of the 187 subprograms in the 22 C/5 document into one of four categories: increase resources, reduce resources, eliminate, or remain unchanged.[1] There were substantial differences between the U.S. positions and those of the Western Group as a whole regarding the question of which subprograms should be eliminated or given reduced funding (see Table 6.2). The substantial differences made negotiating change in specific subprogram activities a bit of a challenge. On the other hand, the discussions over this exercise helped to clarify those areas around which a consensus could be built within WIG. As in the other reform areas, a Western Group consensus played an important role in inducing program change.

Western Group consensus alone, however, cannot account for the magnitude of reform success in the program area. Another factor that played a major role was the combined impact of actual U.S. withdrawal and the threat of British withdrawal at year's end, which forced many hard decisions in UNESCO during 1985. The U.S. withdrawal necessitated an adjustment of 25 percent in the program budget for the 1986–1987 biennium. When linked with the possible loss of another 5 percent, considerable pressure existed for inducing immediate program change. The program prioritization scheme that had been agreed upon in principle earlier in the draft 23 C/5 was now to be implemented; second priority programs would not receive funding unless from voluntary contributions.

It should also be noted that during 1985 the British government had focused on Major Program XIII (peace and human rights) as its most important remaining reform concern. Negotiating change in this major program was exceedingly difficult, even though a general consensus in this regard existed in WIG. The difficulty resulted largely from the importance Soviet officials placed in MP XIII. However, as we have seen, British delegates with active support for other members of the Western Group were quite successful in altering the substance of this program at the 23rd General Conference.

Throughout this period reform negotiations within WIG, as well as within UNESCO more generally, were affected by various international systemic and UNESCO-specific factors.[2] Never far out of mind during internal WIG reform discussions was the realization that in order for major nonmanagerial reform to occur, UNESCO needed at least the passive acquiescence of the Third World majority, but the Group of 77 could be pushed just so far in such a short period of time. The reform package, which had been negotiated by the Temporary Committee, was seen as approaching

Table 6.2
Comparison of Program Prioritization Positions: The United States and the Western Information Group as a Whole (including U.S. positions).

United States Positions

Reduce Program Resources

WIG Program Resources Unchanged:
II. 1.4, II. 2.3, II. 6.2, II. 2.2, III. 3.7, IV. 1.1, IV. 3.1, IV. 4.2, V. 5.1, VI. 2.2, VI. 2.3, VI. 4.1, VII. 1.1, VII. 1.3, VIII. 3.1, VIII. 3.2, VIII. 3.3, XI. 1.4, XI. 2.1, XII. 2.2, XII. 3.3, XIII. 3.1, XIII. 3.2, XIII. 4.3

WIG Reduce Program Resources:
II. 1.1, II. 2.2, III. 1.1, V. 4.3, VI. 3.1, VIII. 1.1, VIII. 1.2, XI. 1.3, XII. 1.1, XII. 1.2, XIII. 1.3, XIII. 1.1, XIII. 2.1

WIG Eliminate Program: (none)

WIG Program Resources Unchanged:
II. 3.2, II. 3.3, II. 3.4, II. 4.1, III. 1.3, III. 2.1, V. 1.1, V. 1.2, V. 2.2, V. 3.1, V. 5.2, V. 6.2, V. 6.3, VI. 3.3, IX. 2.4, XI. 3.2, XI. 3.3, XI. 4.2, XII. 2.3, XII. 2.4, XII. 3.4, XIII. 4.2

Eliminate Programs

WIG Reduce Program Resources:
I. 1.1, I. 1.2, IV. 4.3, V. 4.2, V. 6.1, VI. 5.1, VI. 5.2, VIII. 1.3, VIII. 1.4, VIII. 2.1, VIII. 2.2, VIII. 1.2, IX. 2.1, IX. 2.2, IX. 2.3, IX. 2.5, XI. 4.5, XII. 3.2, XIII. 3.3, XIII. 3.4

WIG Eliminate Program:
I. 1.3, I. 2., III. 1.2, III. 2.3, VI. 5.3, VI. 5.4, XIII. 1.2

Note: In two cases (MP V. 3.2 and MP XI. 2.2) when the U.S. position was to eliminate these programs the WIG position was to increase resources.

Source: Assistant Secretary Newell's 13 July 1984 letter to Director-General M'Bow, an internal Department of State draft writing exercise on platform reform—UNESCO; and a summary prepared by Swedish Ambassador Watz of the program prioritization exercise of the Western Information subcommittee on programs.

the limits of acquiesence from the Group of 77; to continue to push further at that time (that is, October 1984) might jeopardize the entire package. Such sensitivity to the needs of other groups of member states was also illustrated in the language of the face-saving zero-growth budget DR at the 120th Board session, which invited the DG to submit a list of additional proposals of possible development assistance projects, even though the budget provided no funding for the projects.

The personality and role of the Director-General also was closely tied to North-South considerations. WIG delegates, including those from the United States, were very reluctant to attack Mr. M'Bow directly. To do so, they feared, might be perceived as an attack on the Third World, which, in turn, might lead African and other Third World members to become defensive and rigid in their positions. From a more particularistic perspective U.S. officials were very cautious not to say or do anything that might appear as being racist. Thus, it was not overly difficult for WIG to provide a common front in this regard.

In addition, UNESCO's role as a specialized agency within the United Nations system provided important constraints. Many WIG and other delegates viewed the U.S. threat of withdrawal and subsequent demands as an attack on the UN generally. The fundamental structural changes demanded by the Reagan administration were not particular to UNESCO. No other member of WIG was willing to support such broad-ranging reforms. A number of delegates were quick to point out that such sweeping structural changes might lead to Third World demands to restructure the UN Security Council. The British, among others, were quite hesitant to foster such a debate. WIG members displayed substantial consensus in this regard; however, the U.S. position lay well outside that zone of consensus.

Other differences within WIG were also important. The position of the French delegation was especially critical. As host government to UNESCO, France was very reluctant to do anything that might lead to the disintegration of the organization, and they were hesitant to support any WIG action that might weaken what they viewed as their special relationship with the Third World. Throughout the reform period the French position contrasted sharply with the British position. Yet, as discussed in Chapter 5, when it was perceived that the very survival of UNESCO was at stake, as was the case in May 1985, the French ambassador played an instrumental role in negotiating a full set of draft program and budget recommendations, which were widely applauded by other members of WIG, including the British.

An underlying tension also prevailed in WIG with regard to the nature of U.S. participation in the reform negotiations. In interviews conducted in Paris with various Western Group representatives during July and October 1984, the U.S. position was commonly and negatively referred to as a "moving target" strategy. Several Western ambassadors bluntly confided that they believed that no amount of reform in UNESCO would satisfy the Reagan administration. Moreover, on a number of occasions U.S. positions and actions were viewed as barriers, not facilitators, of reform. The nature of U.S. participation would certainly seem to suggest that constructive reform of UNESCO was not a major objective being sought by Assistant Secretary Newell during much, if not all, of 1984. How then can we account for the U.S. withdrawal action?

THE IDEOLOGICAL HERITAGE OF WITHDRAWAL

Reconsidering the findings from the above chapters, a not very flattering picture of the withdrawal process begins to take form. The path to withdrawal appears to have been a rather tortuous one, especially given the Reagan administration's professed objective of enhancing the role of the private sector in international organizational affairs.

Six months before the first formal review was initiated the Reagan administration moved to cut all funding and staffing for the U.S. National Commission, the one private sector organization that had been congressionally mandated the role of helping to facilitate U.S./UNESCO relations. Congress, however, authorized $250,000 for each of the fiscal years 1984 and 1985 to fund the commission's secretariat.[3] The administration went further and divided the National Commission's program responsibilities between two separate bureaus. As a U.S. House of Representatives Staff Report (1984a: 13) concluded, in effect, the commission no longer functioned as Congress had mandated in 1946. If the Reagan administration was to reform UNESCO, it desired to do so without the assistance of the one private body that had been legally constituted to provide the needed assistance and expertise.

The U.S. National Commission was viewed by the Heritage Foundation and its associates in the administration as being a liberal alliance of private interest groups.[4] Despite the fact that forty of the commission's one hundred members, including its chairman, had been appointed by President Reagan to serve in "at-large" capacities, Heritage President Edwin Feulner portrayed the National Commission as part of a "liberal and Third-World UNESCO lobby," which by implication was claimed to be supporting anti-Western ends. Feulner sought support from Heritage contributors to defeat the anti-Western threat.[5]

Other signs also suggest a predetermined move against UNESCO on ideological grounds. Barely one week after Ronald Reagan had been sworn in as president in January 1981, David Stockman, director-designate of the Office of Management and Budget (OMB), had proposed that the U.S. might wish to consider withdrawing from UNESCO. Stockman urged withdrawal in the context of an overall retrenchment in foreign aid, citing "UNESCO's pro-

PLO policies and its support for measures limiting the free flow of information" (Fobes, 1981). Furthermore, he discussed additional cost savings that could be made should the U.S. refuse to pay its legally binding assessments for 1981 and 1982.

These early predilections of withdrawal were quite compatible with a broader ideological approach that was taking form in the White House and elsewhere in Washington, both inside and outside the U.S. government. According to a former high-level White House advisor who was actively engaged in the UNESCO issue, Stockman was merely attempting to exploit deep-seated anti-UN and anti-UNESCO attitudes among right-wing White House officials and advisors in order to slash the budget.[6]

An examination of various of the memoranda, papers, monographs and books, published by Heritage as part of its United Nations Assessment Project, provides insight into administration attitudes and beliefs. The volume, *A World Without a UN: What Would Happen if the United Nations Shut Down?*, edited by Burton Yale Pines (1984), is especially helpful in this regard. In introducing the book Pines, the vice president of Heritage, provides a general overview of the foundation's perspective on the United Nations and multilateralism. He begins by charging that the UN is "exceedingly anti-U.S., anti-West and anti-free enterprise" (Pines, 1984:x). The persistent challenges to the established private enterprise world economy made by various member states in UN delegate bodies are portrayed as challenges initiated by the United Nations itself. Pines (1984:xi) argues,

> The U.N. crusade attacks the very essence and philosophical base of the free enterprise system. It is an assault which condemns, almost without supporting evidence, the notion that the dynamics of growth and economic expansion is individual initiative, creativity and the incentive provided by the opportunity of making a profit. . . . In repudiating free enterprise, and by ignoring capitalism's record of success, the United Nations and its agencies have raised to the level of gospel the tenets of what is called the New International Economic Order. . . . The tenacity with which the United Nations fights for NIEO at every forum, from every rostrum and in every possible publication and statement is awesome.

Moreover, since the UN provides a forum for member states to articulate challenges to capitalism there seems to be a belief that if the UN were to go away, so might the challenges.

In addition, there appears to be an element of anti-internationalism inherent in Pines's ideology. He raises the complaint that local and regional problems become globalized in the UN (Pines, 1984:xi). Dealing with local concerns in a global arena like the General Assembly, according to Pines, unduly complicates the issue resolution process. Universal membership, general purpose international organizations are not viewed as legitimate institutions for solving world problems.

"Dangerous too," writes Pines (1984:xi), "is the legitimacy conferred by the UN on the illegitimate, while discrediting those entitled to respect as members of the world community." He rails against the official status accorded various national liberation movements in the United Nations while "Israel, South Africa, Chile, and the Shah's Iran . . . are or have been reviled as pariah states" (Pines, 1984:xi).

Although some form of muiltilateralism might be acceptable if it facilitates maintenance of the status quo, "the UN is not required for the continuation of such multilateralism" (Pines, 1984:xviii). In fact, he argues that "technical and specialized agencies would benefit if freed from their association with the UN" This brings one to the main theme of the Heritage Foundation's United Nations Assessment Project—"a world without the UN would be a better world" (Pines, 1984:xix).

Beginning in 1982, UNESCO became a favorite target of Heritage writers. Since that time the foundation has issued numerous polemical tracts attacking UNESCO. Heritage had issued five tracts by the time of the December 1983 U.S. decision to withdraw from UNESCO:

1. "For UNESCO, A Failing Grade in Education," October 21, 1982;
2. "UNESCO, Where Culture Becomes Propaganda," December 13, 1982;
3. "The IPDC: UNESCO vs. The Free Press," March 10, 1983;
4. "The U.S. and UNESCO at a Crossroads," October 19, 1983; and
5. "The U.S. and UNESCO: Time for Decision," December 5, 1983.[7]

The first three of these tracts were written by Thomas G. Gulick. In his attack on UNESCO's programs in education Gulick (October 21, 1982) charged that UNESCO had become increasingly biased toward socialist economies and a utopian strain of internationalism that was anti–free enterprise. He called for cutting off U.S. funding to UNESCO educational and social science programs, which he claimed were so oriented. His second pamphlet targeted UNESCO cultural programs and related activities. Gulick (December 13, 1982) claimed that the organization's Secretariat and radical member states were promoting proposals to license journalists and to censor private international news and information services. The U.S. government, he declared, should either fight back or get out of UNESCO. In his third assault Gulick (March 10, 1983) took aim at the Western-created and U.S.-supported International Program for the Development of Communications (IPDC). He asserted that the IPDC was a spearhead of the UNESCO attack on the commercial free press.

The remaining two tracts were written by Owen Harries, who by fall 1983 appears to have become the Heritage Foundation's main assault weapon in its war against UNESCO. Harries had been the Australian permanent delegate to UNESCO for eighteen months during 1982–1983 before joining

Heritage. He argued that the U.S. government should withdraw from UNESCO unless the organization agreed to major institutional and other changes (Harries, October 19, 1983). After the 22nd General Conference Harries (December 5, 1983) charged that nothing in UNESCO had really changed; withdrawal was the appropriate response.

Such an action, he argued, should be taken for two main reasons. First, "it is morally and politically wrong for America to continue to lend authority and legitimacy . . . to an organization dedicated to attacking its fundamental American values and interests." Second, the "existing structure and ethics of UNESCO make it impossible for the United States and other liberal democracies to change things from within" (Harries, 1983b:1). These tracts by Harries were the studies that Heritage President Feulner claimed had served as the basis for the initial U.S. withdrawal decision.[8]

Of course, it is extremely difficult to validate Feulner's claim. Yet, there does appear to have been direct links between such ideologically charged activities and policy processes within the administration and the U.S. mission to UNESCO in Paris. Not least among the links was the move in 1982 of a former Reagan campaign aide and White House employee, Gregory Newell, to the IO bureau as the assistant secretary. Mr. Newell came on board just as the bureau was completing the 1983 State Department Reports to Congress (discussed in Chapter 2), which helps to explain the discrepancy between those reports and Mr. Newell's contradictory claims about conditions in UNESCO. As one IO bureau official has suggested, "the timing of his arrival in relation to these studies is important because it indicates that Newell came to IO loaded with a separate agenda and special mission."[9]

Events subsequent to 1983 have been somewhat less ambiguous regarding a link between the Heritage Foundation's anti-UNESCO activities and U.S./UNESCO relations. During 1984 anti-UNESCO activities continued at Heritage with the production of three additional pamphlets: "An Insider Looks at UNESCO's Problems" (July); "GAO's UNESCO Report Card: A Failing Grade" (October); and "UNESCO: Time to Leave" (December). Of these, the pamphlet on the then still classified GAO report provided some clearer evidence of Heritage influence. A European permanent delegate confided quite disapprovingly that during the GAO report controversy at the 120th Executive Board a U.S. representative had provided him with a copy of this highly slanted Heritage brochure, leading him to assume that it was an accurate representation of the GAO report. The European delegate became quite disconcerted later, when the actual GAO draft report was made available to board members on a confidential basis.[10]

Also, it is important to note the similarity between the anti-UNESCO charges leveled by Assistant Secretary Newell and other administration spokespersons and those made by Harries in his Heritage Foundation tracts. As part of his study of American press coverage of the U.S. withdrawal from

UNESCO, C. Anthony Giffard (1986) conducted such a comparative analysis. "To check the correspondence between Heritage Foundation views and those of the State Department, a content analysis was made of the Heritage documents on UNESCO, and of State Department press releases, briefings, and statements at congressional hearings. The analysis showed that spokesmen for the State Department reiterated both the language and the emphasis provided by the Heritage reports" (Giffard, 1986:197).[11] The similarity might not have appeared so significant had the views not deviated so drastically from the historical record.

In addition, Ambassador Gerard and Owen Harries were jointly engaged actively in London in fall 1984, lobbying for British withdrawal. A favorite theme of right-wing U.S. supporters of British withdrawal was that U.K. representatives in Paris had been "captured" by the UNESCO reform process. Thus, the prime minister should disregard British officials' advice to remain in UNESCO and should listen to Harries and these U.S. citizens who could see UNESCO more objectively.

The Australian ambassador to UNESCO, Gough Whitlam, has documented such transnational lobbying efforts in detail.

> The Commonwealth permanent delegates stationed in Paris were the first to spot what was going on in Britain. . . . They noticed that after the second [120th] Board session the same arguments and attitudes about UNESCO were appearing in the British media as had appeared in the U.S. media at the end of the previous year. The similarity in campaigns was no coincidence. The International Organisation section of the State Department had engaged the same organisation to conduct both campaigns, the Heritage Foundation. . . . To spearhead its campaign against UNESCO, the Foundation employed Associate Professor Owen Harries, who . . . [had been] the Australian Ambassador to UNESCO. After taking up his duties in Paris, he saw much of the new American Ambassador to UNESCO, Jean Gerard, and made three visits to the US, each time visiting the Heritage Foundation in Washington, D.C. In September 1983, he became John M. Olin Fellow at the Foundation. . . . For several weeks after Christmas 1983, Harries was engaged in justifying America's withdrawal. In October 1984, he was engaged in promoting Britain's withdrawal.[12]

Whitlam went on to provide the details of three separate meetings in London, where Harries and Gerard lobbied members of the British media and government to support British withdrawal from UNESCO.

According to Whitlam (1985:11–12), the guests at dinners on October 19 and 22 had included: Lords Bauer, Beloff, and Chalfont; Michael Charlton (BBC); Roger Scruton (columnist, *Times*); Charles Douglas-Home (editor, *Times*); Brian Beedham (foreign editor, *Economist*); Gerald Mansell and Huw Wheldon (ex-BBC); Richard Hoggart; and Dirk Kinane (a U.S. citizen employed by UNESCO). A larger discussion, which included over forty invited guests, was held on October 23. This event was sponsored by the Institute of European Defence and Strategic Studies, a London-based organization funded by the Heritage Foundation and chaired by Edwin Feulner.[13] Among others, guests at this event included *Sunday Times* columnist Rosemary Righter and MP Sir Percy Blaker (Whitlam, 1985:11). In addition, Harries also met with three ministers: Sir Keith Joseph (Education and Science); Timothy Renton (Foreign and Commonwealth Affairs); and Timothy Raison (Whitlam, 1985:12).

These meetings by themselves tell us little. However, as Whitlam suggests, they may well have been rather effective. "Previously there had been very few editorials and signed articles on UNESCO. Between the Gerard/Harries foray and Sir Geoffrey Howe's announcement of withdrawal on 22 November, there was a spate of them" (Whitlam, 1985:12). The Australian ambassador then proceeded to list the dates and sources of twenty-eight editorials and articles of which he had become aware.

Two critical points emerge from the U.S. involvement in the British withdrawal. First, U.S. officials' actions would seem to indicate clearly that a final decision had already been made in the United States. It is noteworthy that Ambassador Gerard was in London meeting with British officials and media people on October 18, 19, 20, and 22, 1984. These were precisely the concluding dates of the 120th Executive Board. Even though the ambassador was a vice chairman of the board and head of the U.S. delegation for which these board meetings were of critical importance, she was in London lobbying for British withdrawal from UNESCO.

Second, U.S. officials' involvement in the U.K. illustrates a transnational political process that was to continue even after the U.S. government had officially terminated its membership in the organization. Furthermore, it served to undermine the position of the U.S. ambassador's British counterpart back in Paris. "Not only did she not tell her British colleagues that she was going to London, but she did not tell them what she had done after she returned. Lack of candour led to lack of trust and lack of progress in the Western group" (Whitlam, 1985:13).

It is questionable whether the ambassador's lack of candor was accidental. Although few public statements are available that illustrate directly the ambassador's perspective, a statement by U.S. Congressman Scheuer (November 19, 1984) articulated a similar general point of view:

> While British politicians and government ministers have taken a firm line on the abuses and failings of UNESCO, Foreign Office civil servants have muffled, diluted and obscured the message repeatedly during the last few months. Mid-level civil servants of the British delegation to UNESCO have, at times, been indistinguishable from Mr. M'Bow's cheerleaders. These civil servants seemed, for a time, to have convinced the politicians at home that real reform was underway at UNESCO. Fortunately, the transparency of the cosmetic reform

program engineered by UNESCO's executive board has not fooled the British public or press, and they, in turn, have begun to put pressure on government ministers to take the next logical step by serving notice. A pusillanimous reaction by the British government will be seen as hypocrisy and weakness by other countries looking for leadership in getting their collective act together.[14]

From such a perspective, someone had to get the truth through to the British people and government ministers. Ambassador Gerard assumed responsibility for undertaking such a mission.

Scheuer's sentiment about the officials at the British mission in Paris were echoed in the U.S. ambassador's actions toward her own official staff. During October 1984, the frustrations of U.S. mission staff members with Ambassador Gerard were quite evident in Paris. Various staff members articulated deep resentment at what they perceived to be the ambassador's practice of circumventing their input into important policy decisions. As discussed earlier, for example, the mission staff had been greatly surprised when Ambassador Gerard suggested to the Executive Board that a special session be convened to consider the draft GAO report.

The transnational effort to get the United Kingdom out of UNESCO continued during 1985, and in November of that year Ambassador Gerard was back in London again meeting with British editors, columnists, and broadcasters.[15] This time, however, the former ambassador's efforts were upstaged by a high-level U.S. government intervention.

At the meeting of the interdepartmental International Policy Committee (IPC) on October 7, 1985, members of the IPC decided to encourage the British to follow through on their withdrawal.[16] It was reported that the IPC agreed to persuade the British "among other reasons to ensure that the Reagan administration would not be isolated in its attitude toward UNESCO. The committee's uncertainty about British intentions arose from the fact that the Foreign Affairs Committee of Britain's House of Commons recommended unanimously . . . that Britain should remain in UNESCO and fight for reforms from within."[17] The IPC decision was followed by a personal note from Secretary of State Shultz to British Foreign Secretary Howe on October 17[18] and reports of other subsequent exchanges between the highest levels of government.[19]

These U.S. interventions stood in direct opposition to the widely held view in Britain and elsewhere that the U.K. should remain in UNESCO. The position that Britain should stay was reinforced by the postconference assessment of the British delegation to the 23rd General Conference;[20] a nearly unanimous debate (only one dissenting voice) in the House of Commons; an overwhelming vote against withdrawal in the British National Commission for UNESCO (with only two dissenters, Rosemary Righter and Roger Scruton, two of Gerard's close contacts in London); a nearly unanimous and unprecedented demarche from the Commonwealth High

Commissioners to the Foreign Secretary in support of Britain's continued UNESCO membership (with only Singapore dissenting);[21] and a united and vocal opposition to withdrawal by the other European Economic Community (EEC) members.

In the face of such overwhelming support for continued British membership in UNESCO, the prime minister insisted that her government complete its withdrawal action. While publicly portraying the action as a consensus cabinet decision, various British sources have challenged the prime minister's assertion. For example, the *New Statesman* reported that "within the Cabinet the Prime Minister alone was strongly in favour of quitting. The Foreign Secretary had been persuaded over the past year that on balance we ought to stay in. The clear majority of the Cabinet were in favour of staying in."[22] It seems likely that various of the ministers might have been reluctant to undertake a unilateral action that was opposed by most other EEC members. Two days prior to the withdrawal announcement the British government had been successful in getting the rest of the European Community to agree to the final act of a treaty, codifying foreign policy coordination among EEC states. This agreement bound members to avoid any action "which impairs the effectiveness of the EEC states as a cohesive force . . . within international organisations."[23]

However, in the last analysis a majority of the prime minister's cabinet did not oppose her on this issue; why remains unclear. It does not seem to be compatible with any rational assessment of reform outcomes in UNESCO during 1985. In fact, as reviewed above nearly all assessments conducted in Britain (for example, U.K. UNESCO mission; U.K. UNESCO General Conference delegation; House of Commons Foreign Affairs Committee; and U.K. National Commission) overwhelmingly supported continued British membership in the organization.

It would appear, as was the case with U.S. withdrawal, that ideology was a significant factor in the U.K. action. As we have seen, the same ideological forces were at play in both cases, as was substantiated by the report of the Commons Foreign Affairs Committee. That report discussed the role that the Heritage Foundation was perceived to have played in influencing British officials and public opinion: "We have subsequently received what appears to be firm evidence of the Foundation being involved in campaigns to attack the UN and its agencies, and have no reason to doubt Mr. Whitlam's allegations of attempts by the Foundation to influence the British press and British opinion leaders."[24]

Back in the United States the relationship between the IO bureau and the Heritage Foundation was brought further into public view in 1985, after the U.S. withdrawal. At that time Heritage President Edwin Feulner was appointed to the high-level U.S. Reform Observation Panel on UNESCO. It is interesting to note that this appointment was made following the wide circulation by Heritage of the ideologically charged fundraising appeal by Feulner, discussed earlier (Feulner, October 8, 1984). Also, Heritage Fellow Roger A. Brooks was appointed to the position of policy planning coordinator in the IO bureau. In interviews with several IO bureau careerists, they voiced great frustration that at least ten "Heritage types" had been brought in by then Assistant Secretary Keyes at the technical level of the bureau. Their function, the interviewees charged, was to act as ward captains to monitor the behavior of the career professionals.[25]

It appears then that, although UNESCO was an immediate target of the Heritage Foundation and Reagan administration officials, the United Nations more generally was the ultimate target. But why target UNESCO, an organization in which conditions had improved since the beginning of President Reagan's term in office? And how could such a relatively small group of ideologues have captured so completely the policy process? What factors and conditions made the outcome possible?

THE CLIMATE OF IDEOLOGICAL TRIUMPH

Three general factors related to the evolution of U.S./UNESCO relations, as well as a set of specific conditions that prevailed within the Reagan administration and its foreign policy process, seem to have been instrumental in influencing the target and tactics. Early in U.S./UNESCO relations disgruntlement emerged in various quarters in the U.S. government and the private sector regarding a perceived unwillingness of UNESCO and its member states to play a major political role in the U.S. struggle against communism. Growing apathy, loss of interest and even alienation ensued in subsequent decades as the predominant orientation of UNESCO was seen to shift from functionalism and intellectual cooperation to development. As the shift occurred, UNESCO programs and activities became less central to the organization's traditional constituency in the United States; serious problems of legitimacy for UNESCO set in.

A second and related factor was a substantial decline in the quality of U.S. participation in UNESCO, especially from around 1969 onwards. Official U.S. participation became largely negative and reactive. Little positive leadership was initiated during these later decades. Thus, U.S. successes in UNESCO seemed to be few and far between. Without active promotion of U.S. programmatic concerns, the main work of the organization moved even further outside the scope of public and private sectoral interests in the United States. Problems of legitimacy intensified and the U.S. public and private base of support for UNESCO was further weakened.

Third, the U.S. public as well as a great many governmental officials were heavily dependent on the private news media for information about

UNESCO. Since the early 1970s American press coverage of UNESCO has been extremely slanted and misleading. By the 1980s press coverage came to focus almost exclusively and negatively on one narrow aspect of the organization's work—the communications issue.

These three factors provided the background for the foreign policy process within the Reagan administration in regard to the withdrawal issue. However, to understand and appreciate fully the nature and dynamics of the process, more thorough examination of these three factors is needed.

Early Frustrations

The early war-time activities in CAME toward educational reconstruction presented U.S. officials with an agenda item that they found difficult to ignore. Movement in the London deliberations toward creating a permanent international organization in education posed a significant challenge. With the U.S. decision to enter fully into international negotiations came a commitment to mobilize an aggressive leadership effort.

United States officials were forced to look beyond the narrow sectoral boundaries that had tended to characterize U.S. planning for post-war educational recovery and to look toward the creation of a more comprehensive global order. International educational, scientific, and cultural policies had to be viewed in an integrative manner and to be coordinated accordingly. To these areas, at U.S. insistence, had been added communications.

At the beginning, as well as later, State Department officials found themselves forced to operate in substantive issue contexts about which they knew little and felt relatively uneasy.[26] Unlike authorities in many other member states, U.S. officials tended to be rather distrustful of national policies in education, science, culture, and communications. Lacking directly comparable sectoral ministries through which to conduct substantive participation in UNESCO, U.S. responsibility for the organization was largely left to the State Department, whose officials generally felt uneasy about dealing in UNESCO areas of competence.

Domestic discord over participation concerns became overt as Congress considered the question of official U.S. affiliation. The UNESCO Constitution required each member state to make arrangements for associating its principal nongovernmental and governmental bodies in education, science, and culture with the work of the organization (Article VII.1). The nature of such popular participation received a mixed reception in Washington. An important element in this debate was the extent to which the National Commission should be associated with or subject to control by the State Department. "Those who argued against identification with State were generally the most vociferous in support of UNESCO programs that aimed directly at peace and security, whereas those favoring an enlarged governmental role were usually the exponents of purely intellectual activities for UNESCO" (Ninkovich, 1981:95). While those forces calling for a large, autonomous and popularly-based commission won the day in Congress (that is, Public Law 79-565), the future relationship between the National Commission and the State Department remained ambiguous.

The ambiguity was never to be completely resolved and served throughout the history of U.S./UNESCO relations as a further complicating element with respect to problems of identity. Over the course of its existence the National Commission was attached to three different bureaus in the State Department: the Bureau of Public Relations (1947–1952), the Bureau of Cultural and Educational Affairs (1952–1980), and the Bureau of International Organization Affairs (1980–1985). Historically, U.S. participation was strongest when the commission was based in the Bureau of Cultural and Educational Affairs, which placed an emphasis on programmatic concerns. Conversely, participation was weakest when the commission was attached to the IO bureau where the overriding concerns tended to be budgetary, political, and administrative issues.[27]

Evolving identity problems within UNESCO itself compounded the situation. Although there was relatively little conflict between the organization and its major funder regarding core programmatic tasks during these early years, problems did arise with respect to UNESCO's more ideologically charged role, as promoter of a liberal democratic world order. At a general political level, frustration existed in the United States over what was perceived as UNESCO's uncooperative posture in the struggle against communism. Irritation grew over the unwillingness of the organization to assume a legitimizing role in a U.S.-sponsored initiative to establish a world-wide radio network designed to broadcast Western messages to the peoples of Eastern Europe (Sewell, 1973:162). From the beginning, communications had been the primary focus of U.S. interest in UNESCO and the organization was perceived to have faltered in regard to its communications mandate.

As discussed earlier, irritation turned to outrage in some quarters in Washington as UNESCO was perceived again to have faltered over the Korean issue. Although UNESCO did actively become engaged in a world-wide educational campaign in support of the U.S./UN action in Korea, a number of important U.S. policy elites perceived UNESCO as not having gone far enough.

It should be noted at this point, though, that U.S. participation in UNESCO did not stand as a central element of post-war U.S. foreign policy. Beginning in January 1947, however, increased attention within the State Department focused on the organization. At the center of this attention were a number of staff appointments made by the Director-General. Some U.S. officials perceived that Huxley was attempting to promote left-wing ideals by appointing communist sympathizers to sensitive UNESCO positions

(Ninkovich, 1981:100–103), thereby threatening UNESCO's mandate in promoting liberal democratic ideals and values.

U.S. officials deemed a response was necessary. They enlisted British assistance, and diplomatic pressure was brought to bear against Huxley. Also, the State Department moved to develop a security system for clearing U.S. citizens applying for Secretariat staff positions (Ninkovich, 1981:103). The controversial issue of Secretariat employees' national loyalty, however, was by no means resolved.

Growing U.S. disillusionment with UNESCO was soon felt in Paris over the organization's budget. The second UNESCO Director-General (that is, Torres-Bodet) and the U.S. delegation found themselves in substantial disagreement. Given the United Nations' ability to pay basis for establishing budget assessments, the U.S. delegation was in a position to threaten and, if needed, apply negative sanctions. The U.S. government's share of the total assessed budget at this time was 38 percent. UNESCO and its Director-General found themselves to be exceedingly vulnerable under the U.S. threat. In large part it was the U.S. delegation's exercise of sanctions that led to Torres-Bodet's resignation at the Seventh General Conference in 1962. The acting Director-General, John Taylor, and his permanent replacement, Luther Evans, were both U.S. nationals. Yet, the U.S./UNESCO relationship remained strained, primarily over questions of Secretariat employees' national loyalty. U.S. government agencies attempted to impose jurisdiction over U.S. citizens in the international civil service of UNESCO, as it related to questions of alleged disloyalty and anti-American activities.

The Director-General failed to respond as quickly and as completely as U.S. officials desired. Evans argued that the rules of procedure of the international civil service and the constitution of UNESCO were explicit in regard to the exclusively international character of the Secretariat staff. Subsequently, the vulnerability of the DG and his organization to U.S. pressure proved to be too great. Evans refused to renew the contracts of seven UNESCO employees who were U.S. citizens and who had declined to appear before U.S. government loyalty boards (Behrstock, 1987). Regardless, the DG and UNESCO were denounced by the U.S. ambassador to the UN, Henry Cabot Lodge, and others for not acting more quickly and more completely. Furthermore, UNESCO came under increased attack from various U.S. civic groups, including the American Legion, the Daughters of the American Revolution, and the U.S. Chamber of Commerce (Sathyamurthy, 1964:159-161).

UNESCO's Growing Loss of Legitimacy

Despite initial disappointments and frustrations, U.S. officials and citizens remained actively engaged in UNESCO. While disenchantment grew, U.S. participation remained active and U.S. nationals who were engaged in

UNESCO remained supportive. Such a posture was reflected in the quality of individuals appointed to represent the United States during these early years (for example, Archibald MacLeish, William Benton, Milton Eisenhower).

As seen in Chapter 3, the nature of U.S. objectives for the organization shifted in the mid-1950s. UNESCO's functional mandates were now the main focus of U.S. attention; the organization's role as a political force was to be minimized. However, the organization's mission in intellectual cooperation was being redefined in practice. There was a growing focus on technical assistance. UNESCO's functionalist programmatic orientation was rapidly giving way to a major concentration on development. Problems of identity grew.

An important problem of legitimacy for UNESCO slowly materialized in the United States. The nature of such legitimacy problems was rather complex. The State Department actively supported UNESCO's emerging technical assistance focus; the organization needed to get into the field, U.S. officials argued, and in Paris a large staff was amassed to do so.[28]

Yet, with this increased focus on technical assistance came a desire in the United States to fund such activities through special funds—for example, the United Nations Development Program (UNDP)—over which U.S. officials had relatively greater control than was the case with the regular UNESCO budget. With such a policy orientation came American initiatives for greater budgetary stringency within UNESCO proper. The ongoing conflict over the budget intensified. Officials voiced complaints in Washington over increased travel and other costs associated with field activities. Funding levels proved insufficient for UNESCO to be effective in the field or to decentralize its activities further. The organization was left with a large staff in Paris, conducting activities that were largely only indirectly related to applied development. Paradoxically, this large imbalance between headquarters and field operations later became an important symbol to Reagan administration officials of management problems in UNESCO.

Finkelstein (1986) and others have suggested that budgetary conflicts helped to fuel a growing sense of indifference in the early 1960s at the political level in Washington. Also, the main governmental and nongovernmental agencies, which served as the organization's main support groups, found UNESCO to be increasingly less central to their primary mandates. The U.S. National Commission continued to function but, after the late 1960s, less and less effectively.

A main turning point in U.S. participation in UNESCO appears to have coincided with the coming into office of the Nixon administration. A frequently told story alleges that the new president scrawled a pejorative note—"let's gut this outfit"—on the corner of a UNESCO-related memorandum. While the validity of this tale has proven difficult to establish, it was about this time that U.S. participation became markedly more reactive and oriented toward damage limitation, rather than being positive and oriented toward projecting a leadership role.[29]

An indicator of such change in participation can be found in the nature and tenure of appointees who have served as U.S. representatives to the Executive Board. As illustrated in Figure 6.1, there was a marked shift in the tenure of U.S. board members following the replacement in 1969 of Katie Louchheim, a Johnson appointment, with Louise Gore. In 1973 Gore was replaced by Edward Sullivan, a relative of Pat Nixon, who attended relatively few Board functions during 1973–1974. This period of U.S. participation in UNESCO was perhaps most notable for its inattention to issues of

Figure 6.1
U.S. Executive Board Members, 1946–1983

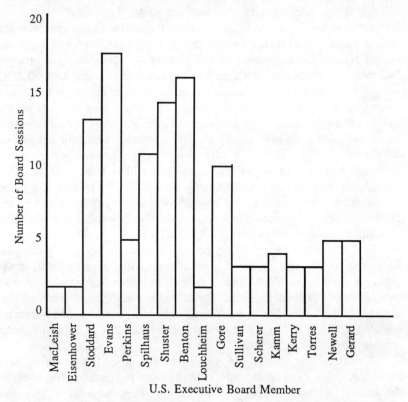

*Jean Gerard served as U.S. Representative to the Board until U.S. withdrawal (i.e., a total of seven sessions).

Source : UNESCO, *The Executive Board of UNESCO* . Paris: UNESCO, 1984.

importance to the U.S. and its ineffectiveness. For example, it was during this time that Arab members were successful in pushing through their anti-Israeli resolutions.[30]

Beginning with Sullivan, the tenure of U.S. board members averaged only four Executive Board sessions. In contrast, between the 5th Executive Board in 1947, following the very brief tenures of Archibald MacLeish and Milton Eisenhower, and the election of Louchheim at the 15th General Conference in 1968, the average tenure of U.S. board members was over twelve sessions. When viewed in the context of the substantial complexity of the organization's program and budget, the average tenure of less than two years per appointee since 1973 has likely inhibited U.S. delegates from assuming serious leadership roles. The manner in which the U.S. government has made its appointments to and used its seat on the board in recent decades has undoubtedly limited U.S. effectiveness in UNESCO.

UNESCO's growing commitment during the 1970s to development and other Third World concerns brought a further channeling of organizational resources and energies away from intellectual cooperation. This, in turn, hastened a growing loss of U.S. interest, as reflected in the discussion above. Those agencies with primary responsibilities in the main substantive sectors of UNESCO (that is, education, science, culture, and communications) for the most part had only marginal interests in development.[31] Thus, as UNESCO program activities reflected more and more a concern with development, the value of sustaining active U.S. involvement in the organization declined. Lack of an active U.S. leadership role in program planning activities in UNESCO, in turn, greatly inhibited U.S. interests in these areas from being forcefully and effectively promoted.

The anti-Israeli resolutions and activities in UNESCO in 1974 led to further U.S. alienation and disengagement. As discussed earlier, these actions brought an almost immediate response from Congress. Public Law 93-559 prohibited U.S. contributions until the situation had been rectified. Although there was a speedy resolution to the situation, the ghost of these anti-Israeli activities continued to haunt U.S./UNESCO relations.[32] One of the most significant long-term impacts was the change in attitude within the Jewish community toward UNESCO. Although historically Jewish scientists and educators, as well as other Jewish intellectuals, had been among the most active participants in U.S./UNESCO relations, many intellectually prominent Jews ceased to participate in UNESCO's work after these 1974 actions. Moreover, while Israeli officials in Paris in 1984 privately voiced trepidation over U.S. withdrawal, Jewish groups in the United States generally voiced strong support of President Reagan's decision.

As we have seen, U.S. officials were actively engaged during this period in the communications debate. Even in this area, though, such involvement tended to be dominated by a defensive and reactive policy posture. Although U.S. officials were largely successful in fending off attacks in UNESCO on the Western media, a quite contrary perspective prevailed more generally within the United States.

It should be recalled that not all U.S. policy initiatives were defensive and reactive. The IPDC initiative represented the clearest example of a case where the policy posture was much more positive. However, like numerous other U.S. pledges of multilateral development assistance, the promise of substantial financial assistance for the IPDC never materialized. "America's repeated promises of assistance were made with great flourishes: $25 million pledged in 1976 for communications development; $25 million promised again in 1978; $100,000 and then $250,000, and then $800,000 pledged when the International Program for the Development of Communications was created . . . virtually none of this has yet materialized" (Sussman, 1984d:6). Flirtations with the positive use of funding as a policy instrument might well have played some role in bringing about generally positive results in the communications area from a U.S. perspective. However, that kind of determination is exceedingly difficult to make.

Although the outcomes of UNESCO communications debates were relatively positive from a U.S. perspective after 1981, the impact of the issue on U.S. policy became increasingly negative. A notable example in this regard was Congressional passage in 1982 of the Beard Amendment (that is, Section 109 of the State Department Authorization Act for fiscal year 1982/83, PL 97-241). Important policy successes in UNESCO, such as those in the communications and human rights areas, tended to be viewed by government officials and the public alike as having been failures. UNESCO's decline of legitimacy in the United States grew.

Thus, when UN Ambassador Kirkpatrick, Assistant Secretary Newell, and their associates decided that the U.S. government should terminate its membership in UNESCO, relatively few strong voices of protest were heard from educational, scientific, cultural, or communications constituencies in the United States. Not only were most UNESCO activities viewed as being somewhat marginal to mainstream sectoral interests in these areas but, as will be discussed below, all but the most astute observers of the organization had been sensitized by the news media in the United States to view UNESCO with disregard.

Flawed Policy Processes

Over the years State Department officials became disenchanted with and lost interest in UNESCO. Many careerists in the IO bureau had a difficult time coping with the large and complex program agenda in UNESCO about which they knew or cared little. These careerists tended to focus their attention on problematical issues related to budgetary expansion and on political debates. U.S. participation reflected U.S. disenchantment.

The internal 1983 State Department draft document, referred to in Chapter 2, began by stating that "the U.S. Government has not had for many years an articulated set of goals and objectives which, linked together constitute a comprehensive policy toward UNESCO." As discussed earlier, this draft document had been prepared as part of the 1983 assessment of U.S. participation in UNESCO. It was based on the contributions from the various governmental agencies that had participated in the overall policy review.

As required by the basic terms of reference for the policy review of UNESCO, each agency was asked to assess U.S. management of its relations with UNESCO. Summarizing those findings, the draft document concluded the following:

> If the U.S. could be said to have any policy for dealing with UNESCO, it is essentially one of damage limitation—intermittent fending off of threatening demands when they appear to be excessive or seriously inimical to U.S. interests. This defensive position is tactical rather than strategic, and results in continuing *ad hoc* crisis management behavior in the UNESCO forum. . . . The sum of this uneven posture towards UNESCO is to leave the United States, as the Heritage Foundation notes, 'poised uneasily between piecemeal damage limitation, expressions of indignation and outrage, and disassociation with what is going on.' The defensive and reactive image of the U.S. is a questionable base from which to project U.S. influence and leadership.[33]

The draft report stated that there was no systematic interagency coordination for UNESCO policy and also criticized the State Department for not exercising a strong central oversight function with respect to UNESCO activities.[34] "In terms of potential, the evidence indicates that U.S. participation in UNESCO has not been well managed. This is attested to by comments from several federal agencies and private sector groups, and is summed up in a comment from an AID observer: 'while we may have good cause to be frustrated with UNESCO, we ourselves bear much of the responsibility for our lack of influence.'"[35] None of the data from this highly critical draft document, however, had been included in the *U.S./UNESCO Policy Review.*

The following statements illustrate some of the specific concerns about U.S. policy management expressed by a number of those agencies most closely linked to UNESCO substantive mandates:

> In short, UNESCO communications matters have been handled from an entirely political perspective, with State's prototypical meeting-to-meeting, crisis-to-crisis, style of management. . . . State, has without intending it, promoted the solely ideological view of this

activity. . . . We should be fair: State has ably pursued communications development as a strategy for political gain. Its deficiency has been in giving little weight to development outcomes in dealing with UNESCO specific issues and programs (U.S. AID, 1983).

The mechanisms necessary to ensure effective U.S. participation in UNESCO are not currently available. While there is reason to believe that many U.S. scientists are active in UNESCO programs, there is no instrumentality either inside or outside of government to ascertain the full dimension of that involvement, let alone to take advantage of it. The demise, for all practical purposes, of the U.S. National Commission for UNESCO and the termination, due to funding cutbacks, of a small NRC group concerned with UNESCO science programs, coupled with the apparent lack of interest and support for science in UNESCO at the State Department, signify the extent to which guidance is lacking . . . (National Academy of Sciences, 1983).

The United States lacks a central mechanism to coordinate and manage all aspects, private and governmental, of U.S. participation in UNESCO. . . . The United States' negative attitude to its commitments, responsibilities, and participation within UNESCO hinders the achievement of U.S. national objectives. . . . The effectiveness of U.S. representation at the U.S. mission to UNESCO is increasingly hampered by the drainage of resources and severe personnel limitations . . . (National Science Foundation, 1983).

In general, UNESCO receives relatively low priority and attention from official U.S. channels except in regard to highly visible, well publicized crisis issues. When the USG does respond to these political issues, it places extraordinary effort on those issues, often at the expense of other issues (e.g., education) which are not crises but do not receive the attention they should because they are more subtle and long-range, and do not attract publicity. These other issues are often just as potentially damaging to U.S. interests. For education, this problem becomes more acute at General Conference and at other UNESCO meetings when U.S. Delegations are inexperienced in the methods of UNESCO, do not receive adequate briefings and are unaware of USG policy (U.S. Department of Education, 1983).

These conclusions echoed those of a U.S. comptroller general report of September 1979, *UNESCO Programming and Budgeting Need Greater U.S. Attention* (pages ii–iii). That report concluded that "U.S. efforts in UNESCO in recent years have been directed more toward political concerns than with Agency programs." The report continued, "the United States . . . has not adopted to best advantage the administrative machinery established to co-ordinate and oversee agency activities." The report found the following flaws:

- Procedures for establishing current and explicit statements of U.S. program objectives and priorities were inadequate.

- Development of a new policy analysis and resources management process designed to improve U.S. effectiveness in UNESCO was lagging.
- Performance of some U.S. representatives at UNESCO forums was reduced because of inadequate preparation times and inexperience.[36]
- Domestic agencies and professional constituencies concerned with the UNESCO program were not involved deeply or early enough in the agency planning process to allow American interests to be clearly defined and promoted (U.S. Comptroller General, 1979:iii).

In short, it seems likely "that U.S. management (mismanagement) of its relations with UNESCO over the years has helped bring on some of the problems UNESCO now faces" (U.S. House of Representatives, 1984:34). Moreover, the U.S. management posture with all of the associated problems, when linked to UNESCO's mounting legitimacy problems in the United States, helped to make UNESCO an easy target.

AMERICAN PRESS COVERAGE OF UNESCO

The very negative public image of UNESCO that had been created by biased press coverage in the United States of the organization's activities served as a third important element that facilitated the withdrawal action. The anti-UNESCO rhetoric of the administration was compatible with the general image of UNESCO that the press had been promoting for some years.

> American press coverage has reflected the *possibilities* of press-controls, not actualities, and that important distinction has never been made clear. For example, the Soviet Union's outrageous draft resolution of 1976 tying all the press to governmental oversight was defeated. Yet the memory of that bitter debate remains, and blackens the name of UNESCO more than the Soviets who initiated the draft. . . . [The] memory of that bitter draft [the *Soviet* 1978 Mass Media Declaration] remains, and UNESCO—far from getting credit for defeating it—is still charged, in memory, with having 'proposed' it. That, of course, was untrue (Sussman, 1984a–e).

Such distorted press coverage has not been an isolated occurrence.

The self-interest orientation inherent in the Western press coverage of UNESCO activities has been well documented. For example, a study of American press coverage of the 21st General Conference in 1980, conducted by A. H. Raskin (1980) of the National News Council, found that all 448 news reports of the conference reported exclusively the communications issue. None of the news articles covered any of the hundreds of resolutions and programs on education, science, and culture, which accounted for over 95 percent of the UNESCO budget.

An analysis of news coverage of the Fourth Extraordinary Session of the General Conference in 1982 by George Gerbner (1983) found similar results. The almost exclusive focus was on communications issues, especially the NWICO issue. "The press constructed a picture of the meetings more from selected speeches and prior information than from the actual resolutions and official actions of the conference. That construction showed a preoccupation with real and imagined threats to private control of the press to the virtual exclusion of other issues."[37] Furthermore, the study concluded that "a defensive, belligerent and often paranoid tone pervaded most editorials published about the conference. There was little recognition of U.S. citizens' points of view other than that of the press and its trade associations and public relations spokespersons."[38]

Press coverage of the 22nd General Conference in 1983 was equally misleading. Sussman's (1984c:9-10) documentation of the conference is instructive: "By any current definition of news, UNESCO communications debates . . . were newsworthy. Of 49 communications resolutions introduced, 33 (including those of the U.S. and its friends) were not objectionable to free-press advocates. Of the remaining 16, the worst—introduced by the Soviet Union and the German Democratic Republic—were withdrawn without ever reaching the floor." Also, as we have reviewed earlier, this conference represented a number of significant successes for free-press advocates. In addition, more resolutions were adopted by consensus at this conference than ever before in the history of UNESCO. Of the thirty highly contentious resolutions submitted to the Drafting and Negotiating Committee, ten were withdrawn and the remaining twenty were substantially amended so that they could be adopted by consensus (U.S. House of Representatives, 1984:27–28).

However, nearly all news reports of the General Conference belie such changes. While large headlines proclaimed the introduction of anti-free-press proposals into the debate by participants like the Soviet delegate, the press usually made little or no mention when such proposals were successfully negotiated out of existence or otherwise killed. The NWICO debates appear to have become the exclusive obsession of most U.S.-based reporters covering UNESCO affairs. General Conference results and other activities in the areas of education, science, and culture were systematically ignored even when satisfactory to the United States. Yet, again such activities represent an overwhelming majority of what UNESCO does. Viewing the UNESCO initiatives as an agenda for censorship, reporters generally ignored the fact that no resolution regarding licensing, monitoring, or journalistic codes had ever been adopted. Moreover, no top UNESCO official has ever called for restrictive actions either.

Biased reporting did not cease with the U.S. withdrawal announcement. An analysis of nearly 4,000 news reports, editorials, and columns that appeared during 1984 found that "taken as a whole, the agency coverage (i.e.,

AP, UPI, New York Times, Washington Post/L.A. Times news services) was strongly anti-UNESCO and supportative of withdrawal. About seventy percent of the themes in the reports were critical of the organization, or supported pullout" (Giffard, 1986:7). News reports that actually appeared in the press were even more negative toward UNESCO.

> Editorials in the press reinforced the anti-UNESCO orientation of the news reports. Surprisingly, many newspapers carried only editorials—twice as many as carried any news reports. The editorials were far more critical of the organization than the news stories. Nearly 85 percent of the themes in the editorials criticized UNESCO, urged the administration to follow through with its intention to withdraw. A handful of large papers called for continued U.S. membership, but even they acknowledged UNESCO's shortcomings. The majority saw no merit in UNESCO, and applauded the withdrawal (Giffard, 1986:8–9).

Giffard found that the Heritage Foundation's views reached the press through three channels: "News reports quoted administration spokesmen, who echoed the Heritage position. Columns and editorials by Heritage Foundation writers appeared under their byline in the press. And Heritage papers, mailed to editorial writers and columnists nationwide, became the basis for numerous opinion pieces urging the U.S. to make good its threat to withdraw" (Giffard, 1986:11). Although opponents of withdrawal also attempted to influence public opinion, the study found that the Heritage Foundation and other supporters of withdrawal were far more successful in gaining access to the press.

Paradoxically, press treatment of UNESCO, in general, and of the communications issue, more specifically, has tended to reflect rather directly the imbalances and distortions in news coverage that supporters of a NWICO have long decried and that U.S. opponents of such a new order have denied. The distorted image appears to have had a significant impact on policy and policymaking processes during 1983–1984. The public at large and most U.S. officials knew little about UNESCO other than what they had read in the press. That image, as we have seen, was a very negative one. Thus, when U.S. officials announced the withdrawal decision, relatively few individuals or groups had an independent information base upon which to make a reasoned judgement regarding the administration's indictment of UNESCO.

Three factors then—growing alienation toward/loss of legitimacy of UNESCO, poor management of U.S. participation in the organization, and greatly distorted press coverage—provided a general context that facilitated the U.S. withdrawal. When supplemented by a few more situationally specific conditions, the elements were in place for a small group of highly committed ideologues to capture and successfully manipulate the policy process.

IDEOLOGY AND BUREAUCRATIC INTERESTS

Within the Reagan administration there emerged a complementarity of interests among three sets of participants that, in combination, appear to have created an environment sufficient to manipulate the policy process. Careerists in the IO bureau outside of the small IO/UNESCO unit, administration budget officials, and right-wing political appointees and their associates all had stakes or interests that would be enhanced by withdrawal from UNESCO.

As discussed earlier, David Stockman and others at the budget office (OMB) were anxious to find ways to cut federal spending. Multilateral agencies in general and UNESCO in particular were seen as good targets, given the deep-seated anti-UN and anti-UNESCO attitudes among right-wing administration officials, advisors, and supporters. These negative attitudes were compatible with the perspectives of many careerists in the IO bureau, as well as the State Department more generally, who were weary over fighting budget and political battles in IGO delegate bodies. Withdrawal would mean that they would have to wage one less set of battles over political issues in UN agencies. Furthermore, State Department careerists seemed to know or care little about the programmatic concerns of UNESCO. Withdrawal would serve to reduce their burdens.[39]

At least one of Newell's superiors at the State Department, Deputy Secretary Lawrence Eagleburger, appears to have understood and was concerned about the largely ideological foundations of the withdrawal decision. Yet, given the weak domestic support base for UNESCO, the general preference at State for bilateral diplomacy, and competing foreign policy needs and interests that were viewed to have much higher priority, the issue of continued U.S. participation in UNESCO was quite simply not viewed as being worth a costly political struggle with Newell and others close to the White House. UNESCO was seen as a no-win issue.[40] Moreover, 1984 was an election year and the Heritage Foundation had raised the matter of U.S. withdrawal from UNESCO to the status of an important symbolic issue of the administration's commitment to the far right.

There was no effective counterbalance to the ideologically based assault on UNESCO either within or outside the U.S. government. The U.S. National Commission for UNESCO, which had been run down for years, had been effectively emasculated by Newell prior to initiating the withdrawal action. The UNESCO constituencies in federal agencies other than State were widely scattered and small in number. Moreover, Newell's never-to-be fulfilled pledge to redirect the $47 million saved from withdrawal to other international activities in education, science, culture, and communications appears to have limited vocal opposition among these groups.[41] Also, the general public's impression of UNESCO was either nonexistent or largely negative and based on misinformation that supported the official justification for withdrawal.

Thus, while few in number, Newell and his associates were able to gain control and manipulate U.S./UNESCO policy processes with few major obstacles. UNESCO was quite vulnerable relative to the United Nations organization and most other UN agencies, whose domestic constituencies were considerably stronger. In retrospect, it appears that they had chosen their target well.

NOTES

1. Twenty-three of the 24 WIG members responded to the subprogram prioritization exercise. The subgroup calculated composite scores for each subprogram. Each subprogram was scored on a 3 to 0 scale, with 3 indicating increased resources, 2 - unchanged resources, 1 - reduced resources, and 0 indicating elimination of the program. An overall composite (mean) score was calculated for each subprogram. For purposes of analysis rankings that fell between 3.0 and 2.25 were considered to merit increased resources; rankings between 2.24 and 1.50 were considered as unchanged; those between 1.49 and 0.76, reduce resources; and rankings below 0.76 were considered as subprograms to be eliminated.

2. Specific observations about the reform process made in the following sections are based on interviews conducted in Paris during October 1984 and September 1985.

3. Although authorized, these funds were not appropriated.

4. The Heritage Foundation is a private, conservative public policy organization, which was established in Washington, D.C., in 1973. In addition to producing written policy papers, reports and statements, the foundation organizes and sponsors seminars, lectures, debates and briefings, as well as operates its own news/editorial service—Heritage Features. Its policy papers are widely circulated to members of Congress and the Executive Branch, as well as to newspaper editors, journalists, and academics.

5. Edwin Feulner, letter, October 8, 1984.

6. Personal interview, spring 1987.

7. This last item was actually a memorandum drafted by Owen Harries.

8. It is interesting to note in this regard that the fundraising letter in which Feulner made this claim also attacked the UNESCO Director-General for hiring a Washington-based public relations firm to improve the image of UNESCO in the United States. As part of their reform recommendations, the British and various other Western governments had recommended that UNESCO move to expand its public information activities in member states. The public relations firm in question—Wagner and Baroody—had been active in support of the Reagan campaign. Moreover, the arrangement with this firm had been worked out by a strong Reagan and Heritage Foundation supporter. Personal observations and interviews, summer and fall 1984.

9. Personal interview, summer 1987.

10. Personal interview, fall 1984.

11. The only significant differences that were found were that the State Department, as a matter of policy, did not echo Heritage's criticisms of

Director-General M'Bow and that U.S. officials also paid some attention to the question of what would happen after withdrawal (Giffard, 1986:197).

12. Gough Whitlam, "Partner or Puppet? The United Kingdom, United Nations and United States." Address to the United Nations Association of Great Britain and Northern Ireland, London, April 13, 1985:9–11.

13. Richard Norton-Taylor, "Where Detente Is a Dirty Word," *The Guardian*, November 26, 1985.

14. "UNESCO's Bunker Mentality," *The Wall Street Journal*, November 19, 1984.

15. Arthur Gavshon, "Washington Raises Pressure on Britain to Leave UNESCO," *The Guardian*, November 22, 1985.

16. "U.S. Urges Britain to Quit UNESCO," *Newsday*, October 20, 1985; "Shultz Urges UK to Leave UNESCO," *The Guardian*, October 30, 1985.

17. "Shultz Urges UK to Leave UNESCO," *The Guardian*, October 30, 1985.

18. Ibid.

19. Gavshon, "Washington Raises Pressure."

20. "UNESCO 'Satisfied' British Objections," *The Guardian*, November 16, 1985.

21. "An Outpost of the Evil Empire," *New Statesman*, December 13, 1985.

22. "Britain Picks Up Its Marbles," *New Statesman*, December 13, 1985.

23. "Britain Dismays EEC by Leaving UNESCO," *The Guardian*, December 6, 1985.

24. Quoted in "MPs Urge Britain to Stay in UNESCO," *Financial Times*, September 25, 1985.

25. Personal interviews, winter and summer 1987.

26. I wish to thank Jack Fobes for these and other insights gained through numerous discussions with him about U.S./UNESCO relations.

27. Personal interviews, winter and summer 1987.

28. This discussion is based on personal interviews with former Department of State officials.

29. I wish to thank former Assistant Secretary of State for International Organization Affairs Samuel DePalma, as well as Jack Fobes, for their helpful clarifications on this point.

30. Also, it should be noted that Maheu was ill at this time and the Secretariat was in a situation of transition between Directors-General.

31. Even in respect to development activities, efforts to secure significant U.S. AID involvement were only minimally successful. Personal interview, summer 1987.

32. Under Section 9(a)(2) of the Foreign Assistance Act of 1974 (PL 93-559), U.S. contributions were prohibited until "The President certifies to Congress that such Organization (1) has adopted such policies which are fully consistent with its educational, scientific and cultural objectives, and (2) has taken concrete steps to correct its recent actions of a primarily political character." In 1975 President Ford certified that UNESCO had taken such steps and Congress partially restored funding in a supplemental authorization (Public Law 95-45).

33. U.S. Department of State, "Management of U.S. Participation in UNESCO," Internal Working Document, IO Bureau, 1983:2.

34. Ibid., p.4.

35. Ibid., p.13.

36. Notwithstanding the clearly articulated findings of this report, the U.S. delegation to the 22nd General Conference did not include either a professional scientist or professional educator. Yet, the delegation did include two former White House employees/associates, the chairperson of the National Resolutions Committee of the Daughters of the American Revolution and a close family friend of the Reagans. These individuals were Wendy Borcherdt, Jean Bergaust, Barbara Taylor, and Ursula Meese. Also on the delegation were: Edmund Hennelly (head), John Irwin, Samuel DePalma, Joseph Rawley, and Leonard Sussman.

37. Gerbner (1983), quoted in Giffard (1986:36).

38. Ibid.

39. Personal interview, spring 1987.

40. Personal interviews, spring and summer 1987.

41. Assistant Secretary Newell's statement before the 48th Session of the U.S. National Commission for UNESCO, "Transcript," December 13, 1984. "As U.S. Quits UNESCO, Concerns Rise about Global Science," *Physics Today* (February 1985):53–55.

CHAPTER SEVEN

Beyond Unilateralism

Several years have passed since the U.S. government terminated its membership in UNESCO. During this period official U.S. involvement in multilateral cooperation in education, culture, and communications has all but ceased. In science U.S. involvement has been quite minimal. The total annual allocation of federal funds for such international activities has been only $2.75 million, as compared with the $47 million in foregone assessed budget contributions to UNESCO, which administration officials had repeatedly pledged would be redirected to alternative programs in these areas upon withdrawal.

Of course, many U.S. citizens still continue to be engaged actively in multilateral endeavors despite the official U. S. government posture. The very nature of modern science, education, and communication, as well as the cultural implications of all international activities, make such relations a necessity. Yet, current U.S. involvement in multilateral relations in these areas remains problem ridden, as in the past; but what about the future? Looking back, what lessons can we draw from the UNESCO experience for informing policy debates over the future of U.S. multilateral relations and for studying such phenomena?

LEARNING FROM UNESCO

From the preceding analysis of the interplay of forces that culminated in withdrawal we can learn much to assist us in the future. Only in small part can the U.S. withdrawal be adequately interpreted as a rational response to a wholly untenable situation. Assistant Secretary Newell and other political officials involved in the initial withdrawal decision might well have perceived conditions as such. The inflexible and highly charged ideological orientation that those participants brought to the policy process created perceptual blinders through which they filtered factual information and expert judgements. The resulting selective bias might well have led these individuals to discount or ignore facts and opinions that did not support their commitment to withdraw. Yet, as we have discussed, the official justification for such an immediate and unilateral action as a total withdrawal was not supported by the very information upon which it was claimed to have been based. In order to explain the withdrawal other factors had to be taken into account. Thus, once the notion of rationality is taken beyond an individualistic level, the official explanation becomes quite dubious.

The U.S./UNESCO relationship was troubled from almost the beginning. U.S. officials were generally successful in gaining support for their policy preferences in the early years and occasionally later when they made an honest and adequate effort. Nevertheless, UNESCO came under attack for its perceived unwillingness to serve as the political organization that it had been designed to be. As an instrument for conducting what conventional wisdom saw as important foreign policy affairs, U.S. officials judged UNESCO to be undependable. A general disinterest in the organization slowly developed in official Washington.

Over time a dynamic interrelationship evolved between organizational constraints and weaknesses in UNESCO and policy and administrative failings related to U.S. participation. As the programmatic orientation of UNESCO changed, problems of legitimacy grew in U.S./UNESCO relations. Disinterest gave way to alienation toward the organization in some important policy circles. The quality of U.S. participation declined and a void in leadership occurred, which was filled by an already strong Directorship-General. Conditions within this already troubled organization grew more problematical.

Functional agencies in Washington eventually became effectively disengaged from UNESCO and its domestic support base diminished among both professional and civic NGOs, in part because of the reduction in the catalytic role of the U.S. National Commission. U.S. participation in the organization was conducted on a largely political basis by the State Department. The policy process became so flawed that high-level officials came to interpret important policy successes as failures (for example, the NWICO and human rights debate outcomes) and to praise significant policy foibles (for example, politics of withdrawal). The situation was such that those U.S. officials and concerned citizens who did seek to reform UNESCO were inhibited from mounting successful policy initiatives for doing so.

Although the original withdrawal decision came as a shock to most participants in UNESCO, it was initially viewed by many as a potentially positive action; the movement to reform the organization had been given new life. Yet, in the face of a relatively receptive political environment in UNESCO within which to negotiate reform, attitudes, actions, and nonactions with respect to U.S. participation in the organization made it all but impossible to seize the opportunity. Notwithstanding U.S. policy foibles, numerous important organizational changes were negotiated and initiated. Other important components of the reform agenda, though, remain to be accomplished and the governments of the United States and the United Kingdom remain out of UNESCO. The crisis of multilateralism in education, science, culture, and communications continues.

A Matter of Identity

One important lesson to be learned from the history of U.S./UNESCO relations is that the programmatic objectives and orientation, which serve to establish identity in any formal institution of multilateral cooperation, need to be continuously clarified and redefined as environmental conditions change. Broad agreement among participants over such objectives and orientation is needed, if the organization is to function effectively. Given the tremendous inequities, disparities, and diversities that characterize a world society in rapid transition, there will always be tensions and conflicts over the exact nature of any IGO's identity and the appropriate means of translating identity into action at the programmatic level. It is the struggle for consensus in purpose and identity that helps to clarify needs, values, and objectives and to drive the issue-specific global value dialectic forward.

There will always be conflicts over identity in organizations like UNESCO, which deal in substantive issues that touch on the essence of ideologies (for example, control over communications and information, culture, the substance of education and who should be educated, human rights). What is important is how we deal with these issues. They need to be viewed and treated as representing opportunities. Ideological struggle is a reality of world politics that needs to be confronted constructively, not ignored or walked away from. Unilateralism is not likely to be an adequate response. One function of universal IGOs is to work through such ideologically sensitive matters of identity (that is, the political forum function of these agencies). In this regard Assistant Secretary Newell and much of the American press, paradoxically, appear never to have grasped the role that the NWICO debate had played in clarifying and promoting liberal democratic values.

At the same time, however, the maintenance of institutional legitimacy requires that multilateral programs and activities be based on broadly shared needs and values, excluding a few problem areas, such has been the case in UNESCO. Yet, in their myopic and nondiscriminating harangues about politicization certain foreign policy elites have tended to confuse the political forum and programmatic functions of the organization.

Reestablishing Legitimacy

In UNESCO too there was much confusion. The organization and its members collectively failed to deal effectively with competing demands for delimiting its organizational identity. UNESCO's base of legitimacy in regard to its major funders, especially the United States, had been allowed to erode.

The decline of legitimacy in UNESCO appears to have been the single greatest problem in U.S./UNESCO relations. A retrenchment from active and constructive engagement in UNESCO accompanied the decline. When the largely political and ideologically driven decision was made to leave the organization, there was little overt opposition in the United States. While substantial needs for international cooperation in education, science, culture, and communications continued, the value of UNESCO in satisfying those needs was not perceived to be great. As we saw in Chapter 2, U.S. officials viewed UNESCO as performing a number of important functions, some of which were performed by few other agencies. Yet, UNESCO was not seen as vital to the satisfaction of fundamental needs and values.

Of course, a strong argument could be made that the organization did fulfill such needs. The point, however, is that perceptions of legitimacy were not widespread in the United States. Without them UNESCO was left quite vulnerable.

U.S. officials have viewed the organization generally as a Third World agency, devoted almost exclusively to providing development assistance. It should be made clear that many U.S. officials, including Mr. Newell, seemed to prefer that UNESCO be just that: strictly a development agency. There appears to have been very little interest in the State Department—either from career diplomats and civil servants or political appointees (with a few notable exceptions)—to reorient UNESCO to deal more fully with intellectual concerns. Indeed, there seems to have been a great deal of suspicion about intellectuals, as well as substantial distrust of national policies in education, science, culture, and communications. At the same time, the nature and structure of the management of U.S. participation in UNESCO largely precluded any specific functional agency from taking its place. Thus, at a time when U.S. preeminence was coming under increasing challenge in various UNESCO functional areas, U.S. policy processes inhibited an effective response.

MULTILATERALISM IN A POSTHEGEMONIC WORLD

In his critique of U.S./UN relations Edward Luck (1984–1985:155) has argued that "the U.S. government does not really want what it needs out of the United Nations and does not need what it wants." There does not seem to be a close connection between needs of U.S. citizens, which could be served through international cooperation, and the policies and actions of U.S. officials in multilateral institutions. These officials tend to use the UN largely to gain support for specific foreign policy actions or to condemn the policies and actions of others. With respect to UNESCO this critique needs to be extended. There exists no clear assessment of what U.S. citizens (public or private) need in regard to international cooperation in education, science, culture, and communications. Although the National Academy of Sciences (1984) and a few other organizations have explored selected aspects of this question, no systematic and comprehensive study has been made. Furthermore, there seems to be little interest in doing so. The logical body for undertaking this project, the U.S. National Commission for UNESCO, has been steadily weakened over time and was made largely ineffective by the Reagan administration.

During the reform period, discussion seldom if ever focused on U.S. citizens' needs. Instead, relatively ambiguous notions of national interest tended to dominate most of the discourse. Given the relatively transitory and situationally defined nature of perceived interests, they generally cannot serve as a firm basis for establishing legitimacy over the long run. Legitimacy is based on the perceived satisfaction of needs and values.

A dilemma results with respect to the traditional conduct of U.S. multilateral relations. While State Department officials might be quite accomplished at defining and pursuing perceptions of interests (viewed in fairly narrow political and economic terms), they have little of the expertise or experience necessary for defining needs in specific substantive sectors, a task that requires the participation of functional agencies and especially nongovernmental bodies. Moreover, the heart and soul of multilateral specialized agencies is their programmatic work. Political agencies, like the IO bureau, generally do a very poor job initiating and managing substantive activities. As we have seen in UNESCO, the full potential of expertise and knowledge in education, science, culture, and communications in the United States has seldom been brought productively to bear in UNESCO, except in those few cases (for example, NWICO debates, scientific cooperation, and world documentation exchange) where vital interests were perceived to be threatened.

Although we have not explored the extent to which these failings extend beyond the UNESCO case, it seems likely that U.S. multilateral relations with other international functional agencies might be similarly affected. To the extent that such is the case, major reform of U.S. multilateral policymaking processes and structures would seem to be a prerequisite to any meaningful long-term reform of international organizations.

Effective participation in multilateral organizations requires substantial will, as well as a well managed policy process. Both of these appear to have been lacking in U.S./UNESCO relations. Although the U.S. government appears not to have lost the ability to influence decisions in UNESCO when the will exists, it is not clear, given the pluralistic nature of U.S. policymaking processes, that a will to do so could currently be recovered or mobilized on a sustained basis.

Also, as Robert Johansen (1985) has suggested, the U.S. government has been operating largely outside the circle of multilateral consensus. It is difficult to judge whether Reagan administration officials are willing or know how to operate effectively within the norms and expectations of multilateral diplomacy. Yet, as we have seen with respect to reform politics in UNESCO, there are potentially substantial benefits from doing so. In the 1980s no single member will be able to control outcomes within any international organization most of the time. However, skillful negotiation within the Western Group and a commitment to developing a consensus therein can greatly reduce developments inimical to U.S. interests. When U.S. officials have been successful in gaining cohesive WIG support for their positions, decisions taken by UNESCO have generally been compatible with U.S. views. In those cases where the U.S. initially finds itself the odd man out, greater care and energy need to be devoted toward arriving at a position that other Western delegations can support.

Finally, it seems that U.S. officials and citizens can learn much from international cooperation. In a complex and interdependent world where military might and associated power politics do not always play significant roles in attaining valued outcomes it is important to observe and learn new styles of interaction. It would seem wise to review unilateral habits and eschew unilateral actions where multilateral approaches would be more relevant.

Before and after the Reagan administration walked away from UNESCO, it focused little serious attention on alternative modes of international cooperation in UNESCO areas of interest. Also, little systematic consideration has been given since withdrawal to mechanisms alternative to UNESCO, either bilateral or multilateral. Educators, scientists, communicators, and other intellectuals in the United States, who had previously participated in or otherwise benefited from association with UNESCO, were largely left to their own devices. It seems that the time has come to clarify needs, objectives, and mechanisms for reestablishing such international cooperation.

SOME INTELLECTUAL AND PRACTICAL CONSIDERATIONS

Returning to a theme underscored in the first chapter, the academic community has a significant role to play in conducting policy-relevant research of the nature and causes of the breakdown in U.S. multilateral relations. An important lesson can be learned from the UNESCO case in this regard. As we have seen, the withdrawal process was far from one that could be meaningfully characterized as a rational policy process. Many of the most important factors underlying withdrawal would have been overlooked had a rational policy model à la Allison (1969) been employed. Clearly withdrawal cannot be explained adequately as a policy resulting from rational choice in response to some strategic national problem; there is little evidence of any static selection process among alternative courses of action.

Allison's organizational process and bureaucratic politics models are also limited in their applicability to the UNESCO case. Although severe constraints existed with respect to information processing, withdrawal cannot be meaningfully explained as organizational output resulting more from routine than from the leaders' direction. The withdrawal action came rather abruptly, not incrementally as a function of sequential action toward organizational goals. Nor can withdrawal be adequately explained as a function of bureaucratic infighting or of some bargaining process. Furthermore, it was not the result of a bureaucratic foul-up or of actors attempting to "muddle through" (Lindblom, 1969).

Withdrawal was an intentional action initiated and carried out largely by a small group of ideological zealots. Several important characteristics of the policy process can be identified. First, only one course of action (that is, withdrawal) appears to have been seriously considered. It is not clear that from mid-1983 onward remaining in UNESCO was seriously contemplated. Second, selective bias determined what information was deemed relevant; information that did not support withdrawal appears to have been either ignored, distorted, or assumed to be inaccurate. Newell and his associates sought information primarily from those external experts who they believed would not challenge the withdrawal action. Thus, the Monitoring Panel for UNESCO and the Reform Observation Panel were both heavily stacked with individuals who brought with them strong anti-UNESCO feelings and attitudes. Newell and other administration officials endeavored to manipulate the press and other media in such a way as to assure a favorable climate of opinion for their desired course of action. Convinced of the righteousness of their policy action, they moved to isolate or discredit significant actors who opposed their policy objectives.[1] Also, strong pressures (either real or psychological) were applied to subordinates who disagreed with the withdrawal policy; any challenge to or deviation from the policy was totally unacceptable. Thus, at least one very important piece of information—the 1983 draft document critical of U.S. policy management in UNESCO—was subverted within the IO bureau. In addition, some IO/UNESCO careerists apparently felt compelled to become involved in acts of bureaucratic sabotage.

Readers familiar with Irving Janis' (1972) *Groupthink* might sense substantial congruence between the above characteristics and many of the symptoms of groupthink, as identified by Janis.[2] Indeed, many elements are quite similar. The major conditions that enable groupthink to occur— pressures for group cohesion, insulation of the in-group from external expert judgement, and active promotion by the leader of his or her own preferred policy action—were all present in the small in-group that initiated and oversaw the withdrawal policy. Yet, the groupthink approach focuses rather narrowly on a small cohesive group of decisionmakers as the basic unit of analysis. In the case of U.S. withdrawal from UNESCO the critical aspect of the analysis is the set of conditions that enabled the small group of ideologues to capture and manipulate the larger policy process. Thus, an ideological process model requires that the analyst be willing to incorporate and deal simultaneously with a variety of units of analysis—individuals, small groups, or larger collectivities (such as Congress, the U.S. National Commission for UNESCO, or the American press). It is the nature of the interrelationships among such entities that either facilitates or hinders the ideological group in its attempt to capture the policy process.

When is the foreign policy process susceptible to ideological control and manipulation? That question cannot be answered with any degree of certainty based on the findings of this one case study. However, several hypotheses can be offered based on the U.S./UNESCO experience. The prime condition is the existence of a cohesive core group committed to some self-righteous cause and convinced of the inherent morality of the group and its actions. The members of that core group must be strategically located within positions of authority or influence as related to the particular policy process in question. Placement is facilitated by an administration that places primary importance in staffing on political ideology, as opposed to either competence or political reward.

Second, that group must be in a position to control or otherwise direct the flow of relevant information to other critical participants within the larger foreign policy decisionmaking process. Control can either be direct (for example, manipulation of information via memoranda, reports, or briefings) or indirect (for example, press releases, news articles, editorials, or seeking outside "expert" advice only from those who are already committed to the correctness of the preferred policy action and/or the inherent evil of the target of such action). Not only do individuals in the core group become insulated from judgements of qualified experts who might take a critical perspective, but so do other important participants within the larger policy process.

Third, the issue must be one over which there exists general ambivalence or even antagonism within the policymaking bureaucracy and low saliency outside the bureaucratic structure. The outcome of the policy action must not represent a crucial loss to a politically important and vocal domestic constituency. International institutions, which suffer from serious legitimacy problems, appear to make good targets.

A few observations with respect to practical policy applications also appear to be in order. It would be extremely presumptuous, however, to assume that any single scholarly study could serve as an adequate basis for reordering and/or redesigning U.S. multilateral relations, even in rather narrowly defined functional areas. Speculate as we might, we must not forget that such phenomena are products of a global dialectic, informed to some extent by attempts at informed design. We must view our own participation as part of that social process, with all of its opportunities and constraints.

With this stated, it seems appropriate in concluding this study to raise a number of questions that must be addressed in rethinking multilateral cooperation in education, science, culture, and communications. First, should we necessarily address these four areas in combination when we think about the future? Fobes (1986:2–3) has posed the question this way, "Is there synergy to be gained by close working relationships on programs and projects in education, science, culture and communications? Are there practical political considerations (for governments) in retaining . . . [them] in one organizational context? Does such a grouping have merit for coordination and interaction with other parts of the UN system? Could any one or more of the UNESCO fields be usefully separated from the others, totally or partially?" In a way answering questions presupposes a consensus regarding the goals and objectives of multilateralism in general and international cooperation in these four substantive areas in particular. The existence of general agreement is not clear. Yet, these questions must be confronted; doing so in a collegial manner with all interests represented may well lead to further goal clarification.

In this regard the formation of a cabinet-level committee, similar to that established in the ILO case, would seem to be in order. The primary orientation of an interagency committee would be functional, not political, and it would be chaired by a cabinet-level official from a functional agency (for example, secretary of education). The committee would be charged to develop long-term goals for U.S. multilateral cooperation, as well as to assess the needs of U.S. citizens within the various spheres of interest. Furthermore, experience would seem to indicate that a functional agency, not the IO bureau, should be assigned the primary responsibility for maintaining expertise and staff support for U.S. multilateral relations in education, science, culture, and communications.

Second, we must confront directly an issue related to UNESCO problems of identity. Are there advantages to pursuing both intellectual cooperation and development assistance in the same organization? Or, given that the institutional mechanisms required for each differ, would they best be handled in separate agencies? Making a determination requires a sound understanding by participants of competing needs and values to be fulfilled through multilateral cooperation. Again, any multilateral institution must be based on legitimacy if it is to be viable in the long term.

Also, other stakes and relative influence capabilities must be carefully taken into account; we must remain cognizant of what is achievable in the contemporary international environment. Federico Mayor, newly elected Director-General of UNESCO, has posed an interesting query in this regard.

> What seems more advisable? To try to adapt UNESCO to the requirements of the world as it is now, forty years after its foundation, or to design and build up ex novo another organization or organizations able to fulfill today its permanent aims? Is it really worth undertaking the profound transformation needed? Is it still possible? And, first of all, do the leit motifs, the spirit and needs which led to the creation of UNESCO within the framework of the UN remain unchanged, with the same strength, or have they lost, even partially, their pressure, usefulness and/or expectations? (Mayor, 1986:1).

Such questions strike at the core of a near-term dilemma for the U.S., as well as the British, government. If a moderately reformed UNESCO continues to exist without further defections, are the needs and values of U.S. citizens (or alternatively the British) better served with their governments in or out of UNESCO? Given current trends, scholars and practitioners need to begin to address this question much more seriously than in the past.

Finally, given the preeminence in the United States of the private sector in most of the areas of concern in UNESCO, how can nongovernmental entities (that is, the private sector) be more effectively engaged in the planning, design, selection, implementation, and evaluation of such multilateral activities? What should the role of NGOs be both at the national and international levels? Perhaps not surprisingly, since withdrawal it has been the private sector in the United States that has kept U.S. citizens informed about and actively engaged in the value dialectic over reform in UNESCO. This situation does not seem likely to change in the near future.

Yet, there currently does not exist a mechanism through which U.S. private sector entities can systematically become engaged in planning and/or carrying out official multilateral policy initiatives in education, science, culture, and communications. Whether the U.S. government rejoins UNESCO or not many of the basic functions of the old national commission need to be served. A private sector body is needed to coordinate and promote internationally the views of the professional communities in the United States and to inform those communities about relevant programs from UNESCO and other international institutions. "The [State] Department has neither time nor competence to perform this function; nor does it have the staff. The U.S. Government is not structured to tap private sector resources in American society which could contribute to UNESCO program formulation and implementation in accordance with American-perceived priorities and experiences."[3] A major function of such a private entity would be to assure that professionals, intellectuals, and the public at large in the United States have access to complete and accurate information about multilateral activities and programs. As we have seen, it should not be assumed that the American press will fulfill such a function objectively.

Congress would seem to have an important role to play in assuring a well managed multilateral policy process with sufficient private sector involvement. As such, Congress needs to consider the reestablishment of a private sector advisory body for international cooperation in the areas of education, science, culture, and communications (either collectively or individually). If the decision is taken to rejoin UNESCO, a new national commission will need to be established. If and when the occasion arises, the recommendations for structural changes adopted by the Executive Committee of the previous U.S. National Commission in November 1983 might serve as a basic working document around which to structure discussion.[4]

Additionally, as implied above, Congress might desire to assume a more active role in assuring that U.S. participation in multilateral institutions is properly managed. The congressional activities related to the U.S. withdrawal from UNESCO were extraordinary and helped to lay bare the misinformation campaign and policy failings of various administration officials. Congressional involvement, if sustained and regularized, could serve to enhance policy management, as well as to militate against the effects of ideologically motivated incursions into the foreign policy process.

A crisis of multilateralism in education, science, culture, and communications continues. Yet, there is a spark of hope. The events of 1984–1985 in UNESCO raised the issue of reform to the status of a major agenda item, not only in UNESCO but in the United Nations more generally.

Organizational change has occurred and more seems likely. The new Director-General has made continued organizational reform a top priority, and is committed to bringing the United States and the United Kingdom back into the organization as soon as possible. What is less certain is the response from the United States. While multilateralism in general does not appear to be at bay, U.S. involvement in institutions of international cooperation seems to be.

NOTES

1. For example, strong pressure was brought to bear to prevent Ambassador Designate Edmund Hennelly from being officially confirmed after he returned home from the 22nd General Conference in Paris with the assessment that the conference had been a clear plus for the United States. Freedom House also became a target when its Executive Director, Leonard

Sussman, began to speak out aggressively in opposition to withdrawal. The assault focused on the financial base of private contributions upon which Freedom House depended. Personal interviews, spring and summer 1985.

2. Groupthink refers to a "mode of thinking that people engage in when they are deeply involved in a cohesive in-group, when members' strivings for unanimity override their motivation to realistically appraise alternative courses of action" (Janis, 1972:9). Mental efficiency, reality testing, and moral judgement deteriorate, as does critical thinking.

3. U.S. Department of State, "Management of U.S. Participation in UNESCO," Internal Working Document, IO Bureau, 1983:21.

4. U.S. National Commission for UNESCO, "Future of the U.S. National Commission for UNESCO: A Framework for Action." Report adopted by the Executive Committee, November 30, 1983. This report called for a reconstituted national commission, which would be more "lean and muscular." While the membership base of the commission would be broadened to be more representative of those NGOs most involved in UNESCO's programs, the actual number of commissioners would be limited to a maximum of forty (fifteen at-large commissioners appointed by the secretary of state and twenty-five appointed upon nomination by the general membership of the commission). The new commission would maintain close working relations with the State Department, but the responsibility for conducting the day-to-day operations would rest in a more private sector-oriented secretariat, financed both by private and public sector funds.

Appendixes

APPENDIX 1 UNATTRIBUTED [U.S.] LIST OF THIRTEEN POINTS

1. Creation of a committee of the Executive Board (similar in concept to the DNG) to which proposals that lack broad support could be referred at the request of several members. Such issues would not be returned to plenary in the absence of general agreement by the committee.

2. Agreement on concentration of resources in those core program areas whose central importance is universally recognized. . . .

3. Creation of a mechanism to ensure that . . . UNESCO decisions and programs enjoy the support of all geographic groups. . . . no budget would pass without the support of members who together contribute a large percentage, say 51 percent, of the funds.

4. A broadened mandate for the external auditor . . . to authorize and require the auditor to . . . respond to inquiries from the geographic groups on the financial aspects of program execution, expenditure, etc.

5. Adoption of . . . zero real growth for the 1986–1987 biennium with maximum absorption of inflationary costs and exchange rate fluctuations.

6. A recommitment to the fundamental importance of individual human rights, while maintaining an open mind regarding the development . . . of new concepts which might further strengthen respect for them.

7. Swift and wholehearted initiation of question-and-answer sessions between the Executive Board and Assistant Directors-General on matters of their program responsibilities. . . .

8. Clearer definition, by the board, of authority and responsibility for both Deputy- and Assistant Directors-General in their contracts. . . .

9. Establishment of procedures whereby member states . . . [can] change or eliminate programs presented in the draft C/5. . . .

10. Establishment of a policy forbidding employment by the Secretariat of Executive Board members until "x" number of years after they have ceased their function as Executive Board members.

11. Greater flexibility and ease of recourse to the secret ballot. . . .

12. More frequent and longer private sessions of the Executive Board to cover a multitude of subjects and not just the appointment of senior-level personnel.

13. Establishment of . . . procedures to improve and accelerate the consideration given individual member states . . . when they request information on matters related to program execution and planning.

Source: "Unattributed List of Thirteen Points," Paris, March 1984.

APPENDIX 2.1 UNESCO REFORM DECISIONS AND ACTIONS: MANAGEMENT

	WIG	UK	US
It was agreed that more attention would be paid to quality as opposed to geographical origins in filling staff positions (2).	x	x	x
Secretariat consultations with member states in preparing the C/5 document and Medium-Term Plan is to be greatly enhanced (122 EX/4) (3).	x	x	x
Fewer documents are to be produced (3).	x	x	x
Increased effort is being made to improve collaboration with other UN bodies to increase overall effectiveness of the UN (3).	x	x	x
A review was carried out and report made to 122nd Board identifying major areas where collaboration with other UN bodies takes place (3).	x	x	x .
Number and grading of proposed meetings was studied and suggestions for improvements made (1).	x	x	x
A separate Central Evaluation Unit was set up under direct authority of DG (2).	x	x	x
Increased use is to be made of outside expertise in program planning, implementation, and evaluation and in seeking management improvements (2).	x		x
More intersectoral cooperation has occurred (3).	x		x
Numerous changes were made in internal bureaucracy of the Secretariat to increase efficiency (2).	x	x	
Evaluation techniques that already exist, including self-evaluation, are being implemented and more fully utilized. (2).	x	x	
A review was conducted of Office of Public Information and it was reorganized (2).	x	x	
Targets and progress indicators were specified for each subprogram in the draft C/5 (2).	x		
Administrative and personnel costs were reduced and so reported in the C/5 document (4).	x		
Recruitment standards and procedures were improved and are to be speeded up (2).		x	x
Spending on outside consultants has been severely reduced (2).			x

Proposals not addressed:

	WIG	UK	US
A study, drawing on outside experience, ought to be carried out on management of fellowship programs for presentation at the 122nd Executive Board.	x	x	x
All evaluation reports should be made available to member states and board members on request.	x		
The external auditor should devote more attention to the "value of money" aspects of his work.		x	
Fixed term appointments should be just that, fixed term, and should not be rolled over year after year indefinitely.		x	x
Competence and experience should be given more weight in the promotion process.			x
Establishment of a policy forbidding employment by the Secretariat of Executive Board members until "x" number of years after they have ceased their function as Executive Board members.		x	x
Unbiased implementation of personnel regulations and proper delegation of decisionmaking powers are needed, with due attention to the concerns of employee unions and associations.			x
More U.S. citizens need to be appointed to UNESCO positions, especially at senior levels.			x
Contracts of high-level personnel should contain clear and specific provisions regarding the degree and nature of their authority and responsibilities.			x

Notes: (1) 122 EX/3 (Part I); (2) 122 EX/3 (Part II); (3) 121 EX/39 Annex; (4) 23 C/5 - Approved; (5) UNESCO, "Results of the 23rd General Conference," nd.; (6) 120 EX/3; (7) U.S. Department of State, *Report of the Monitoring Panel on UNESCO*, 1984; (8) 23 C/Resolutions, Vol 1; (9) 123 EX/Decisions; and (10) 121 EX/3.

APPENDIX 2.2 UNESCO REFORM DECISIONS AND ACTIONS: BUDGET

	WIG	UK	US
— The 1986–1987 budget was prepared on the basis of zero real growth (4). (Geneva Group)	x	x	x
— Improvements were made in the method of calculation and presentation of the budget as requested (3).	x	x	x
— After U.S. withdrawal, proportional cuts were made in budget (6).	x	x	

	WIG	UK	US
— The Director-General returned 1981–1983 Part VIII currency fluctuation gains to member states.		x	x
— DG submitted study to 122nd Board on need to set up committee of experts on budgetary matters (3).		x	x

Proposal not addressed:

More accessibility is needed to budgetary data.			x

Note: (1) 122 EX/3 (Part I); (2) 122 EX/3 (Part II); (3) 121 EX/39 Annex; (4) 23 C/5 - Approved; (5) UNESCO, "Results of the 23rd General Conference," nd.; (6) 120 EX/3; (7) U.S. Department of State, *Report of the Monitoring Panel on UNESCO*, 1984; (8) 23 C/Resolutions, Vol 1; (9) 123 EX/Decisions; and (10) 121 EX/3.

APPENDIX 2.3 UNESCO REFORM DECISIONS AND ACTIONS: PROGRAM

	WIG	UK	US
— A shift of resources was made "from reflection to action" (fewer studies) (4).	x	x	x
— Studies are to be better planned and more relevant to urgent needs of member states and to action oriented elements of the programs (4).	x	x	x
— Program priority was given to activities aimed at assisting member states to find solutions to urgent problems through international collaboration (4).	x	x	x
— The Media Declaration of 1978 was not enlarged (4).	x	x	x
— Views expressed in program commissions are to be considered when implementing the program (4).	x	x	x
— Program has been more highly concentrated into the core elements in education, science, culture, and communications where a consensus exists (4).	x	x	x
— In establishing 23 C/5 priorities resource inputs were weighed against potential benefits (4).	x	x	x
— 23 C/5 gave greater priority to core programs in education, science, and culture; lower priority to MP I, Programs III.1 and XIII.1 (4).	x	x	x
— 23 C/5 included prioritization of subprograms (4).	x		x
— UNESCO programs have been streamlined and number of subprograms and program actions reduced (4).	x	x	x

	WIG	UK	US
— Support for establishment of NWICO was reduced (4).	x		x
— In introducing 23 C/5 at 121st Board DG addressed questions on adjustments to major programs.	x	x	
— Board identified subprograms that should seem to warrant increased resources, those that should be unchanged, and those that should be eliminated for lack of general support (121 EX/DR 11).	x		
— Clearer criteria were drawn up by the Secretariat for selection of appropriate forms of action (3).	x		
— A recommitment was made to fundamental importance of individual human rights (4)		x	x
— A review of provisions of the Second Medium Term Plan with regard to MP XIII (peace and disarmament and human rights) will be carried out (8).		x	
— Emphasis in communication will be directed toward the basic objectives of UNESCO (e.g., IPDC) (4).			x
— A distinction between traditional human rights and peoples' rights has been articulated (4).			x
— Zero real growth was achieved through a reordering of program priorities (4).			x
— In draft 23 C/5 a choice of proposals was provided on contentious major program issues (3).			x

Proposals not addressed:

	WIG	UK	US
A reduction is needed in program spending in the biennium (1984/85) by the elimination of obsolete programs, programs that are really underfunded.	x		x
Activities for which UNESCO spends less than $100,000 should be examined for their viability.		x	x
Clarification is needed regarding the degree of responsiveness to program suggestions from the UNO.			x

Note: (1) 122 EX/3 (Part I); (2) 122 EX/3 (Part II); (3) 121 EX/39 Annex; (4) 23 C/5 - Approved; (5) UNESCO, "Results of the 23rd General Conference," nd.; (6) 120 EX/3; (7) U.S. Department of State, *Report of the Monitoring Panel on UNESCO*, 1984; (8) 23 C/Resolutions, Vol 1; (9) 123 EX/Decisions; and (10) 121 EX/3.

APPENDIX 2.4 UNESCO REFORM DECISIONS AND ACTIONS: STRUCTURAL

	WIG	UK	US
— Full use will be made of the presence in Paris of permanent delegations as representative of the governments of other member states (2).	x	x	x
— Special Committee of the board will be invited to comment on methods used within the Secretariat for monitoring progress of program implementation (3).	x	x	x
— Various decentralization steps were undertaken (2,5).	x	x	x
— The practice of the DG undertaking a full scale consultation of member states and NGOs in the first six months of the biennium will be retained (3).	x	x	x
— Consultations between the DG and member states will continue and be intensified while the C/5 documents are being prepared (3).	x	x	x
— The Special Committee of the board has been charged with oversight of evaluation activities (9).	x	x	
— Full consultation is to occur between Secretariat and member states during preparatory stage of the medium–term plan and discussion is to be enlarged regarding the possibilities for amendments (2).	x	x	
— A more effective role has been established for and by the Executive Board in monitoring and evaluation of each major program (1).	x	x	
— The existing practice of informative sessions with the DG and his closest collaborators on the eve of meetings of the governing bodies is to be expanded during preparatory stage of C/5 documents (3).	x		x
— Permanent delegations will be allowed to strengthen their informal contacts on short term and longer term issues of a general interest to UNESCO (2).	x		x
— Debate was kept focused on program and budget issues rather than on political issues.	x		x
— Basic decisions about the method of preparation and timetable for the next medium term plan were taken at 23rd General Conference and include improved consultation mechanisms (2).	x		
— Assistant DGs will appear before the program commission on a periodic basis for program hearings (7).			x
— The role of the General Conference in determining general policy and in considering and approving the program of activity will be reinforced (2).			x

WIG UK US

— Reservations expressed at the time of the adoption of a
decision are to be attached to the text of any decision
adopted by consensus (10)   x

— Consideration, at or before the autumn board session, of
means by which the effectiveness of the Executive Board's
subunits might be increased (6).   x

Proposals not addressed:

Stress importance of in-depth study, to be carried out by the
Special Committee, on dissemination of results of studies
and research.   x   x   x

A review of the formal consultation practices of other UN
bodies should be undertaken by the DG.   x

There should be fewer meetings.   x   x

A broadened mandate for the external auditor should
authorize and require the auditor to receive and respond to
inquiries from geographic groups.   x   x

The Executive Board should be given the opportunity to
discuss in-depth the work of the Inspectorate General in
monitoring Secretariat activities.   x

Particular means should be found of ensuring that the
General Conference benefits to a greater extent than
hitherto from the policy guidance produced by the Executive
Board and by the various specialist intergovernmental
bodies.   x

UNESCO periodical publications should, so far as possible,
be self-financing.   x

The board should reaffirm the decision of the 113th session
of the board that UNESCO standard setting activities should
concentrate on areas in which consensus appears possible
and in which the need for universal norms is widely felt.   x

A drafting and negotiating committee of the Executive
Board should be created to review proposals and resolutions
that have political overtones. The committee will operate
under the strict rule of unanimous consent. Thus, it could
prevent contentious proposals and resolutions from coming
before the entire board.   x

A subcommittee of the Executive Board should be created to
focus on budget and program matters before they become
locked in.   x

A procedure for voting on the budget that would ensure that
no budget would pass without the affirmative support of
members who together contribute at least 51% of the
organization's funds should be established.   x

	WIG	UK	US
There should be more frequent and longer private sessions of the Executive Board to cover numerous subjects.			x
The drafting and negotiating group (DNG) of the General Conference should be strengthened.			x
Increased use of secret ballots needs to be made in the Executive Board where possible.			x
Establishment of some mechanism of procedures to insure that individual member states are given appropriate influence and are accorded due respect and consideration by the Secretariat.			x
The board should more clearly define the roles, authority and responsibilities of senior officials on matters of their program responsibilities.			x
Mechanisms through which member states are given real decisionmaking power, including the ability to change or eliminate programs presented in the draft C/5.			x

Note: (1) 122 EX/3 (Part I); (2) 122 EX/3 (Part II); (3) 121 EX/39 Annex; (4) 23 C/5 - Approved; (5) UNESCO, "Results of the 23rd General Conference," nd.; (6) 120 EX/3; (7) U.S. Department of State, *Report of the Monitoring Panel on UNESCO*, 1984; (8) 23 C/Resolutions, Vol 1; (9) 123 EX/Decisions; and (10) 121 EX/3.

Bibliography

Allison, Graham T. *Essence of Decision: Explaining the Cuban Missile Crisis.* Boston: Little, Brown, 1971.

Behrstock, Julian. *The Eighth Case: Troubled Times at the UN.* Lanham, MD: University Press of America, 1987.

Brooks, Roger A. "The United Nations at 40: Myth and Reality." Washington, D.C.: The Heritage Foundation, August 9, 1985.

Buergenthal, Thomas, and Judith V. Torney. *International Human Rights and International Education.* Washington, D.C.: U.S. National Commission for UNESCO, 1976.

de Cuellar, Javier Perez. "What Future for Multilateralism?" Speech delivered before the Geneva Diplomatic Club and the Centre d'etudes practiques de la negociation internationale, Geneva, July 3, 1984.

Calder, Ritchie. "A Pork Barrel on a Cloud," *News Chronicle,* December 16, 1944.

Church, David. "UNESCO, Review of the First Meeting of Temporary Committee of the Board." Paris, July 17, 1984 (mimeo).

Coate, Roger A., and Jonathan Davidson. *Assessment of the Draft Programme and Budget for 1986-1987 of UNESCO.* Washington, D.C.: U.S. National Commission for UNESCO, December 1985.

Cox, Robert W., and Harold K. Jacobson et al. *The Anatomy of Influence.* New Haven: Yale University Press, 1973.

Elmandjra, Mahdi. "U.N. Organizations: Ways to Their Reactivation." Address presented to the Tokyo International Round Table, September 24-27, 1986.

Faulkner, Ronnie, and Michael Gunter. "The New Relevancy of an Old Philosophy: Ambassador Moynihan's `Calhounian' Strategy at the United Nations." Paper delivered at the Annual Meeting of the American Political Science Association, Washington, D.C., August 28-31, 1986.

Feulner, Edwin, Jr. "Letter," Washington, D.C.: The Heritage Foundation, October 8, 1984.

Finkelstein, Lawrence. "The Political Role of the Director-General of UNESCO." DeKalb: Northern Illinois University, August 18, 1986.
————. "The United States and UNESCO: The Lines are Drawn." DeKalb: Northern Illinois University, 1984.
————. "The United States and UNESCO: Is the Past Prologue?" Paper prepared for the U.S. National Commission for UNESCO Annual Meeting, Columbia, South Carolina, June 1-3, 1982.
Fobes, John. "UNESCO: Management of an International Institution," in Robert Jordan (ed.), Multinational Cooperation. New York: Oxford University Press, 1972.
————. "OMB Suggestion of U.S. Withdrawal from UNESCO," Memorandum to members of the Executive Committee and task force of the U.S. National Commission for UNESCO, February 1, 1981.
Gerbner, George. "The American Press Coverage of the Fourth Extraordinary Session of the UNESCO General Conference, Paris, 1982." Philadelphia: Annenberg School of Communications, 1983.
Gerard, Jean. "Written Response to a Congressional Inquiry by the House Committee on Foreign Affairs," June 1984.
Giffard, C. Anthony. Through a Lens Darkly: Press Coverage of the U.S. Withdrawal from UNESCO. Seattle: University of Washington, 1986.
Gulick, Thomas G. "For UNESCO; A Failing Grade in Education." Washington, D.C.: The Heritage Foundation, October 21, 1982.
————. "The IPDC: UNESCO vs. The Free Press." Washington, D.C.: The Heritage Foundation, March 10, 1983.
————. "UNESCO, Where Culture Becomes Propaganda." Washington, D.C.: The Heritage Foundation, December 13, 1982.
Harries, Owen. "The U.S. and UNESCO at the Crossroads." Washington, D.C.: The Heritage Foundation, October 19, 1983.
————. "The U.S. and UNESCO: Time for Decision." Washington, D.C.: The Heritage Foundation, December 5, 1983.
Hoggart, Richard. An Idea and Its Servants: UNESCO from Within. London: Chatto and Windus, 1978.
Hughes, Thomas L. "The Twilight of Internationalism," Foreign Policy (Winter 1985-1986):25-48.
Janis, Irving L. Victims of Groupthink. Boston: Houghton Mifflin Company, 1972.
Johansen, Robert C. "The Reagan Administration and the U.N.: The Costs of Unilateralism." World Policy Journal, Vol. 3, No. 4 (Fall 1986):601-642.
Jordan, Robert. "Boycott Diplomacy: The U.S., the U.N., and UNESCO," Public Administration Review (July/August 1984):283-291.
————. "Why a NIEO? The View from the Third World." In Harold Jacobson and Dusan Sidjanski (eds.), The Emerging International Economic Order: Dynamic Processes, Constraints, and Opportunities. Beverly Hills: Sage Publications, 1982.
Karns, Margaret, and Karen Mingst. "Power and IGO Participation: Changing Patterns of Instrumentality and Influence," in Karns and Mingst (eds.), The Crisis of Mulitlateralism: Continuity and Change in U.S.–IGO Relations. New York: Allan and Unwin, 1988.

Keohane, Robert. *After Hegemony: Cooperation and Discord in the World Political Economy.* Princeton: Princeton University Press, 1984.

Laves, Walter H.C., and Charles A. Thompson. *UNESCO: Purpose, Progress, Prospects.* Bloomington: Indiana University Press, 1957.

Lengyel, Peter. *International Social Science: The UNESCO Experience.* New Brunswick, NJ: Transaction Books, 1986.

Lindblom, E. "The Science of `Muddlingthrough.' In A. Etzioni (ed.), *Readings on Modern Organizations.* Englewood Cliffs, NJ: Prentice-Hall, 1969:154-165.

Luck, Edward. "The U.N. at 40: A Supporter's Lament," *Foreign Policy* (Winter 1984-1985):143-159.

Massing, Michael. "UNESCO Under Fire," *The Atlantic Monthly* (July 1984):89-97.

Mayor, Federico. "Restructuring UNESCO?" Paper delivered at the conference on "Perspectives on the Crisis of UNESCO," Rancho Santa Fe Inn, San Diego, California, January 31-February 2, 1986.

————. Address on the occasion of his installation as Director-General of UNESCO. Paris, November 16, 1987.

McFarlane, Robert C. "National Security Council Memorandum on Withdrawal from UNESCO," Washington, D.C., December 23, 1983.

————. "National Security Council Memorandum on a Strategy for UNESCO," Washington, D.C., February 11, 1984.

McHugh, Lois. "U.S. Withdrawal from the International Labor Organization: Successful Precedent for UNESCO?" Congressional Research Service Report No. 84-202, Library of Congress, Washington, D.C., November 8, 1984.

Meltzer, Ronald. "Restructuring the United Nations System: Institutional Reform Efforts in the Context of North-South Relations," *International Organization* 32(4)(1978):993-1018.

National Academy of Sciences. Contribution to the U.S./UNESCO Policy Review, untitled, 1983.

————. "UNESCO Science Programs: Impacts of U.S. Withdrawal and Suggestions for Alternative Interim Arrangements; A Preliminary Assessment." Washington, D.C.: NAS Press, 1984.

Newell, Gregory. "On-the-Record Briefing on United States Withdrawal from UNESCO," U.S. Department of State, Washington, D.C., December 29, 1983.

————. "Letter to the Director-General of UNESCO," July 13, 1984.

————. "Official Statement of U.S. Withdrawal," December 23, 1984.

————. "The United States Confirms Withdrawal," U.S. Department of State, Washington, D.C., December 14, 1984.

Ninkovich, Frank A. *The Diplomacy of Ideas: U.S. Foreign Policy and Cultural Relations, 1938–1950.* Cambridge: Cambridge University Press, 1981.

Pines, Burton Yale. *A World Without the U.N.: What Would Happen if the U.N. Shut Down.* Washington, D.C.: The Heritage Foundation, 1984.

Raison, Timothy. "Letter to the Director-General of UNESCO," April 2, 1984.

Raskin, A.H. "Report on News Coverage of the Belgrade UNESCO Conference." New York: National News Council, 1981.

Richardson, Elliot. "United States' UNESCO Policy: 1985 and Beyond." *Christian Science Monitor*, December 17, 1984:17.

Ripley, Randall B., and Grace A. Franklin. *Congress, the Bureaucracy, and Public Policy*. Homewood, IL: The Dorsey Press, 1980.

Ruggie, John. "The United States and the United Nations," *International Organziation* 39(2)(Spring 1985):343-356.

Sathyamurthy, T.V. *The Politics of International Cooperation*. Geneva: Libraire Droz, 1964.

Scheuer, James H. "UNESCO's Bunker Mentality," *The Wall Street Journal*, November 19, 1984:32.

Senarclens, Pierre. "Fiasco at UNESCO: The Smashed Mirror of Past Illusions," *Society*, September-October 1985.

Sewell, James P. *UNESCO and World Politics*. Princeton: Princeton University Press, 1975.

———. "UNESCO: Pluralism Rampant," in Robert Cox and Harold Jacobson (eds.), *The Anatomy of Influence*. New Haven: Yale University Press, 1973.

Shultz, George. Letter to UNESCO Director-General M'Bow, December 28, 1983.

Smithsonian Institution. Contribution to the U.S./UNESCO Policy Review, untitled, Washington, D.C., 1983.

Sussman, Leonard. "Access: An American Perspective." Presentation at the Annual Conference of the American Library Association, June 25, 1984a (mimeo).

———. "A Review of the UNESCO Decision." Discussion with Gregory Newell, Assistant Secretary of State at the National Conference on "Global Crossroads: Educating Americans for Responsible Choices, Washington, D.C., May 17, 1984b (mimeo).

———. "Testimony," before the Joint Hearings of the U.S. House of Representatives' Subcommittee on Human Rights and International Organization and Subcommittee on International Operations, April 26, 1984c (mimeo).

———. "UNESCO and the New World Information Order." Presentation at the School of Journalism of the University of Missouri, April 17, 1984d (mimeo).

———. "The U.S. Withdrawal from UNESCO -- A Case Study for the Public Relations Specialist." Presentation before the International Committee of the Public Relations Society of America; the International Committee of the N.Y. Chapter of the Public Relations Society of America; and the New York United States Council of the International Public Relations Association, United Nations Delegates Dining Room, April 12, 1984e (mimeo).

UNESCO. *The Executive Board of UNESCO*. Paris: UNESCO, 1984.

U.S. Agency for International Develpoment. "AID Contribution to the Department of Education Statement on UNESCO," 1983a.

———. "UNESCO Communications Sector Evaluation: An AID Viewpoint," Washington, D.C., 1983b.

U.S. Comptroller General, *UNESCO Programming and Budgeting Need Greater U.S. Attention*. Washington, D.C.: GPO, September, 1979.

U.S. Department of Education. "U.S. Policy Review of UNESCO and U.S. Participation in UNESCO; Education Sector," Washington, D.C., 1983.

U.S. Department of State. "Perspectives on the U.S. Withdrawal from UNESCO," Washington, D.C., October 31, 1984.

————. "Reports to the Congress Requested in Sections 108 and 109 of Public Law 97-241." Washington, D.C., February 24, 1983.

————. "Report to Congress on UNESCO Policies and Procedures with Respect to the Media Requested in Section 109 of Public Law 97-241." Washington, D.C., January 1984.

————. *U.S./UNESCO Policy Review.* Washington, D.C., February 27, 1984.

U.S. Government Accounting Office, *Improvements Needed in UNESCO's Management, Personnel, Financial, and Budgetary Practices.* Report to the Committee on Foreign Affairs and Committee on Science and Technology of the House of Representatives, Washington, D.C., November 30, 1984.

U.S. House of Representatives. "Assessment of U.S.–UNESCO Relations, 1984." Report of the Staff Study Mission to Paris-UNESCO to the Committee on Foreign Affairs, January 1985.

————. "U.S. Participation in International Scientific, Educational, Cultural, and Communications Fields in the Absence of U.S. Membership in UNESCO." Report prepared by the Congressional Research Service for the House Committee on Foreign Affairs Subcommittee on International Operations, Washington, D.C., March 1, 1985.

————. "U.S. Withdrawal from UNESCO." Report of a Staff Study Mission to the Committee on Foreign Affairs, Washington, D.C., April 1984a.

————. "Summary," Joint Hearings of the Committee of Foreign Affairs' Subcommittee on Human Rights and International Organization and Subcommittee on International Operations, April 1984b.

U.S. Monitoring Panel on Reform. *Report of the Monitoring Panel on UNESCO.* Washington, D.C.: U.S. Department of State, 1984.

U.S. National Commission for UNESCO. *What Are the Issues Concerning the Decision of the United States to Withdraw from UNESCO?* Washington, D.C., 1984.

U.S. National Science Foundation. "Natural Sciences in UNESCO, A U.S. Interagency Perspective," Washington, D.C., 1983.

Weber, Nathan. "UNESCO: Who Needs It?" *Across the Board,* Vol. XXI, No. 9 (September 1984):11-17.

Western Information Group. "The Final Western Group Paper on UNESCO's Problem," Paris, March 12, 1984.

Whitlam, Gough. "Partner or Puppet? The United Kingdom, United Nations and United States." Address to the United Nations Association of Great Britain and Northern Ireland, London, April 13, 1985.

Index